Praise for *Entrepreneurial Solutions for Prosperity in BoP Markets*

"Poised to become a key reference, *Entrepreneurial Solutions for Prosperity in BoP Markets* will change the way we think, act, and teach about emerging markets. Kacou provides just the right blend of framework and hands-on examples to those committed to transforming the Bottom of the Pyramid."

—**Dean Thomas R. Robertson**, The Wharton School, University of Pennsylvania

"Kacou's insight that many low-income countries are stuck in a Survival Trap whose solution lies in mindset change and entrepreneurship is a powerful one. *Entrepreneurial Solutions for Prosperity in BoP Markets* is a timely book that will influence development policy and business for years to come."

—**Dr. Donald Kaberuka**, President, African Development Bank Group (AfDB)

"Kacou, powered by his deep, on-the-ground experience in developing countries, argues convincingly that the most powerful infrastructure for development lies between the ears of the citizens of these poor countries—their mindsets. He provides insightful analysis of the mindset challenge and numerous case studies to illustrate how mindsets can be modified and enhanced to open the path for development in the most intractable problem areas in the world."

—**Dean Roger Martin**, Rotman School of Management at the University of Toronto; author of *The Design of Business*

"It is becoming increasingly clear that enterprise with moral purpose can be a solution to poverty. What was missing until now was a practical blueprint to make the potential of business in prosperity creation a reality. Eric Kacou, one of Africa's emerging thought leaders, fills this important gap. This book is a must-read!"

—**Dr. Manu Chandaria**, Chairman, Comcraft; Founding Chairman, East African Business Council

"BoP markets represent manifold opportunities for considerable growth. However, business-as-usual will neither help companies succeed nor trigger regional social wealth. Kacou's *Entrepreneurial Solutions for Prosperity in BoP Markets* provides the insights needed for far-thinking strategists to succeed in these emerging markets."

—**Professor Ian MacMillan**, Dhirubhai Ambani Professor of Innovation and Entrepreneurship at The Wharton School; author of *The Entrepreneurial Mindset*

"By integrating mindset, business, and development, Eric Kacou ignites a candid debate around a forbidden, though fundamental, underlying issue that keeps African nations poor. The result is a poignant and practical way to engage businesses in Africa's quest for prosperity."

—**Andrew Mwenda**, Founding Managing Editor, *The Independent*

"This book is a refreshing perspective on how business can transform Africa and the rest of the developing world. It offers practical wisdom for those who are serious about expanding prosperity in the developing world."

—**Professor Calestous Juma**, Professor of the Practice of International Development, Harvard Kennedy School

"A practitioner, business strategist, and gifted storyteller, Eric Kacou provides a unique window into the reality of entrepreneurs in developing countries. His solutions lead the way to success not only for businesses but also for the communities that depend on them."

—**Allon Raiz**, Founder and CEO, Raizcorp; author of *Lose the Business Plan*

Entrepreneurial Solutions for Prosperity in BoP Markets

Entrepreneurial Solutions for Prosperity in BoP Markets

Strategies for Business and Economic Transformation

Eric Kacou

Vice President, Publisher: Tim Moore
Associate Publisher and Director of Marketing: Amy Neidlinger
Wharton Editor: Steve Kobrin
Executive Editor: Jeanne Glasser
Editorial Assistant: Pamela Boland
Operations Manager: Gina Kanouse
Senior Marketing Manager: Julie Phifer
Publicity Manager: Laura Czaja
Assistant Marketing Manager: Megan Colvin
Cover Designer: Chuti Prasertsith
Managing Editor: Kristy Hart
Project Editor: Betsy Harris
Copy Editor: Geneil Breeze
Proofreader: Kathy Ruiz
Indexer: Lisa Stumpf
Senior Compositor: Gloria Schurick
Manufacturing Buyer: Dan Uhrig

ISBN-10 0-13-707926-5
ISBN-13 978-0-13-707926-1

Pearson Education LTD.
Pearson Education Australia PTY, Limited.
Pearson Education Singapore, Pte. Ltd.
Pearson Education Asia, Ltd.
Pearson Education Canada, Ltd.
Pearson Educación de Mexico, S.A. de C.V.
Pearson Education—Japan
Pearson Education Malaysia, Pte. Ltd.

Library of Congress Cataloging-in-Publication Data

Kacou, Eric.

Entrepreneurial solutions for prosperity in BoP markets : strategies for business and economic transformation / Eric Kacou.

p. cm.

Includes bibliographical references.

ISBN-13: 978-0-13-707926-1 (hardback : alk. paper)

ISBN-10: 0-13-707926-5 (hardback : alk. paper)

1. Small business—Developing countries—Management. 2. Poverty—Developing countries. 3. Poverty—Developing countries—Prevention. 4. Sustainable development. 5. Social responsibility of business. I. Title.

HD2346.5.K33 2011

338'.04091724—dc22

2010031130

For Chantal Yoboua Djedje

Contents

Foreword

Eric Kacou builds upon the ideas of Michael Porter, Larry Harrison, C.K. Prahalad, and many others. These are the eminent people we read not just because of what is in their books, but because they wrote it. Now we will begin to study and comprehend Eric's work.

Eric grew up in a poor country, found his way to a world-class education, and competed with elite students and professionals to finally co-lead a management consultancy firm focused on helping post-conflict nations.

You will note from his biography that Eric is an expert in creating informed choices and getting others willing to be guided by him, that he is results-oriented, that he is one of the world's best practitioners of competitiveness. What may be harder to see is that Eric was a great colleague and mentor to scores of young professionals, that clients from Washington to Kigali asked for him specifically, and that he has become, over ten years of working on four continents and stints at Wharton and Harvard, a master integrator of the ideas that support enterprise solutions to poverty.

Porter innovated on the range of strategic choices but focused only on rich countries and left the idea of mindset or culture out of his synthesis. Harrison helped us to focus on the notion of trust and pro-innovation thinking but had nothing to say about how innovation occurs at the level of the firm. Prahalad helped us to value the size and quality of emerging markets but had few normative frameworks to enable company-level choices. My own research and writing comes up short because I don't find and write about iconic local entrepreneurs who could become role models for so many others, which is an important basis of change.

Eric's work remedies and reconciles many of these shortcomings. But that is not entirely what is important here. It is very significant that a citizen of Africa writes about mindset, that he illustrates his thinking with homegrown entrepreneurs, and that he is not only eloquent about the principles of indigenous innovation, but that he embodies the virtues and principles of innovation himself.

It is time for this book. Strategic thinking should not be the sole province of the Ivy Leagues; policies that affect trade and growth in the Majority World are not better when they are constructed in the metropoles of North America and Europe. Role models are not those who travel from these affluent places and espouse innovation and prosperity to others, only to return, as I do, to the comfort and safety of rich institutions, predictable careers, and leafy suburbs.

Eric writes about many who really had to worry about the education, shelter, and medical care for their families and still build businesses in tough places that create unique value for consumers, workers, and future generations.

He has spent many of the last ten years working in Rwanda. The country has grown 8% per year during that time and will grow to 10% this year due to a culture of self-determination, transparent policies, and a firm level focus. Eric has as much to do with this success as any outsider can claim. He has warm, trustful relationships at every level of society, taught hundreds of seminars, presented to cabinet and parliament, and informed the policy debates in numerous sectors of the economy. He has also learned from the Rwandans, and this book has much to say on what outside advisors can learn from local innovators and role models, if and when they lose their arrogance.

Eric borrows, modifies, and builds upon the work of numerous mentors, colleagues, and clients, especially the Rwandans, but finds ways to make the work more practical, tangible, and meaningful. This book will find a wide audience and have impact in far-flung places for years, not just because of what it says, but because of who wrote it.

—Michael Fairbanks
Founder of the OTF Group

Acknowledgments

Every book is a collaborative effort. Each idea, insight, and story contained in this book can be traced back to specific people, conversations, and lives. I would like to thank each person, for they contributed to this project sometimes more than they imagined.

My editors Stephen Kobrin and Jeanne Glasser at Wharton School Publishing deserve special thanks not only for their painstaking editorial support but also their forbearance.

I would like to recognize the importance that Rwanda, its leaders, and its people have played in shaping not only this book but me as well. As a young African, I have been proud and privileged to witness first-hand Rwanda's metamorphosis. The unique brand of leadership of His Excellency President Paul Kagame and his team demonstrates how BoP markets can leverage entrepreneurial strategies to foster greater prosperity and write a more hopeful story for their future.

My special gratitude also goes to Michael Fairbanks, OTF Group founder, for planting and nurturing the seed for this book. This entrepreneur, pioneer, and integrative thinker developed many of the ideas I explored. His landmark 1997 book *Plowing the Sea: Nurturing the Hidden Sources of Growth in the Developing World* introduced mental models and entrepreneurship to the development discussion. The Pioneers of Prosperity program, which searches for indigenous private sector role models and gives them rocket fuel, and from which many of the examples in this book are drawn, was his brainchild. Having Mike, one of the world's exceptional development practitioners, as a mentor has shaped my career and transformed my life.

An entrepreneurial firm, OTF Group provided the platform for this book. My special thanks go to Ken Hynes, my comanaging director at the firm, for his support. Swimming in the river with other inspiring colleagues such as Malik Fal, Andreas Widmer, Rob Henning, James Foster, Mike Brennan, Carole Chapelier, and Elizabeth Hooper crystallized most of the insights here. I am indebted to many colleagues, though nameless and faceless, who came before me and established the foundations for the ideas embedded in this book. A special thanks to Kaia Miller whose original work inspired The Survival Trap concept.

The lives and choices of the outstanding entrepreneurs, managers, and leaders profiled in this book served as an inspiration and a testimony to the impact of entrepreneurial solutions. Dr. Manu Chandaria must be highlighted as the archetype of entrepreneurs who can succeed and transform BoP markets.

Ashani Alles, Charity Kabango, Anna Sowinski, Shannon Hunt, and Amin Gafaranga stand out for their editorial work. Their insights and friendship were invaluable.

My participation in different knowledge networks helped refine some of the ideas in this book. The Wharton School at the University of Pennsylvania, the Harvard Kennedy School, the Young Global Leaders community at the World Economic Forum, and the African Leadership Initiative served as testing platforms for the various ideas exposed in this book.

I am especially grateful to my parents, Chantal Yoboua Djedje, Germain Kacou, and Louis Djedje, for teaching me the importance of mindsets and self-determination. Finally, I am grateful for the grace bestowed on me by the Lord throughout this endeavor and always.

About the Author

Born and raised in Cote d'Ivoire, **Eric Kacou**'s passion is enterprise solutions to poverty. Eric is actively engaged in consulting and investing across Africa. In 2010, Eric was honored by the World Economic Forum as a Young Global Leader.

Eric Kacou is currently completing a Mason Fellowship in Public Policy at the Harvard Kennedy School. Prior to this fellowship, Eric served as Managing Director of OTF Group, a competitiveness consultancy focused on emerging markets. An expert in postconflict economic reconstruction, he led the Rwanda National Innovation and Competitiveness (RNIC) Program, an initiative sponsored by President Paul Kagame. The RNIC is credited with helping Rwanda revitalize its economy, fostering the renaissance of the country's private sector, and fueling the growth of the country's main exports.

At OTF Group, Eric served leaders of a dozen developing countries and consulted with international development partners.

Prior to joining the OTF Group, Eric worked a strategy consultant with Monitor Company in Toronto and Paris advising Fortune 500 executives. Eric earned his MBA at the Wharton School.

Prologue: Transformation in BoP Markets: Learning from Rwanda

What is Africa's biggest success story?

Skeptics claim it is impossible to find a success story in Africa; even optimists struggle to answer the question. One might consider high-profile African leaders, like Nelson Mandela, for fathering a peaceful post-Apartheid South Africa. Observers might highlight a business achieving fast growth and record profits: Cell phone companies, social entrepreneurs tackling health or education, or fast-growing banks may emerge.

Yet many highlight the country of Rwanda and its leader President Paul Kagame, also referred to as Rwanda's "entrepreneurial president" for his focus on private sector reforms and investment as the centerpiece of that nation's growth.

In the summer of 2009, CNN's Fareed Zakaria called Rwanda Africa's biggest success story. Mr. Zakaria was the latest in a series of global commentators recognizing Rwanda's metamorphosis. In the last year alone, CNN, *Fortune*, *The New Yorker*, *Fast Company*, and other global media outlets have given Rwanda accolades for its remarkable journey. Rwanda's success represents change and growth processes that will interest businesspeople and leaders striving for dynamic transformation in Bottom of the Pyramid (BoP) markets.

In *Entrepreneurial Solutions for Prosperity in BoP Markets*, I look closely at Rwanda as one key case study that represents an entrepreneurial microcosm in which we can understand the impact of mindset on prosperity creation in difficult operating realities.

In 2001, the country was at its breaking point. The infrastructure was shattered and investments in human capital limited. The private sector was practically nonexistent. Businesspeople working across key sectors faced seemingly insurmountable challenges. From power shortages to customs delays, every step in doing business was a grueling process.

By contrast in 2009, the World Bank in its *Doing Business Survey* named Rwanda the world's leading nation in private sector reforms. A battery of media coverage told the nation's inspiring story to a growing, interested worldwide audience.

Much of the media attention on Rwanda highlights the physical transformations the country has undergone, offering a stark contrast with the images the world saw in *Hotel Rwanda* or global media in 1994, with a large percentage of its population living in poverty, at the bottom of the pyramid. New buildings stand in lieu of ruins, beautiful gardens have taken the place of mass graves, and order has replaced chaos.

It is widely recognized how the nation's leadership team proactively shapes its economic, social, and political destiny. Rwanda sets the terms of its own engagement on the global stage. Rwanda's leadership, vision, and targeted investments in mindset change have driven the rebirth of the country's private sector.

Rwanda took on the difficult task of building its economic growth from within and in an incredibly short amount of time. Vision 2020, the roadmap guiding the entire process, prioritizes pillars such as good governance, private sector-led growth, knowledge-based industries, market-oriented agriculture, and integration into regional markets. In articulating their Vision 2020, Rwandan leaders open by asking themselves: "How do Rwandans envisage their future? What kind of society do we want to become? How can we construct a united and inclusive Rwandan identity? What are the transformations needed to emerge from a deeply unsatisfactory social and economic situation?"

Rwanda's startling journey was defined by the people's vision for their own futures—and supported by innovative thinking and an unconventional approach. The nation's approach is rooted in entrepreneurial thinking. The parallels between the questions Rwanda's Vision 2020 asks and that of a good business plan are apparent.

Rwanda has managed to articulate and implement a unique strategy based on entrepreneurial solutions for prosperity.

The rest of the world is starting to recognize the opportunities and want to be part of the country's bright future. The small African nation has captured the imagination of some of the world's top businesspeople. Chicago businessman and investor Dan Cooper told *Fortune* in a 2007 interview that on his first visit to Rwanda, "We came away saying: this is the most undervalued 'stock' on the continent and maybe in the world." Rwanda's success showcases what Africa and other BoP regions can accomplish.

Entrepreneurial Solutions for Prosperity in BoP Markets examines the opportunities available to businesspeople and leaders in BoP markets. The book explores one of the foremost challenges inherent in these regions encapsulated by a vicious cycle I call "The Survival Trap" and outlines how holding the same, outdated mindsets perpetuate this cycle. After this diagnosis, the book then proposes Seven Opportunities, along with supporting principles and practices, for breaking out and creating prosperity.

This book equips entrepreneurs, managers, and leaders with a better understanding of the challenges of operating in BoP markets. It also provides the necessary tools to identify the pitfalls that keep them stuck in The Survival Trap, and practical solutions to achieve success in business and beyond in emerging markets.

While most of the businesspeople and leaders profiled here hail from Africa, this book also draws insights from leaders in India and the Caribbean, showing the global applicability of the entrepreneurial solutions articulated here in the real life across emerging markets. It also provides governments with the framework necessary to embrace and implement "private sector-led development." Development partners and nongovernmental organizations (NGOs) gain the necessary understanding to challenge business and government to play their respective roles in fostering prosperity in BoP markets.

In the following chapters, *Entrepreneurial Solutions for Prosperity in BoP Markets* draws from the experience of businesspeople and leaders across the globe to draw lessons that can be used to change not only businesses, but other institutions and entire countries that are struggling to find their place in the global market.

1

Identifying the Problem— And the Solution

Every generation faces a challenge, the answer to which shapes how it is remembered in history. Poverty has emerged as the foremost challenge facing our generation. A great many approaches have been tried in the fight against poverty. Despite limited progress, most citizens in developing countries still live at the bottom of the economic pyramid (BoP).

In *Fortune at the Bottom of the Pyramid*, C. K. Prahalad makes a strong case that the vast majority of people living on under two dollars a day in the developing world represents an opportunity for businesses to make money while having a social impact. Finding ways to solve poverty while tapping into economic opportunity at the BoP requires that we discover why this challenge persists.

Whether in business, government, civil society, or just simple citizens, most individuals operating at the BoP face myriad challenges. These challenges not only affect productivity but also confuse attempts to unearth the root cause of poverty. Getting to the root cause requires moving beyond theory as we look at the problem from the perspective of typical individuals in BoP markets. Let us consider such individuals.

Pretoria, South Africa: Themba, CEO Who Can't Collect

It is early Monday morning in Pretoria, South Africa. In the bustling capital city, workers head into their offices. It is the last

5

week of the month. The excitement is tangible: It is month-end, with a coming three-day weekend. High spirits incite an eagerness to close deals, secure payments, and swiftly conclude the month's business.

But the coming weekend is the least of Themba's concerns.

When poverty led others to join gangs, Themba decided to start a business. The story of his firm, ITC Africa, started as the business equivalent of a fairy tale. Themba won a large multimillion rand contract to supply his national government with IT equipment and training. The deal made headlines. It was the first time a black-owned firm had won such a large tender.

Yet, nine months later, Themba feels as though he is standing in quicksand. Themba is exhausted. The government officer who is supposed to pay him hasn't done so and has not returned his repeated telephone calls of late. Failure to make payroll would deal a devastating blow to employee morale.

To make matters worse, he has malaria and his fever is rising. As he walks out of his office, he prays that his illness doesn't make a difficult situation impossible.

Kibera, Nairobi, Kenya: Mariam, Microentrepreneur Who Must Choose between Feeding Her Children and Feeding Her Business

Mariam is among millions of microentrepreneurs living hand-to-mouth. Stuck at what C. K. Prahalad called the Bottom of the Pyramid (BoP), these entrepreneurs struggle daily to create economic opportunities that enable them to escape crushing poverty.

The mother of three young children, Mariam faces a dilemma in Nairobi's Kibera slum. *"Cash or credit?"* she thinks, taking out her last 5,000 shilling.

Cash will allow Mariam to return home a hero, with food for her children. Credit, in the form of cell phone airtime, or M-Pesa which doubles as local currency, will sustain her business.

Mariam takes a resolved step toward an airtime retailer, where she loads 5,000 shillings onto her phone. She elects to invest in her business. One thousand shillings in M-Pesa mobile money is one day of cash flow for her business.

Mariam takes the forward-looking view to increase her ability to earn a living: She's investing in her future potential for commercial transactions, rather than the security of tangible goods in hand. Mariam sees opportunity over risk.

When asked about her decision, Mariam says she is opening her own doors. "Everyone keeps doors closed to businesspeople! That is unless you have a bribe. Otherwise, they force you to go under the door, around the door, or even create your own. Why have doors if we cannot go through them?"

One of a legion of struggling BoP entrepreneurs, Mariam's frustration is palpable. Her only hope is that her children avoid her fate through the education and quality of life she strives to give them.

Santiago, Chile: Jaime, International Executive Who Has to Please Everyone

It is close to midnight in Santiago. Jaime sits alone in his office, finalizing the presentation for his meeting with the company's CEO who is visiting Chile. The data tells a clear story, the graphics are compelling, and the actions are clear.

Yet, Jaime cannot help but feel something is missing. Last year, mineral giant MineGroup acquired a major minerals concession. Analysts applauded the firm for scooping a jewel. The company's public relations team scored a coup by diffusing the good news represented by this acquisition.

A rising star at MineGroup, Jaime, a native of Bolivia, was overjoyed to lead the new entity: His international experience, managerial skills, and a Wharton MBA prepared him for this assignment.

After 100 days on the job, Jaime's initial excitement is gradually turning into apprehension. MineGroup faces major union disputes. Protests from the community and environmental activists are multiplying.

The next morning, Jaime delivers his presentation to a full room including senior government officials, MineCorp's CEO delegation, and the local management team. The CEO congratulates Jaime on his progress addressing strategic issues around community engagement, while ultimately stressing financial targets.

Despite a near-perfect performance in the boardroom, Jaime senses that something is still wrong. The demeanor of the Chilean counterparts tells Jaime he failed to convince them to buy into MineCorp's vision. Jaime feels he won a small battle in a long and protracted war, but fears the situation will get much worse before it gets better. He only hopes his Latin American heritage will help him broker peace.

Kingston, Jamaica: Lisa, Business Leader Whose Industry Is Struggling

It has been a long time since Lisa had a good night's sleep. Behind her poise, honed by a lifetime as a top hospitality entrepreneur, Lisa feels powerless to help most members in her industry association. She accepted the position of president of the hotel owners association because she believed another way was possible for Jamaica's tourism industry. Today she is not so sure.

After studying English literature at Oxford, Lisa returned to her native Jamaica to support her parents in running their hotel. The family business has grown from a single property venture into one of the prominent chains on the island.

Over the past decade, Jamaica's tourism industry has struggled. The island has become hostage to a cartel of large travel wholesalers selling sand and sun packages to low-paying tourists. Most hotel owners are now reduced to working to barely pay the mortgages on their properties. Larger international or regional chains with integrated distribution networks are taking over the industry.

The sector has reduced both the number and the quality of jobs, fuelling the unemployment crisis and increased violence on the island. This has resulted in the local tourism industry losing significant ground. With its limited resources, the government has not been able to offer any assistance to struggling properties. Relations across the industry have deteriorated as the pressure on stakeholders increases.

A recent hurricane damaged several properties on the Northern part of the island. A crisis meeting has been called with government. Lisa knows that several of her members will not fail to raise the unsustainable state of the industry and is not quite sure how to answer these valid concerns.

Abuja, Nigeria: Ijeoma, Government Leader Who Can't Help Feeling Like a Beggar

After graduating top of her class at Princeton, Ijeoma had a distinguished career on Wall Street and followed by a stint in academia. Two years ago, Ijeoma agreed to serve in the government of her native state in Nigeria. Ijeoma knew she made the right decision when she visited her village and saw that people were living in worse conditions than those she experienced growing up there in the 1970s.

Ijeoma's house was flooded by relatives begging for money to send their children to school, get medical treatments, and bury loved ones. While she understands that handouts are not the solution, she can't just let her relatives fend for themselves.

As Minister of Finance and Economy in her state, Ijeoma is at a loss about what to do. As an economist, she believes her state needs a "big push" that would see billions of dollars invested in infrastructure, education, and private sector development.

For a variety of reasons, internal resources make up only 30 percent of her budget. Ijeoma is now reduced to begging from the central government, development partners, or anyone who will listen to get money.

Yet, Ijeoma feels stuck. She espouses the view that aid will not get African nations out of poverty. But she must alleviate the suffering of millions of her fellow citizens. From where she sits, aid seems the only pragmatic, and often possible, solution. As she sits on the plane for her ninth trip to Washington, DC, Ijeoma feels sick to her stomach. Unless she can find a solution out of her life as a beggar, she knows her personal sacrifice will have been in vain.

Washington, DC: Rob, Development Partner Can't Work Self Out of Job

Rob has had the "development bug" for as long as he can remember. His dream has always been to work himself out of a job.

After a stint in government, Rob traveled the world as an economic development consultant. He fondly remembers traveling to remote parts of Africa, Southeast Asia, and Eastern Europe to talk about business strategy and entrepreneurship.

Thirty years later, when the new USAID administrator asked him to head its economic transformation department, Rob saw this as an opportunity to revolutionize the development conversation. At long last, he controlled the purse strings.

Rob has always believed that money was not the problem in development. Now, he knows. After injecting hundreds of millions of dollars into key initiatives over the past two years, the program review his team just completed suggests even more money is needed.

As he contemplates the next phase of his program, Rob knows something has to change. While he has some radical proposals such as enforcing a definite deadline for all his programs, he begins to wonder whether he will have the political know-how to maneuver his way out of this bind.

The Core Problem: Caught in The Survival Trap

Stories of individuals like Themba, Mariam, Jaime, Lisa, Ijeoma, and Rob play out daily in any of a hundred developing nations, from islands in the Caribbean to the landlocked heart of Africa. Entrepreneurs, managers, and leaders in BoP markets alike experience deep frustration.

It would be easy to look at these scenarios and put them into categories of common business or development issues, and prescribe "tried and true" approaches: cash flow management for Themba, access to a microfinance program for Mariam, a corporate social responsibility (CSR) strategy for Jaime, marketing efforts for Lisa, a resource mobilization drive for Ijeoma, and a new development strategy for Rob. This is exactly what development experts have done for decades.

There is real value in these initiatives. Cash flow management is critical for any business; microfinance creates opportunities to improve livelihoods at the bottom of the pyramid; and strategies matter both in business and development. But none of these initiatives are sufficient to succeed in the complex operating reality of developing nations. When we see scenarios such as the ones described above, we spring into action. These are important issues to tackle. However, all too often, the actions only offer temporary relief.

Three key gaps illustrate the unique nature of doing business in emerging markets. The first is the tension between meeting the vast unmet demands for basic services, while confronting the reality that existing businesses struggle for access to fundamentals such as educated staff and suitable infrastructure.

The second gap is the existence of The Survival Trap. The Survival Trap is a cycle that entraps those at the BoP. Its effects can be felt at all different levels throughout the nation, including the reality that the poorest nations face complete bankruptcy in their inability to meet their operating and investments needs.

Finally, conditions are such that a high proportion of potentially productive pockets of society, especially women and youth, are underutilized at significant costs to society. Acknowledging these realities is fundamental to defining a new approach to doing business and creating prosperity in BoP markets.

The question becomes, why do we keep using the "tried and true" approaches? Have we become so accustomed to them that we automatically reach to these solutions, knowing they will at least produce some results, rather than breaking with convention and stepping out into the unknown?

As Albert Einstein allegedly remarked once, "the definition of insanity is to do the same thing over and over again and expect a different result." While "tried and true" approaches are important and can yield results in some instances, there is an even bigger problem than knowing what approach to apply. The bigger problem is this: People become stuck in a Survival Trap.

The Survival Trap is a vicious cycle that keeps individuals, business-people, and leaders in the developing world pursuing the same strategies in the face of chronic problems. This habitual process robs them of the power to solve their problems and catalyze significant change.

In his *Action Science* theory, Chris Argyris gives us a key to understanding The Survival Trap.[1] The breakthrough in Argyris' model is the recognition that operating reality (or context) and mindset matter dramatically in achieving results.

As illustrated in Figure 1.1, stakeholders stuck in The Survival Trap become overwhelmed by their operating reality and its difficulties. As a result, they develop reactive mindsets that fail to imagine solutions beyond their immediate challenges. These mindsets inform reactive actions which provide short-term relief but fail to address the real problems. When things fail to change, they repeat the same actions only with redoubled efforts.

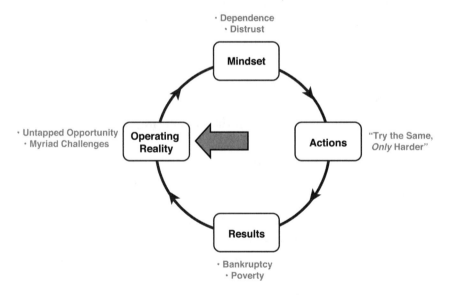

Figure 1.1   Stuck in The Survival Trap

Leaders, whether business, national, or development, are increasingly recognizing the success of individual firms as key to economic growth. However, when faced with a challenge, leaders often apply outdated thinking, or "winning formulas" that worked in the past. As a result, each time people fail to obtain a desired outcome, they implement the same strategy: "doing the same thing, only harder."

Firms fail to thrive, governments continue to rely on aid, and poverty is perpetuated. Results don't change given that the actions are fundamentally the same, and informed by previous mindsets, mental models, or beliefs. These mindsets are further shaped by the operating reality, or business environment, in which these stakeholders operate.

This situation erodes trust while increasing dependence. Trust erodes because stakeholders compete against each other to access limited and unreliable sources of aid. As a result, dependence increases, as individuals rely on somebody else to solve their problems. With effort, an expectation is created, and with each repeated failure, disappointment grows. Continuous disappointment eventually leads to distrust, resentment, and allocation of blame.

As this approach fails to generate results, ownership slips away, and the locus of responsibility shifts, breeding a culture of dependency and mistrust. This eventually evolves into endemic problems with direct implications for business. Eventually, all stakeholders operating in developing countries come to the conclusion that the "context" is to blame. Massive efforts such as the World Bank's Doing Business Survey and the World Economic Forum's Global Competitiveness Index are undertaken to evaluate change in the operating reality or context of countries.

Yet focusing exclusively on myriad challenges present in the operating reality often clouds the judgment of stakeholders. Instead of looking for sustainable solutions, massive, urgent action is taken that ultimately fails to deliver real solutions. Again, this approach means that a lot of work is wasted on efforts that only solve part of the problem and leaves out some of the essence.

Getting at the Essence of The Survival Trap from a Stakeholder's Perspective

Themba, Mariam, Jaime, Lisa, Ijeoma, and Rob profiled at the beginning of this chapter illustrate the pervasiveness of The Survival Trap, which draws its power from its intangible impact on leaders operating in the developing world. No one is immune to the impacts of The Survival Trap. While the stakeholders introduced at the beginning of the chapter each come from different sectors, they are all facing the impacts of operating in The Survival Trap. In the following sections we look at specific characteristics influencing each of the five stakeholder groups introduced at the beginning of the chapter.

Mariam and Other Bottom of the Pyramid Citizens

The vast majority of citizens in the developing world are stuck in The Survival Trap on a daily basis. To fully understand their predicament, one has to have an authentic and strong sense of their daily experience:

- Living hand-to-mouth with no savings or assets
- Powerlessness to realize their ambitions and make their plans work
- Lack of input in the policies and decisions that affect them the most
- Struggling to survive today and simultaneously worrying about the future

Formidable Challenge for Themba and Other Entrepreneurs

Developing world entrepreneurs have a strong ability to overcome difficult conditions. Nonetheless, The Survival Trap is a formidable challenge even for these achievers. For instance, a relationship with government requires translating business needs into political lingo, something that is hard for entrepreneurs to grasp given their level of stress. For entrepreneurs, The Survival Trap robs them of their power to excel in the following ways:

- Status quo merely maintained while great energy is expanded to survive in what seems like quicksand
- Have trouble delegating right now

- Meet closed doors everywhere to expand their businesses
- Do not feel understood by other stakeholders, especially government

Jaime and Managers

Managers, especially international executives, come with talents and brains as well economic might. Yet, even for these stakeholders, The Survival Trap is a force to be reckoned with. Their experience is analogous with being stuck between the hammer and the anvil:

- Sense of not being focused where they could have maximum impact
- Growing pressure to meet the needs of an ever-expanding list of stakeholders
- Frustrated at not being able to control or understand forces at play
- Feel like an outsider that is not trusted by key stakeholders

Lisa and Industry or Cluster Leaders

Industry or cluster leaders have vast real-life experience and relationship networks. However, The Survival Trap compounded by globalization makes several fear for the future of their business in particular and their industries in general. Industry or cluster leaders have lost control of the key drivers in their fields:

- Growing conflicts within the industry that fail to solve the real problem
- Sense of loose financial control with dwindling profit margins
- Customers, competitors, and suppliers that are outside one's circle of influence
- Constant need to innovate without resources and knowledge to do so

Ijeoma and Government Leaders

Beyond the appearance and trappings of power, most government leaders feel immobilized by The Survival Trap. This vicious cycle curtails their power. In hindsight, leaders point to the Trap as a major limitation to their impact:

- Lack of focus on the "real mission" dealing instead with problems without solutions
- Inordinate amounts of energy and time dispensed to make things happen
- Persistent feeling of being assailed with innumerable urgent and important issues
- Experience being at the mercy of outside forces

Rob and the Development Community

Most development workers truly want to make a difference. The Survival Trap makes this righteous objective untenable by becoming frustrated by government. And government blames business for being overly demanding and greedy.

- The BoP point fingers to the elite, who in turn blame the international community.
- The international community decries the irresponsibility of local leaders.
- Blame escalates, communication breaks down, and the status quo persists.
- Everyone feels a certain level of powerlessness and frustration.

Everyone experiences their own version of The Survival Trap. As a business leader once said, "the truth is that we are stuck in a situation where the elite sees its asset base deplete while the rest of the population lives in utmost misery. The situation is getting worse for all of us."

His insight points to a good metaphor to illustrate The Survival Trap, that of the Greek's mythical Sisyphus who is compelled to roll a huge rock up a steep hill. But before he can reach the top of the hill, it always rolls back down, forcing him to begin again. The gods thought that there was no greater punishment than futile work that ultimately did not change the final result. Many stuck in The Survival Trap would agree.

BoP Markets as the Biggest Untapped Business Opportunity

As illustrated by the case of Mariam, most people living at the bottom of the pyramid are in The Survival Trap and forced to make difficult choices.

While awareness of opportunities in BoP markets has increased following C. K. Prahalad's work, these opportunities remain unclear to the majority of business executives and leaders.

It is therefore important to revisit the global importance of BoP markets. Those most affected by The Survival Trap are those at the BoP, those that Prahalad has characterized as an untapped and potentially highly profitable market segment.

The base of the pyramid has productive and entrepreneurial capabilities, as well as representing a massive purchasing force with significant unmet needs for goods and services. If the productivity of this group is harnessed, the impact could be the game changer needed to once and for all alter the dynamic whereby the majority of humanity remains poor.

Characterized by income below $3,000 per annum, BoP citizens number four billion people throughout the world. The four billion people who live in relative poverty have purchasing power representing a $5 trillion market, according to a report by the IFC, the private sector arm of the World Bank Group, and World Resources Institute (WRI).[2] Figure 1.2 offers a breakdown of this market across regions.

The second thing to consider is that the BoP has spending preferences reflected in how it allocates its budget on different services. While food comes on top with almost $3 trillion or 60 percent of all spending, energy ($433 billion), housing ($332 billion), and transportation ($179 billion) represent big opportunities.[3]

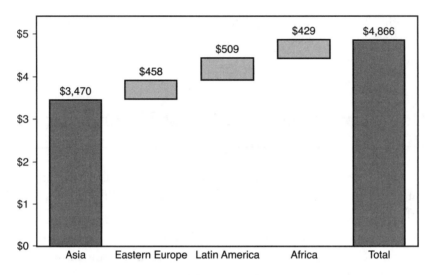

Figure 1.2   BoP income by region

The Case of Africa: Islands of Opportunity in a Sea of Challenges

"Africa is humanity's last frontier in the search for development," President Jakaya Kikwete of Tanzania recently remarked.[4] This last frontier mentality encapsulates the need for a catalyst, for fundamental change, to the manner in which business and development are approached in all BoP markets.

Understanding the unique nature of BoP markets, especially Africa, enables us to identify and address the barriers to transformative change. The important component is to see opportunities where others see the need to fix problems.

To understand the case of Africa, consider the empirical evidence. The economic and human indicators are dire. Over the past 42 years, $568 billion (in today's dollars) has flowed into Africa, yet per capita growth of the median African nation has been close to zero.[5] Despite massive efforts, the number of people living on less than one dollar a day barely changed between 1990 and 2005, declining just 5 percent to 41.1 percent. An important factor to consider is that economic flow is diluted by population growth. Further, the share of the poorest 20 percent has not increased over the 1990-2005 period.

Over the same 15-year period, mortality rates for children under five dropped by less than 3 percent, and only an additional 5 percent of the population have gained access to basic sanitation, leaving 37 percent of people without this necessity.[6] One composite for general progress across all categories, the Human Development Index, placed sub-Saharan Africa's rank in 2007 at 0.514, showing little improvement over the life of the index and ranking well below other regions.[7]

However, there is promise too. Africa is increasingly recognized for the breadth of commercial opportunities it provides. Its population numbers almost a billion with an estimated 42 percent under 18.[8] The low level of development, combined with rapid population and economic growth, means opportunity for the taking.

The story of Africa's cellular operators is one compelling example. Africa is the fastest growing mobile market in the world with mobile penetration in the region ranging from 30 percent to 100 percent and in most countries exceeding the fixed line penetration.[9]

In 2005, the $3.4 billion Zain's acquisition of Celtel was one of the largest deals in emerging markets. In the process, African entrepreneurs like Mo Ibrahim have made fortunes. Similar opportunities exist in sectors such as financial services, healthcare, and infrastructure.

Africa's opportunities are stifled by the continent's performance as a business destination. African nations lag the rest of the world in economic competitiveness. Forty-eight out of the last fifty nations in the World Bank's Doing Business survey hail from Africa.

The gloomy picture painted by these rankings reflects a daily struggle for businesses. Routine procedures, such as the time to file corporate tax returns, take on average three times longer in Africa than in the West. Most businesses cannot count on consistent and affordable supplies of power, water, and other basic infrastructure.

The Survival Trap has also had an impact on Africa's standing in international trade. According to a recent World Bank study "Despite continued commitment to reduce tariff and non-tariff barriers to trade, Africa's share of world exports is on a downward trend. African countries have been unable to gain strong presence in the global manufacturing market and thus remain highly dependent upon a narrow range of primary commodities for their export earnings, leaving them vulnerable to market shocks."[10]

International aid strategy has failed to create sustainable prosperity, largely due to a failure to support business. A debate is currently raging between the proponents of more aid with Jeffrey Sachs as the lead spokesman and, on the other side, those who want Aid Dead, to borrow from the title of Dambisa Moyo's book.

The Solution

Escaping The Survival Trap requires answering this question: What do we do when doing *more* of the same is not enough? When *more* ceases to be enough, a *different* approach is required.

Unlike Sisyphus's predicament, the good news is that we have a say on whether we remain stuck in The Survival Trap. What if one solution—one issue— is the central concern in this trap, with many different manifestations?

What if we went beyond that and discovered not only that there is one solution, but a solution that affects not only economic implications of The Survival Trap but all other issues related to this vicious cycle? Is there one answer that can integrate all of that?

What is that one answer driving all of these other problems?

"Mindsets."

Mindsets provide the key to escaping The Survival Trap.

In each one of these scenarios, there is one common issue—the stakeholders above harbor mindsets that impact their actions. We must start with *mindsets* and ask hard questions about the thinking underlying our actions. We are then able to engage in what Argyris and Schön call double-loop learning. In a nutshell, double-loop learning occurs when stakeholder or organizations correct errors by revisiting the underlying norms, policies and objectives.[11] We expand this idea in our discussion of mindsets in Chapter 3, "Why Mindsets Matter."

When we engage in double-loop learning, we are able to change our mindsets and as a result take new actions that go outside established patterns. Such double-loop learning is the key to escaping The Survival Trap.

Focusing solely on "operating reality" leads stakeholders to consider generic or massive solutions, to shift the locus of responsibility, and ultimately to reinforce feelings of powerlessness. Instead of confronting reality, one ends up shifting responsibility for the challenges one faces. Focusing on mindset, however, invites stakeholders to recognize the central role *individuals* play in bringing change to massive systems. That realization is powerful because it makes substantial change possible.

Figure 1.3 illustrates how stakeholders can lead the escape out of The Survival Trap by focusing on mindsets instead of being overly reactive to the context. It makes us question our assumptions about the situation we are facing while bringing forward hard questions about context, actions, and results that can help move us out of this vicious cycle.

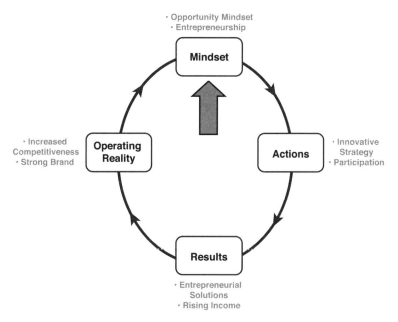

Figure 1.3   Escaping The Survival Trap

Why Business Must Lead BoP Nations out of The Survival Trap

So far, we have established that The Survival Trap is an experience shared by all stakeholders in the developing world. We have also discussed how escaping The Survival Trap requires mindset change.

The next step is to identify the stakeholders best positioned to lead the change process. Business, both entrepreneurs and managers, must be at the forefront of the struggle for prosperity in BoP. First, because the core of the challenge in these regions stuck in The Survival Trap is economic. Both individual experiences and empirical evidence highlight this challenge. When inspired by the right values, firms are better equipped to solve economic challenges. This is not to say that government and development partners have no role to play. Indeed, their foremost responsibility is in improving the operating reality for firms to compete.

Among businesspeople, entrepreneurs are prime candidates to serve as change agents and have a unique perspective. By definition, entrepreneurs are problem solvers. They also have an excellent track record of producing results in BoP markets.

Second, business has an incentive to solve the challenges in BoP markets. In *Africa Rising*, Dr. Vijay Mahajan redefines Africa from a collection of countries with varying agendas and conflicts, to a unified pan-African consumer base of one billion with tremendous purchasing power. Africa is awaiting its entrepreneurs to build fortunes while helping the continent escape The Survival Trap.

Finally, there is a strong moral imperative for businesspeople to transform their communities. While such successes are commendable and inspiring, they highlight the sharp contrasts that exist within BoP markets. To succeed in these environments, it is important that entrepreneurs realize that they cannot live in castles in the midst of slums without repercussions. The moral case for business to lead the escape out of The Survival Trap is compelling.

In leading BoP markets out of the Trap, it matters a great deal that businesses understand the value of collaboration. This is particularly important because the difficult context of BoP markets has taught businesses to be self-reliant. While this self-reliant mindset is critical to prevail over the tough challenges in BoP markets, business must understand that it is not enough to change the context alone.

When operating in BoP markets, most businesses are faced with a host of apparent problems: market inefficiencies, production difficulties, and global competition. Yet a sole focus on those can be misleading. The deepest challenge, mindset, is not apparent.

A distinguishing feature of most successful executives in BoP markets is their superior ability to go beyond the apparent and confront the reality of the mindsets that inform unproductive behavior. A key to prospering in BoP markets is the capacity to change these mindsets and foster new behavior. The business leaders discussed in this book are good illustrations.

The magnitude of the challenge requires that businesses come together if they are to succeed. Business must leverage partnerships, associations, and clusters to address their business challenges in a sustainable manner. Beyond cooperation with other businesses, firms must also collaborate with government and development partners to solve some of the structural issues in TST countries including infrastructure, rule of law, and so on.

Building Partnerships That Transcend The Survival Trap

Businesspeople are but one, albeit one of the most important, set of stakeholders that can help BoP nations prevail over The Survival Trap. Other change makers include political leaders and development financing institutions.

Political leaders often define the playing field where entrepreneurs operate. Through their vision (or lack thereof), political leaders perpetuate bad strategies that have kept developing countries poor. The fundamental mindset shift required here is the acceptance that business must drive prosperity creation, which runs opposite the classic development model.

While this model made tremendous sense when the elites needed to focus on politics to build new nations post-independence, new global conditions require a different approach. Instead, citizens living in countries characterized by The Survival Trap must be empowered to take responsibility and exercise self-determination at all levels.

Most BoP countries are emerging nations with young and growing populations that aspire to live a prosperous life according to their own definitions. These aspirations translate into business opportunities such as selling new products, which for-profit businesses are in the best position to provide.

One of the crucial mindsets to overcome is zero-sum thinking—a belief derived from economic theory and game theory that suggests that one's neighbor and oneself cannot prosper at the same time. Such thinking makes public sector leaders and development partners loathe entrepreneurs.

As a result, these groups often assume that helping business executives is helping the rich instead of focusing on the poor. These groups need to acknowledge that their focus to help the poor has been misguided and needs to shift in order to get the sought-after results—alleviating poverty and creating prosperity.

Practical Solutions for Escaping The Survival Trap

As discussed above and further explored throughout this book, varied stakeholder groups have unique roles to play in the process of escaping The Survival Trap. Stakeholders must realize that business creates opportunities for all citizens as players, especially the poor. Business has the know-how to deploy capital effectively for all involved. *Entrepreneurial Solutions for Prosperity* frames the debate for each of the key players.

- **Business** Businesspeople must equip themselves to "name the elephant in the room" in their businesses and at the national level. By identifying The Survival Trap and its characteristics, entrepreneurs are then able to identify practical actions within their control to address its pervasive effects. Managers must develop an improved understanding of the challenges of operating in BoP markets, in particular the unique challenges of an environment as nuanced as emerging nations especially Africa. All business leaders will learn how to leverage the Seven Opportunities to conduct "good" and profitable business in BoP markets.

- **Government** Governments sometimes embrace "private sector led development" without the tools to effectively fuel this change. Failure comes from the lack of a structured approach linking mindset change to day-to-day actions. *Entrepreneurial Solutions for Prosperity* helps government leaders identify the mindsets and actions required to enable businesses operating in BoP markets to have a positive societal impact, while maintaining optimal profitability. Government further learns to foster an entrepreneurial mindset in their midst and break continuous dependence on development partners.

- **Development partners** Development partners gain the tools to challenge both business and governments to play their respective roles in fostering prosperity in BoP countries. Partners also develop a better understanding of the systemic reasons BoP markets remain mired in poverty, and identify the mindsets and actions to enable businesses in BoP markets to operate effectively. Finally, development partners gain the resources necessary to challenge the existing entrepreneurship/private sector development model that puts the onus on development partners and government as opposed to the entrepreneur.

The Approach

This is primarily a book about prosperity creation in business and society. It is about your business, your institution, your nation, and your sense of control over your economic destiny. Hopefully, it will help you *think* and *act* differently so that we together can escape The Survival Trap.

The initial focus is on defining mindsets and their impact on business. Mental models are measurable and changeable. Good frameworks exist across disciplines to change mindsets. The next chapter addresses these issues.

Themba, Mariam, Jaime, Lisa, Ijeoma, and Rob consider this new perspective; they realize how uncomfortable they are with the idea of mindset. I explore a few underlying concepts to understand these mindsets and the implications on their lives.

Next, we move to identify and provide specific opportunities for entrepreneurs, managers, and leaders to not only change the mindsets that inform their economic strategies but also act differently. Throughout I offer case studies of businesspeople and leaders who have successfully confronted The Survival Trap in their lives, transforming their businesses, and in some cases their nations.

Endnotes

[1] Chris Argyris explicits his Action Science theory in his book *Action Science, Concepts, Methods, and Skills for Research and Intervention* (San Francisco: Jossey-Bass, 1985). These concepts are further applied to organizations in his bestseller *Knowledge for Action: A Guide to Overcoming Barriers to Organizational Change* (San Francisco: Jossey-Bass, Inc. Publishers, 1993). This is also discussed in C. Argyris and D. Schön, *Organizational Learning: A Theory of Action Perspective* (Reading, Mass: Addison Wesley, 1978). Michael Fairbanks and Stace Lindsay applied this model to developing countries in *Plowing the Sea* (Cambridge: Harvard Business School Press, 1997).

[2] "The Next 4 Billion: Market Size and Business Strategy at the Base of the Pyramid," World Resource Institute, 2007, Executive Summary, page 7 http://pdf.wri.org/n4b_executive_summary_graphics.pdf.

[3] Ibid.

[4] Remarks by President Jakaya Kikwete at the World Economic Forum in Africa in Tanzania, May 2010.

[5] *Journal of Economic Perspectives*, http://www.atypon-link.com/AEAP/doi/pdfplus/10.1257/aer.97.2.328

[6] Ibid.

[7] The Millennium Development Goals Report, United Nations, 2007, http://www.un.org/millenniumgoals/pdf/mdg2007.pdf.

[8] Human Development Reports, UNDP, http://hdr.undp.org/en/statistics/data/.

[9] 2008 African Population Data Sheet, Population Reference Bureau, http://www.prb.org/pdf08/africadatasheet2008.pdf.

[10] *African Mobile Handbook 2008* (Blycroft Publishing, 2008), http://www.w3.org/2008/MW4D/wiki/images/9/9c/FrontPage%24Africa_Mobile_Fact_Book_2008.pdf.

[11] Philip English, Bernard Hoekman and Aaditiya Matoo, "Development, Trade, and the WTO: A Handbook," WorldBank, 2002.

2

Rwanda's Metamorphosis

Travel Warning

Boston, August 2001. Toward the end of dinner, Mary pushed an envelope across the table: "I told my dad you were moving to Rwanda. He made me promise to give you this!" I took the package without second thoughts. I was off to Kigali in less than a week.

The next morning, I opened the envelope. Under the seal of the United States, the title read: TRAVEL WARNING. "The US embassy has confirmed continued insurgent activity in Northern Rwanda," it began. The warning almost suggested that Rwanda was still at war. An Internet search confirmed that other western nations had similar travel warnings in place.

The international media coverage confirmed the bad news on Rwanda. Even in 2001, articles dealt primarily with the 1994 genocide as if suggesting that the country's progress had stopped seven years before. The few articles that did not focus on this terrible situation covered the instability in Eastern Congo.

Rwanda's international image was mired in conflict. War correspondents, relief agencies, and civil right groups took up public relations on behalf of the African nation. Notably, there was a complete lack of information on business opportunities and the economy. The result was a disastrous international image that kept investors and tourists alike at bay.

The story was clear: Rwanda was an unsafe country with limited economic prospects stuck in a volatile region. All of this was extremely alarming.

False Alarm

Kigali, September 2001. Rwanda was nothing like what the travel warning suggested. Kigali was beautiful, safe, and clean. Upon the OTF team arrival in Kigali, our visits to ten regions of the country to meet with local leaders confirmed that the beauty, safety, and cleanliness applied to the whole of Rwanda. Surprisingly, the rolling green hills and nice weather put Rwanda closer to the Garden of Eden than the distressing caricature painted internationally.

Yet, Rwanda faced many hardships. Quickly we realized that Rwanda shared very strong similarities with other poor nations with a large BoP population. The fact that Rwanda was a post-conflict nation makes most of these characteristics more pronounced.

The relief community was present in full force. A fleet of 4X4s harboring nongovernmental organizations (NGOs) workers incessantly patrolled the country's roads. This community was engaged in righteous and important work, especially around the management of the country's refugee crisis, healthcare, and other critical social services. To support their activities, these relief organizations invested a vast amount of resources outside the national government's budget.

While this situation created some opportunities for the local private sector, it also brought socioeconomic challenges. Rwanda's economy was still overreliant on the international community. An estimated 80 percent of budget was funded through aid. A large community of relief workers pushed rents beyond the means of the average Rwandan.

The physical and social infrastructure had only started being rebuilt after the 1994 genocide. Power and water shortages were frequent and the road network limited. Human and institutional capital was relatively scarce. Laws, statistics, and processes for getting things done were not clear.

The real problem Rwanda faced was to rebuild itself without any obvious natural or institutional assets. The challenge was to create a sense of nation in a state where the population had seen its rulers turn against the minority. Of notable instance, the historical context of colonial heritage shaped the postcolonial leadership. Poor leadership led to ethnic hatred that produced waves of refugees that had finally come back home in some case after having been gone since 1959. The difficult question was how to create the long-term conditions to migrate from a cycle of violence, poverty, and mistrust to a cycle of peace, prosperity, and trust.

True innovation came from an unexpected place: the Rwandans themselves. There was something fundamentally different about Rwandans. The series of meetings with key government leaders were refreshing. Posturing was replaced by frank discussion. It became clear that no subject that could move the country forward was taboo. The focus on progress could not be mistaken.

A key inheritance from 1994 was a strong belief in the power of mindset to change reality. President Kagame, dubbed "the entrepreneurial President," and his leadership team faced a litany of urgent and important challenges. In appearance, these issues were mostly social—food security, reconciliation, and justice. Nonetheless, the President and his team put a great emphasis on private sector development and competitiveness.

A Fractal of BoP Markets

Acclaimed Nigerian writer Chimamanda Adichie points to the danger of the single story: "The single story creates stereotypes. And the problem with stereotypes is not that they are untrue, but that they are incomplete. They make one story become the only story. The consequence of the single story is this: It robs people of dignity. It makes our recognition of our equal humanity difficult. It emphasizes how we are different rather than how we are similar."[1]

The single story is sometimes the sole information we think we have access to, which sadly leads us to critical misunderstandings. Back in 2001, the single story the world held about Rwanda was one of chaos, destruction, and danger. Somehow, Rwanda had come to epitomize the worst of Africa, a continent already facing a serious perception deficit. The real problem was not about security. In fact, security was not the issue at all. Rwanda was safe.

Executives with experience in Africa will recognize a similarity between Rwanda's challenges and that of the rest of the continent. However, it is important to clarify ways in which the Rwandan experience is representative of and relevant to the rest of the African continent and other BoP markets.

First, the shape of Rwanda's private sector (with a majority of micro-entrepreneurs, a small but growing SME segment, and few large firms) mirrors that of most African countries. A 2003 Study by the World Bank on small and medium enterprises (SMEs) around the globe showed this to be the case throughout developing countries, thus explaining why SMEs are often referred to as the missing middle.[2]

The challenges faced by Rwandan entrepreneurs in 2001 are consistent with those of the rest of the continent—including a difficult business environment; access to finance, capital and inputs; and lack of qualified staff being their top constraints.

While different countries face unique challenges, the essence of being an entrepreneur in Africa is a shared experience. Executives and leaders across the continent must be practical, compare notes, and leverage what works. This book attempts to provide such practical tools.

Finally, while the Rwandan genocide is one of the worst human tragedies the world has witnessed, conflict is not uncommon in Africa—38 out of 53 African nations have had some form of conflict since the 1960s. Most conflicts in Africa are intrastates wars that destroy the fabric of society.

Implications for executives looking to master business in Africa are numerous. First, on average, an economy will be 15 percent smaller at the end of a war.[3] Learning to seize opportunities after conflict is important. This also means that executives have to be willing to work with governments to rebuild nations. In the case of Rwanda, the articulation of Vision 2020 provides a key element of the framework to rebuild the nation.

Traditional methods of measuring poverty are inadequate—a dollar a day does not give us the full picture of an individual's circumstance. While efforts to alleviate poverty are well-meaning, such initiatives can only be a stepping-stone toward the ultimate objective of prosperity creation. What Africa needs is a drive toward prosperity. Such a drive will hinge on a discontinuous productivity leap.

Prosperity creation must become the preeminent issue in every African nation. The struggle for prosperity is a quest for productivity. Productivity matters a great deal in economic development. Harvard

strategist Michael Porter suggests that a nation's prosperity is deter-
mined by the efficiency with which it mobilizes its human, capital,
and natural resources to drive productivity.

However, many BoP nations ignore the product in productivity—
at their own peril. Entrepreneurial solutions for prosperity are about
empowering the stakeholders in society with the best track record of
creating competitive products or solutions. Rwanda has made a bid to
rewrite its history with a focus on prosperity.

Rwanda's Operating Reality

The primary challenge Rwanda's leadership faced was the country's operating reality. The operating reality is best defined as the
unique set of circumstances forming the context under which one
operates a unique combination of cultural, microeconomic, macroeconomic, financial, institutional, environmental, political, and
human capital that defines the set of possible outcomes for any entity.

This operating reality shapes the opportunities and challenges
available to entrepreneurs. It is shaped by internal pressures and
external constraints, as well as the intrinsic sense of possibility or the
prevailing story and accompanying mindsets about the stakeholders.
As such, this operating reality is a powerful force to contend with.

Any real process to bring positive and sustainable change must
begin with a clear understanding of the individual, the business, or
the national operating reality. Such an operating reality is particularly
important in BoP markets, because it provides a clear understanding
of the essence of the situation and sets the stage for what is possible.

Second, operating reality also shapes the mindsets that are at
play, through a continuous feedback loop that integrates data about
the broader environment and the results of certain actions with an
individual's understanding of their ability to shape the environment
through future actions.[4]

In addition to one's impressions, the operating reality can be
measured. In the case of countries, a good way to conduct such
measurements is to start with existing frameworks that seek to provide a holistic view on the state of a nation's development. The World

Economic Forum Global Competitiveness Index offers a great framework.

The framework assesses countries on dimensions such as the effectiveness of public and private institutions, the condition of general infrastructure, and macroeconomic stability. It also measures human factors such as health, education, and economic factors such as the presence of competition, the state of the labor market, and the levels of sophistication of business, finance, and technology.

In summary, Rwanda's operating reality was one of the most difficult in the world for a set of reasons that had nothing to do with the country still being engulfed in genocide, but because it was still recovering from the broader impact of the crisis and, as a result, was stuck in The Survival Trap.

Introducing SOAR

Businesspeople and leaders finding ways to thrive in Rwanda's difficult operating environment had to leverage every arrow in their quivers. In a sense they had to find a way to "soar" out of challenges and the difficult operating reality. Specific actions can be understood within the context of the SOAR framework.[5]

As illustrated in Figure 2.1, effective execution requires a balance among and equal emphasis on strategy, operations, and assets. SOAR can be broken down into the following components:

- **Strategy** Businesspeople must leverage strategy as a rigorous choice-making exercise under difficult circumstances. When resources are limited and the operating environment is complex, strategy takes on a penultimate importance. When resources must be deployed in a bare-bones environment to achieve extraordinary results, good strategy becomes a key differentiator.

- **Operations** Operations is the day-to-day business of executing on the business's mission and vision. Firm-level operations include manufacturing products, moving products between locations, getting those products to customers, marketing and outreach, and essential details such as billing and customer service. With limited resources at a firm's disposal, operations must be lean and efficient.

- **Assets**   When assets are limited, the process of stewardship is both vital and not enough. Businesspeople must work simultaneously to maximize the impact of available assets, while pushing beyond the limitations. In addition to the traditional definitions of assets, other assets include management and business planning capabilities. Human capital is a vital asset that features in both strategic planning and execution.

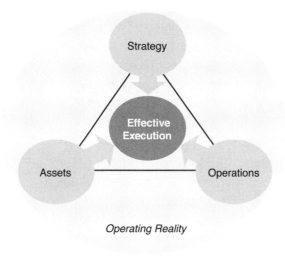

Operating Reality

Figure 2.1   The drivers of effective execution

While a balance of strategy, operations, and assets is necessary to build competitiveness, it is not sufficient. Executing competitiveness strategies successfully requires strategies that are aligned with the prevailing enabling environment.

- **Reality**   Reality represents the context—literally, the operating reality in which a firm does business. Stated differently, this context includes factors such as political, environmental, financial, macroecononic, as well as accounting for microfactors such as infrastructure, human capital, and financial markets. On a deeper dive, reality accounts for the underlying mindsets and the impact they have on other areas of the business.

Many Battles, One Struggle

In 2001, Rwandan stakeholders were engaged in various economic battles. The majority of coffee farmers were severely affected by declining world commercial coffee prices. Most businesses especially those outside of trading were struggling because of a small market combined with high costs. Despite their high moral purpose, government leaders struggled to balance the budget and deliver much needed services to their citizens.

All these individual struggles of Rwandan citizens pointed to one reality: The Survival Trap was in full play in Rwanda. Levels of interpersonal trust were low. There were few businesses, and few exemplified an entrepreneurial mindset. Most traded in undifferentiated products to low-end customer segments. Access to capital was limited. Human and institutional capital was scarce. Businesses were so focused on basic survival that they lacked the resources to think about the long-term societal or environmental impact of their operations. Yet something had to change.

In 2001, the leadership of Rwanda invited OTF Group, a U.S.-based competitiveness firm to assist its efforts in rebuilding its economy. As a member of the OTF Group team, I met JP during our first week in Kigali. A taxi driver, JP became indispensable to us. I came to love JP: He was one of the most opinionated and inquisitive human beings I have met. We quickly became friends. Later, I learned JP was a genocide survivor.

An entrepreneur, JP had managed to own his cab beginning with just three cents after the genocide. When he learned the reason of my presence in Rwanda, JP told me: "Do you know what the problem with most international development experts is? They wish for us what they would not want for themselves!" In true JP fashion he continued: "Seriously who should aspire to make *only* one dollar a day?"

In two sentences, JP had summed up one of my frustrations with the development conversation. To escape the Survival Trap, Africa must embrace entrepreneurial solutions for prosperity. In my experience, one of Rwanda's greatest achievements, one the rest of the continent can emulate, is embracing entrepreneurial solutions for prosperity.

In 2001, the nation's leadership faced a momentous decision—one that President Paul Kagame and his team seized. President Kagame and his team sensed that the nation needed a different approach. Their liberation struggle gave them an intuition backed up by true experience that mindsets were a critical factor in bringing transformation. From this basis, they set out to reinvent Rwanda.

Vision 2020

Visions are often to countries what New Year's resolutions are to individuals: lofty goals pushed aside as soon as reality sets in. Most African countries boast these grandiose visions, often ambitious statements denuded of any practical implications.

Rwanda's leadership is steering the country on a different path: It demands that policy, strategies, programs, and investments actually be measured against Vision 2020.[6] In Vision 2020, Rwanda's leadership sets ambitious goals for the nation's development: to grow its per capita GDP from $250 to $900 between the years 2000 and 2020. Achieving this goal would require Rwanda to expand its economy seven times between 2000 and 2020.

If achieved, Rwanda would be transformed. The Greek word for transformation, *metamorphosis*, is used to describe the amazing change a caterpillar goes through in becoming a butterfly. This powerful metaphor illustrates the transformation Rwanda would undergo under Vision 2020.

The most obvious benefit of this metamorphosis is economical. Vision 2020 will make it possible for the average Rwandan to live in a decent home, access quality healthcare and basic infrastructures (i.e., water and electricity), and educate his or her children. The 80 percent of Rwandans living in rural areas stand to benefit the most from this transformation.

Rwanda's defining conditions in setting an aggressive pace of growth is the shift in mindset from a focus on the country's myriad challenges to future possibilities. The nation's biggest innovation is its reframing of the discussion around wealth creation as opposed to poverty alleviation. Business and enterprise are seen as the engines of prosperity creation.

The Rwandan leadership is less worried about Rwanda's challenges than about its ability to conquer those challenges. Scientists often stress that metamorphosis requires a unique combination of favorable factors. While the caterpillar's metamorphosis is a natural effortless process, transforming Rwanda requires the best the nation can muster.

People are sometimes reluctant to believe in progress. But the evidence is unmistakable. Rwanda's economic performance has already markedly improved since 1994. Most importantly, Rwandans themselves have been at the forefront of the ongoing metamorphosis. We revisit Rwanda's metamorphosis later in the book. In the next chapter, we focus on mindsets and their importance in escaping The Survival Trap.

Endnotes

[1] TED (2009). "The danger of a single story: Chimamanda Adichie on TED.com," http://blog.ted.com/2009/10/the_danger_of_a.php (accessed July 22, 2010).

[2] Kaufman 2005.

[3] Paul Collier, *The Bottom Billion* (Oxford University Press, 2007).

[4] Chris Argyris explicits his action science theory in his book *Action Science, Concepts, Methods, and Skills for Research and Intervention* (San Francisco: Jossey-Bass, 1985). These concepts are further applied to organizations in his bestseller *Knowledge for Action: A Guide to Overcoming Barriers to Organizational Change* (San Francisco: Jossey-Bass, 1993). This is also discussed in C. Argyris and D. Schön *Organizational Learning: A Theory of Action Perspective* (Reading, Mass: Addison Wesley, 1978). Michael Fairbanks and Stace Lindsay applied this model to developing countries in *Plowing the Sea* (Cambridge: Harvard Business School Press, 1997). This article was originally published by OTF Group. The insights discussed are based on the firm's work.

[5] Strategy, Operations, and Assets is an OTF Group framework conceived by Michael Fairbanks. *Execution*, by Larry Bossidy and Ram Charam (2002) provides a discussion of how the balance between strategy, operations, and people is critical to implementation. In addition, Harvard's Merilee Grinde and John Thomas stress the importance of context in developing countries in their book *Public Choices and Policy Change: The Political Economy of Reform in Developing Countries*. The present model is the exclusive property of OTF Group. It is reproduced here with permission of OTF Group.

[6] Government of Rwanda, Ministry of Finance and Economic Planning, http://www.minecofin.gov.rw/squelettes-dist/vision2020.html.

3

Why Mindsets Matter

The Battle for the Minds

I had just landed in Kampala, Uganda, where I was invited to speak to a business and government leaders' colloquium in East Africa. On my way out of the airport, I noticed the familiar sight of billboards. They are pervasive throughout the developing world. Leaders, especially in business and public health, use them to shape our perceptions.

Interestingly, billboards often come in proximate pairs: one portrays attractive models enjoying a beer, presumably using sex to sell the alcohol; and, next to it, a billboard gives the number of the nearest HIV Volunteer Counseling and Testing (VCT) center.

This billboard war phenomenon illustrates the competition to influence how people think about an issue. Business and public health pay top dollar to win this battle.

Businesses seek to influence us to buy a product or a service. Successful public health campaigns result in us changing our behavior. The change in behavior is all the more powerful and lasting when people believe they have reached the conclusion themselves, and billboards work especially well as they seemingly allow people to do that.

The battle for mindshare in BoP markets is raging, with no signs of receding; in fact, competition is intensifying because both business and public health professionals realize that without winning the battle for the mind, no real progress is possible. In Chapter 13, "Societal Innovations Through Mindset Change," we further analyze what businesspeople and other leaders in BoP markets can learn from public health about mindset change that induces new behavior.

In the present chapter, we first explore mindsets and why understanding them is fundamental to escaping The Survival Trap. Our exploration focuses on relevant theoretical underpinnings of mindset and mental models as they relate to prosperity creation in BoP markets. We then offer a framework that is leveraged throughout the book to leverage entrepreneurial solutions for prosperity.

Minister Diallo's Outburst

The next morning, I spoke to an audience of over 250 African business and government leaders and was faced with a situation that made me realize how what a person thinks can bring progress to a screeching halt. When I opened the floor to questions and comments, Minister Diallo grabbed the microphone from the facilitator's hands and loudly and angrily stated: "Why should business lead a country's economic development? That is the government's role. Business is only interested in profits." Like most people in the room, I was surprised by the outburst. The chairperson of the organization sponsoring the meeting responded with, "Minister, your reaction underscores the point made by Mr. Kacou: It is culture that we want to change!" The nods from the seasoned executives in the audience showed their agreement, which only served to aggravate the minister further. I quickly grabbed the microphone back to stop the situation from escalating.

This event solidified my hypothesis that mindsets are the foundation that drive people toward either a successful outcome or keep them stuck in the same place.

The Biggest Elephant in the Room

Businesses know how important mindset is to success. They know that they need to influence customer choice to sell their products, and they invest a lot in delivering marketing plans to gain and retain customers.

Yet, businesses consistently underestimate the impact of mindset on other aspects of their operations. The mindsets of employees, investors, and the community at large shape the playing field for business. The choices made by key stakeholders define business performance and form the broader operating reality. In an era in which no one knows what is the most effective way to build political democracies in the developing world, freedom of choice in the market can be a place where dignity and the democratic exercise of free choice can be promoted. If we can democratize access to prosperity, we increase society's ability to build institutions and increase the potential impact of leaders such as Minister Diallo.

The set of beliefs that people hold about their environment, their culture, social issues, and so on might seem ancillary but are primary factors that affect the local business environment. For example, the difficulty foreign investors face in acquiring land in Africa might at first appear to be due to unreasonable laws but more probably stems out of a long-standing belief that land is the most valuable asset and must be kept in the community. Even when mindsets emerge as an obvious problem, discussion about mindsets is taboo. Such a discussion is difficult and uncomfortable and can cause defensiveness. However, stakeholders interested in change must address mindsets. As illustrated in Figure 3.1, mindsets are powerful in shaping our actions. They drive our outcomes, which in turn affect our operating realities.

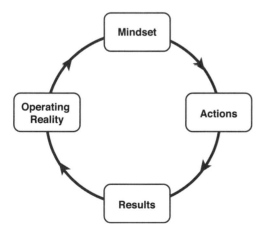

Figure 3.1   The power of mindsets

Defining Mindset

Reasons exist for not discussing mindset in BoP nations, yet the unintended consequences of this behavior are quantifiable. Each reason costs money: It costs firms business; it costs nations foreign investments. It costs the world billions of dollars invested in aid. Each of these reasons contributes to keeping BoP markets stuck in The Survival Trap.

Failure to confront underlying mindsets is the single biggest contributor to perpetuating the status quo. Remember Themba, Mariam, Jaime, Lisa, Ijeoma, and Rob. Each one of these leaders must confront the fact that they harbor mental models that perpetuate their being stuck in The Survival Trap. As long as stakeholders hold the same mental models, they will continue taking the same actions and getting the same results, and the cycle of poverty goes unbroken.

Yet in reality, globalization and increasingly competitive business environments demand complex and flexible strategies from individuals, firms, and governments alike. Competition that was once local or regional has gone global; firms in Ghana are likely to compete with firms in Brazil and China for local business. Firms must contend with complex, global supply chains. Demanding customers must be served from afar. Doing things the way it has always been done is no longer an option.

This is not a challenge only for businesspeople. For instance, government leaders such as Ijeoma must realize that overreliance on aid without steady investments to create a favorable operating reality for business and reinforce the capacity of indigenous firms are not sustainable. Development partners must also operate a similar mental model shift. Businesspeople and other leaders need a user manual to handle something as powerful as mindsets. The ability to "clearly name the elephant"—that is, to define, discuss, and understand mindset—is an important first step to addressing mindsets.

Few have been exposed to the terms *mental models*, *paradigms*, or *frames*. Instead, a host of other terms exist in our vocabulary related to mindsets such as *assumptions*, *attitudes*, *attributions*, *beliefs*, *norms*, *stereotypes*, *and values*. For the purposes of this book,

I use the terms *mental models* and *mindsets* to reflect on or convey these concepts.

Our discussion of mental models borrows heavily from Jonathan Donner's article *Making Mental Models Explicit: Quantitative Techniques for Encouraging Change*.[1] Building on the literature on mental models, Donner defines mental models, offers specific techniques to leverage them for change in the developing world based on the experience of the OTF Group working with mental models throughout the developing world.

Donner reminds us that "mental models," is a term attributed to sociologist Walter Lippmann who, in the early 20th century, suggested that "to traverse the world men must have maps of the world."

Lippman suggests that human beings use fictions to help them deal with and interpret the complexity of the real world, its subtlety, variety, and permutations. Mental models are the shortcuts we routinely use in our choices and decisions: they are both the structure and the strategy. They shape how we think about the world, which in turn drives the actions that we take.

In psychological terminology, mental models represent both paradigms and frames. Paradigms are general notions about what's important, and how things relate to one another. Frames are situation-specific scripts that guide expectations and behavior choices. Specific examples are useful in better comprehending both paradigms and frames.

Let's revisit the case of Themba, where a host of paradigms and frames are at play. For instance, Themba holds the paradigm that his responsibility is to provide for his firm. While this paradigm is at the heart of Themba's entrepreneurial drive, it can also prevent him from finding collaborative solutions.

Specifically, Themba's suppliers and the staff of ITC could do more to support Themba in his struggle. Suppliers may be able to reorganize payment terms provided that certain assurances are given. Some employees may be willing to accept delayed payrolls or temporary salary reductions, thereby spreading the financial burden to make it more bearable.

Themba operates under the frame that to sell new business will enable him to address pressing cash flow issues. This reaction is natural, as new business generates cash that can help keep the business afloat. However, selling new business to address past problems is akin to throwing good money after bad.

Both examples illustrate how paradigms and frames contribute to giving Themba the experience of standing in quicksand, as his responsibilities to deliver increase without a corresponding increase in the resources needed to get this done. In both examples, escaping The Survival Trap is only possible if Themba can understand and subsequently change his mental models and the resultant behavior. Themba's mental models—both paradigms and frames—are making a difficult situation worse.

Characterizing Mental Models

Now that we have established a common vocabulary about mindsets, we can develop a common understanding as to what they mean by looking at their characteristics. These characteristics provide a useful lens through which to understand the importance of mental models in escaping The Survival Trap.

Again, building on the article of Donner, mental models have numerous characteristics, seven which are important in our quest to escape The Survival Trap:

1. *Mental models are individual in nature.* At an essential level, each person holds mental models that are personal and specific in nature. The individual must be the focus in any process aiming to change mental models. Individuals, even from common backgrounds, hold different mental models.

    Minister Diallo holds a very personal belief about the need for government to drive economic development. Furthermore, he appears skeptical vis-à-vis the motivations of business toward society. This belief may be substantiated with his experience dealing with certain businesspeople in his country.

2. *Mental models have a social dimension.* Mental models are learned through interactions with other individuals. As such, mental models tend to be correlated or shared across groups or societies. This has direct implications for firms, industry

clusters, nations, and the global community—for any group that is centered on economic transactions.

At the meeting, Minister Diallo may be expressing aloud what many government or even business leaders think. One of the effects of colonialism in Africa is a paternalistic view of government where it assumed that the public sector must provide for the entire society.

3. *Mental models are active.* Mental models influence the choices we make and provide our blueprint for action. By extension, they dictate our impact and results in the world. It is only by changing our mental models, therefore, that we are able to really effect change.

   One example that mental models are active is the fact that Minister Diallo acted to express his disagreement about the notion of private sector led development. If this belief prompted him to act in this specific case, we can well imagine that he would also trigger other choices such as how to structure potential projects.

4. *Mental models often become implicit.* We are frequently not aware of our mental models on specific issues. Implicit mental models put us on automatic pilot, and undermine our ability to choose, scrutinize, discuss, or change them. Implicit mental models are often at play in vicious cycles. This characteristic is of particular relevance for The Survival Trap.

   This trap borrows most of its power from its implicit nature. The Minister may not have been aware of how strong his belief on government leadership was until he heard it mentioned twice in two different speeches at the meeting two days in a row.

5. *Mental models shape our context and vice versa.* As mental models are learned, they are a direct result of our context. Simultaneously, our mental models shape our context through the results our actions generate. The interactions between mental models and our context provide us with a new and powerful lever to change the business environment in Africa.

   As discussed before, Minister Diallo may be expressing aloud what many government and even business leaders think. One of the effects of colonialism in Africa is a paternalistic view of government where it assumed that the public sector must provide for the entire society.

6. ***Mental models can be measured.*** If the intangible or implicit nature of mental models makes them difficult to comprehend, that mental models can be measured is a relief. The objective quantification of mental models is essential to changing them, particularly in institutional environments. Measuring mental models allows us to assess the effectiveness of any intervention by showing their change over time.

7. ***Mental models can be changed.*** Envision a world where our mental models never changed. We would never experiment, innovate, or grow. Mental models are not static; they evolve over time as result of outside influence, external circumstances, or an active effort to alter our mindset.

More than any other characteristic, this last one holds the key to escaping The Survival Trap. The potential for change means that being caught in The Survival Trap is not a fatal. We do not have to be victims.

Instead, we can choose to escape this vicious cycle, we can choose to change our mental models, and in the process increase our chance at regaining control. The rationale behind my speech was an attempt at making the mental explicit. It was also perhaps to try to change the mental models of the leaders present.

Armed with a clear definition and clear characteristics of mental models, we examine how misconceptions about mental models contribute to perpetuating The Survival Trap.

Misconceptions about Mindset Change

Misconceptions about mindset hinder the ability of stakeholders in BoP markets to escape The Survival Trap. Such misconceptions create defensiveness which makes stakeholders less likely to collaborate or to upgrade their behavior. Fairbanks and Lindsay identify defensiveness as one of the foremost patterns undermining prosperity in developing nations.[2]

My interaction with Minister Diallo provides a good example of the main misconceptions at play.

The first misconception is that mental models equal culture. In his response to Minister Diallo, the Chairperson claims: "It is this culture we want to change." While mental models are a core aspect of one's identity, collapsing mental models and culture can set off landmines in the conversation about mindset change.

We must be explicit that mindset transcends culture. Mental models are not about food, marriage customs, or the validity of heritage. Instead, they are individual assumptions you hold about how the world works. Anyone would resist changing their belief and attitude if they thought their culture was at stake.

In the context of most BoP markets with a colonial history, this misconception presents a formidable barrier. One of Africa's biggest worries is that of becoming assimilated five decades after gaining independence. This very real fear spurs defense mechanisms. Authority, media convergence, and cultural integration often provide a basis for these fears.

It is important to draw a clear distinction between mental models related to business and prosperity creation, and culture and identity. A useful approach here is to frame the discussion as an inquiry into whether a specific belief is conducive or obtrusive to a specific outcome.

In responding to Minister Diallo's comments, a useful framing is the official stance of his government's stated vision to foster economic growth through investments and exports. Looking at our exchange through this prism makes his belief in government dominance of the economic debate a position that could be challenged. It also gives him the opportunity to change his mind without losing face.

The second notable misconception is the idea that everyone must agree before change can occur. While a consensus is desirable, what is truly important is an understanding of the different points of view. It is necessary for businesspeople seeking to foster mindset change to be able to operate in the face of disagreement.

Divergence in mental models is useful and desirable in facing difficult problems such as The Survival Trap. Innovative solutions emerge when one seeks to reconcile such divergence. In the exchange with Minister Diallo, one way to communicate with him was to share specific cases of enterprise-based solutions to poverty. Moving out of survival requires embracing new tool sets that don't undermine what is best serving human capital in a certain culture.

It is helpful to get at least a common ground to leap from so disagreement is transcended and trust can be built. Everyone agrees on growing wealth so disagreement should be overcome even if it is superficial and will require belief to be sustained by later proven results.

The third misconception is divorcing mindset change from action and results. Leaders must be clear about their objective in fostering mindset change and define it as a measurable result achievable through specific actions. Businesspeople and other leaders should thus think of specific attitudes and beliefs that hinder stakeholders from taking the required actions. Identifying stakeholders' fears could be a place to start. This distinction is important in avoiding a situation where mindset campaign becomes hollow and fails to produce specific results. The clearer the leader can be and the greater capacity the leader has for dismantling stakeholders' fears by listening to their concerns and addressing what comes up, the more effective the outcome will be.

With hindsight, I must bear some of the responsibility in triggering Minister Diallo's defensiveness because my statement lacked specificity. Engaging in a more targeted analysis of the situation in his country to unearth specific behavior and ancillary mindsets may have gone a long way toward increasing his receptiveness to my presentation.

Having established an understanding of what mindsets are and what characterized them, the next section outlines targeted actions entrepreneurs can take to escape The Survival Trap. Each of these actions, called the Seven Entrepreneurial Solutions for Prosperity, addresses a specific underlying mindset or series of assumptions that impact the way in which an entrepreneur does business, particularly in the emerging markets context.

Seven Opportunities to Escape The Survival Trap

Escaping The Survival Trap requires a change in mental models at two levels. On the one hand, government, development partners, and civil society must appreciate the role of business in prosperity creation. On the other hand, businesspeople must embrace different beliefs and attitudes to create human and stakeholder value while generating profits.

Several cross-cutting mindsets stand in the way of the change described previously. The entrepreneurial solutions to escape The Survival Trap must begin by recognizing these cross-cutting mindsets. To transcend these barriers, these solutions must offer a concrete new behavior that is rooted in a different mindset. Briefly, these seven opportunities are listed here and in Figure 3.2.

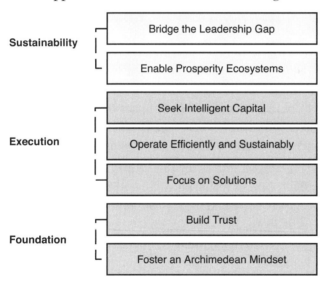

Figure 3.2   Seven opportunities to escape The Survival Trap

Foster an Archimedean mindset: Around 200 BC, Archimedes made a formidable dare: "Give me a lever long enough and a fulcrum on which to place it and I shall move the world." Archimedes remains unchallenged. Two thousand years later, the world still is searching for the lever and the fulcrum to lift a large proportion of the population in BoP markets especially in Africa out of poverty.

An Archimedean mindset recognizes that businesspeople and other leaders have an imperative to create human value while generating adequate risk-adjusted returns. Such value translates into businesses that strive to address the needs of all stakeholders innovatively. Such a mindset goes beyond business as usual in BoP markets.

An Archimedean mindset addresses zero-sum thinking, a cross-cutting mindset in developing nations. People with this mindset believe that their gain or loss is exactly balanced by the losses or gains of other stakeholders.

Dr. Manu Chandaria of Kenya and Talabi Tokunbo of Nigeria are archetypes of two Archimedean business leaders discussed in two separate vignettes in the second part of the book. **Build trust:** Trust is one of the highest forms of business capital. Yet, it is one of the scarcest resources in BoP markets especially in Africa. The prevalence of the zero-sum mindset often means that everyone seeks to take advantage of other stakeholders. The absence of sound institutions aggravates this lack of trust.

Executives must strive to build trust with all stakeholders through specific behavior that demonstrates their trustworthiness. Such behaviors must be rooted in integrity and empathy. Building trust reduces the cost of doing business and the impact business can have at the bottom of the pyramid and elsewhere. This is especially important in environments where governance is a critical issue.

While trust is created at the individual level, its impact goes beyond the individual to affect firms, clusters, and national business environments. In Chapter 6, "Build Trust," we look at ways in which Jean Kacou Diagou of Cote d'Ivoire has built one of West Africa's leading insurance groups by leveraging trust and discuss implications for other business leaders.

Focus on solutions: Focusing on solutions is about drawing inspiration from the reality of a business's stakeholders to articulate offerings that don't just create value for all involved. Focusing on solutions is about defeating the cross-cutting mindset of copycat where businesses believe the key to success is to replicate a successful offering and compete on price. The Survival Trap exacerbates this copycat mindset.

Firms play a critical role in developing products and services that can create human value. The success or failure of products must stop being seen exclusively as a private problem. The private sector is uniquely positioned to identify critical market needs: It has both the skills and incentives to create such solutions.

Such offerings require a different way to apprehend innovation as well as the process of product development. Discussed in separate vignettes, Nuru Light in sustainable energy and Kaelo Consulting in healthcare are two separate businesses who demonstrate how a focus on solutions can translate into innovation and business success.

Operate efficiently and sustainably: This is about delivering solutions to customers in the most resource-efficient and environmentally friendly way possible. If strategy focuses on what do we sell to whom, then efficient and sustainable operations is about how do ensure the best possible process, systems, and activities.

The Survival Trap often means that businesspeople and other leaders must focus on the short term. This short-term focus is the main cross-cutting challenge they must address in achieving efficient and sustainable operations. BoP businesspeople must demonstrate foresight to improve both operational effectiveness and environmental sustainability.

Rwanda tourism industry illustrates how a focus on efficient and sustainable operations can happen beyond the border of one firm to encompass an entire industry or cluster. We also learn from Nuru Light whose businesspeople are anchored in operating efficiently and sustainably.

Enable prosperity ecosystems: The prevalence of defensiveness and lack of trust in BoP markets is a barrier to collaboration. Yet, the myriad challenges inherent to the operating reality in developing countries require that the best minds pool resources to find collaborative and inbred solutions to the challenges posed by The Survival Trap.

Enabling prosperity ecosystems is about creating the conditions and networks for businesspeople and other leaders to leverage entrepreneurial solutions for prosperity. Such conditions and networks begin with accepting that the unique operating reality in BoP markets requires customized solutions as opposed to a one-size-fit-all model.

By creating the first profitable chain of business incubators in Africa, South African Allon Raiz demonstrates that businesspeople can make money out of enabling prosperity ecosystems.

Seek intelligent capital: Business often cites a lack of access to capital as a major constraint to growth and ongoing operations. Empirical evidence shows that money can be hard to come by in BoP markets. At the same time, the perception of risk versus reward is as a powerful mindset that acts as a barrier to the efficient allocation of the limited pool of capital. Seeking intelligent capital goes beyond looking for money. Selecting the right capital partner who is focused on providing solutions, rather than just on achieving a specific return, will enable entrepreneurs to grow businesses wisely. Intelligent capital will help a business not only access financing but also realize its business objectives and deliver human value. India's IT giant, UST Global, is an illustration of the power of intelligent capital in fostering the birth of vibrant businesses.

Bridge the leadership gap: Businesspeople and other leaders alike often look elsewhere for solutions to their problems. Ownership of one's opportunities and problems is a critical mindset for prosperity creation and is at the heart of leadership. Leadership is vital to driving mindset change across all levels of society.

Such leadership combines critical elements: a shared vision that recognizes business as an engine of growth, redefined leadership that includes all stakeholders, a focused agenda for growth based on agreed-upon priorities, a culture of implementation and execution, a sense of ownership, and clear opportunities for capacity building.

Alexandre de Carvalho and Eva Muraya are examples of a corporate manager and an entrepreneur operating in different contexts yet having tremendous business success and social impact through their ability to bridge the leadership gap.

The diagnostic in Table 3.1 offers an at-a-glance toolbox for businesspeople and other leaders to begin identifying which mindsets may be impacting firms:

TABLE 3.1   Key Diagnostic Questions for Entrepreneurial Solutions for Prosperity

Opportunity	Related Questions
Develop an Archimedean mindset	What value are you seeking to create for which stakeholders through your business?
	How does your business model balance profits against stakeholder value?
Build trust	What specific challenges do you face with your stakeholders that could be addressed through greater trust?
	What practices do you have in place that improve stakeholders trust?
Focus on solutions	How innovative is your current product offering?
	How do you have to learn from your customers and stakeholders in developing products and services?
Operate efficiently and sustainably	What resources does your business take from or put into the environment?
	How can you minimize these wastes and resource extractions?
Seek intelligent capital	Do you have access to adequate financial capital?
	What do your financial partners contribute beyond financial resources?
Enable prosperity ecosystems	Do you currently face any business challenges that could be solved through collaboration?
	What key relationships are in place with your stakeholders and how do they impact your business?
Bridge the leadership gap	How does your business define good corporate citizenship?
	Does your organization possess the necessary human capital?

Building on individual case studies of specific businesses, the next section of the book offers practical insight on how businesspeople can leverage each one of those opportunities to succeed in BoP markets. We further illustrate these with vignettes of actual entrepreneurs, manager and other leaders who have succeeded using the seven opportunities. In Chapter 14, "Rwanda's Homegrown Solutions," we come back to Rwanda to learn how the African nation has leveraged the seven opportunities above to transform its economy.

The Essence-Principles-Practices Framework

How do businesspeople and other leaders leverage the seven entrepreneurial solutions for prosperity? The Essence-Principles-Practice framework provides a useful key (see Figure 3.3). The Survival Trap draws its power from stakeholders focus on the challenges inherent to the operating reality.

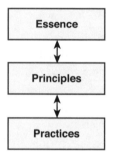

Figure 3.3   The Essence-Principle-Practice framework

The Essence illuminates the core issue at play, the underlying mindset affecting that particular strategic area, and underscores the piece of the operating reality that is out of balance. The Principle outlines the key mental models and nuances at play around each entrepreneurial solution, enabling businesspeople or other leaders to understand and ultimately change the beliefs and ideas impacting her own performance at a deeper level. Finally, Practices represent proactive and pragmatic actions the businesspeople or other leaders can take to correct deficits and have a strategic impact in critical areas of her business.

Let's explore each component in greater detail.

Essence: Understanding the essence of each opportunity enables us to understand the way in which a particular area, such as building trust or the leadership gap, negatively impacts a business. As outlined previously, firms caught in The Survival Trap must contend with a plethora of urgent issues. The essence represents the ability of businesspeople or other leaders to step back from the background noise of day-to-day operations and articulate the key strategic challenge facing them. Stated another way, essence allows us to answer the following question: What particular insight will help identify underlying mindsets that are not working and subsequently enable behavior changes that lead to different results?

Principles: The principles provide additional grounding and explanation of the nuances of the essence, enabling the businesspeople or other leaders to understand and ultimately change the beliefs and idea impacting their performance at a deeper level. Each opportunity, such as focusing on solutions or operating sustainably and efficiently, can be broken down into a subset of supporting ideas that enable us to focus more specifically on areas for further consideration, improvement, and action.

Practice: Practices represent proactive and pragmatic actions businesspeople or other leaders can take to correct deficits and have impact in critical areas of their operations. Here it helps to be able to trace the impact of each practice on the Strategy, Operations, Assets, and Operating Reality of the business or organization. When businesspeople and other leaders understand the essence of an opportunity and have taken a deeper dive into the underlying mindsets by exploring the principles, they are then able to initiate change by focusing on specific practices that represent behavior change. Over time, principles and practices interact through a virtuous cycle—as practices in play yield different results, mindsets change, which in turn leads to a more permanent change or transformation in actions.

Building on the Essence-Principle-Practices framework, Chapter 4, "A Framework to Escape The Survival Trap," provides an overview of the process that businesspeople can leverage to escape The Survival Trap. We use the example of Jaime, our mining executive operating in Latin America, to guide executives on the way to not only unearth but also address core mindset at play in most business situations.

Winning the Battle for the Minds

Billboards offer only a glimpse at the battle of the minds currently underway. The Survival Trap suggests that the real battle of the minds is happening. The core of the battle happens within the individual. As personal and abstract constructs, mental models can only be changed at the individual level.

This realization is both good news and bad news. The bad news is that mental models are not considered by most stakeholders. Taboos exist about discussing them, and techniques for changing and measuring them are not well understood.

Embracing entrepreneurial solutions for prosperity is a challenging process; the ongoing debate between the proponents of more aid and those who want aid dead is an illustration of this challenge. Yet it is an important process for BoP markets especially Africa and the world needs to undertake it to escape The Survival Trap.

Winning the battle for the minds is key to escaping The Survival Trap. In the second part of the book, we offer a framework to leverage the Seven Entrepreneurial Solutions for Prosperity. We then discuss each opportunity in turn building on typical cases to illustrate the specific tools and techniques at the disposal of businesspeople and other leaders to escape The Survival Trap.

Vignette 1—Haiti: Reclaiming the Citadelle

A small group of nations seem to have a monopoly on hard knocks. The January 12th earthquake increases Haiti's position on this infamous list. Since its independence some two hundred years ago, many disasters have struck Haiti. Yet, most astute observers would suggest that the worst ones are manmade.

Almost a year before the earthquake, there was great news in Haiti that went under-reported. A coalition of Haitians leaders from business, government, and civil society came together under the Groupe de Compétitivaté (GC), a presidential working group on competitiveness to articulate a shared vision for prosperity for all in Haiti.

On December 9, 2009, addressing the President and country's leadership, Gladys Coupet,[3] the GC Coordinator, remarked: "After much consultation and analysis, we now have an inclusive prosperity agenda to create five hundred thousand jobs in three years. We owe it to our citizens to achieve this vision through implementation."

Reclaiming the Citadel

Completed in 1820, Haiti's Citadelle La Ferrière has come to symbolize Haiti's struggle for independence. Started right after the independence this massive fort engulfed vast resources and claimed the lives of 15,000 Haitians. Interestingly, the fort never served its military purpose but it demonstrated the enduring spirit of Haitians.

Since the Citadelle, many of Haiti's efforts to build a better future have been misguided. The nation's elites perpetuated the same exploitative model resulting in the vast majority of Haitians living hand to mouth. The failure of the country's elite to empower the BoP only digs Haiti deeper in the Survival Trap.

To illustrate, Haiti's per capita GDP was 405USD in 2006, with a drop of nearly 50% from 1981 levels. Eighty percent of Haitians today live on small-scale subsistence agriculture. Bernard, a Port-au-Prince business owner remarked once: "We all live behind huge walls and drive in bullet proof cars because our economic model has failed. We need a new model."

The Real Problem—Escaping The Survival Trap

Bernard has said aloud what most businesspeople in BoP markets sense. Outdated economic models keep the BoP in misery, while threatening the elite with bankruptcy as the developed world continues to inject development aid to keep economies afloat. What are business leaders to do in such cases?

Similar private sector led vision efforts have taken place throughout the developing world. In April 2010, the Private Sector Apex body launched a visioning exercise entitled Cote d'Ivoire 2030. In the early nineties, South Africa's business leader supported the Mont Fleur scenario to craft the nation's post-Apartheid agenda.

These efforts are the exception rather than the rule. When confronted with economies that are stuck in The Survival Trap, business leaders prefer to behave like "disgruntled tax payers," complaining to whoever will listen, evading taxes when they can get away with it and pursuing short term opportunities.

Successfully changing the private sector's mindset toward prevailing challenges begins with owning the problem. As discussed throughout this section of the book, The Survival Trap is the real culprit. Escaping The Survival Trap begins with a clear characterization of its pernicious effects.

Stuck in The Survival Trap

Haiti is the archetype of the nation stuck in The Survival Trap. At 330 people per square kilometer, Haiti is one of the world's most densely populated nations. With approximately 80 percent of Haitians living from small-scale subsistence farming, erosion has become not only a major environmental but also a survival issue for Haiti.

Simultaneously an equally detrimental erosion of trust and social capital is spreading throughout the country. In a recent survey, 61 percent of respondents suggested other Haitians were not trustworthy.[4] Furthermore, Haiti's history is a testimony that only a small elite can prosper at the expense of the BoP. This also creates a zero-sum mindset.

Combined lack of trust and zero-sum mindsets have done more damage to Haiti than any military attacks could have inflicted upon the Citadelle. Haiti's model failed its citizens at all levels of the economic pyramid. In 2009, empirical evidence provided a sobering picture on how The Survival Trap was affecting Haiti:

Haiti's export sectors are depressed with garment, agriculture, and tourism under price pressure which is leading to an erosion of the asset base throughout the island.

Sixty-three percent of SMEs surveyed reported that their profits had declined.[5] Owners had to invest their savings to keep operating.

A vast majority of educated Haitians emigrated in search of greener pasture mostly to the US leaving the nation under-capitalized humanly.

The overall business environment was fraught with challenges that hindered economic activity.

Toward a Shared Vision for Haiti

The GC knew that it faced an uphill challenge when it accepted its mandate from President René Préval. Under the leadership of Gladys Coupet, the twenty-member GC enlisted the help of OTF Group to facilitate the national change process and enable informed decision through rigorous analysis.

The group articulated a bold shared vision statement: "Haiti creates opportunities for the majority of Haitians through a competitive, sustainable, and diversified economy. Jobs, income, and entrepreneurship are the cornerstone of the modernization of the economy. Haiti regains its economic strength by unifying its society and genuine integration into global economy."

Specifically, this translated into three concrete goals. First, Haiti creates 500,000 jobs mostly in SMEs and rural areas. Second, the nation reduces its dependency on aid. Finally, trust is rebuilt in Haiti as the nation's various stakeholders begin to work together to implement the shared vision.

Rebuilding Haiti

Almost a year after the January earthquake, the international community is still struggling to find its mark in Haiti and deliver much-needed relief. It has taken many meetings to come to the point where Haitians through the GC were in December 2009: Priority number one for Haiti to escape The Survival Trap is quality jobs.

Haiti's greatest hope lies not in the pity of the international community but in the commitment of Haitians from all walks of life to articulate, share, and implement a shared vision of prosperity for all. The enduring spirit of Haiti that prevailed when the Citadelle was built is the same that must prevail today.

Endnotes

[1] Jonathan Donner, *Making Mental Models Explicit: Quantitative Techniques for Encouraging Change, Seeds for Change,* OTF Group, 2001. This article was originally published by OTF Group. The insights discussed are based on the firm's work.

[2] Michael Fairbanks and Stace Lindsay applied this model to developing countries in *Plowing the Sea* (Cambridge: Harvard Business School Press, 1997).

[3] Chairperson of the Groupe de Compétitivité, Gladys Coupet is a prominent private sector leader in Haiti and the country officer of Citibank.

[4] OTF Group National Competitiveness Survey, Haiti, May 2009.

[5] Ibid.

4

A Framework to Escape
The Survival Trap

Crisis Time

It has been 43 weeks since Jaime slept more than four hours per night. His worst fears have come true. The protesters have mounted a formidable effort with significant support from the local and international press.

What makes Jaime truly sad is that despite the billions of investments and taxes paid by MineGroup, the government has given its tacit support to the protesters, rather than coming out to signal the positive impact of one of the largest businesses in the country.

Free One-Way Ticket Survival

When confronted with an opportunity or a crisis, most executives resort to their winning formula. Salesmen sell. Engineers optimize. Managers streamline. Fundraisers raise more money. Talent pickers upgrade their teams. More becomes the motto.

Smart leaders resort to a combination of actions adapted to their organizations. Managers of large businesses look for wide ranging action plans. Entrepreneurs scout for the next opportunity. Managers of public institutions restructure. Political leaders build coalitions. Development partners inject more money.

As executives spring into action, resorting to strategies that have worked well in the past they often fail to assess whether a new or different strategy would be more effective given the operating reality. Resorting de facto to comfortable strategies can complicate things. In fact, it can make executives and their organizations vulnerable to The Survival Trap.

This reflex, of action untempered by strategic thought, has dire consequences in bottom of the pyramid markets. It keeps businesses struggling, makes clusters uncompetitive, and locks nations in a dependency mode. Ultimately, it keeps a large proportion of the population at the bottom of the pyramid. In short, it perpetuates The Survival Trap.

The real question executives must ask when confronted with critical situations is: What do we do when more of the same action is not enough?

Action Framework, Mindsets, and Business Models

Chris Argyris's action framework[1] provides a powerful tool to begin answering this question. In Chapter 2, "Rwanda's Metamorphosis," we explored the relationship between results, actions, mindsets, and operating reality. The Survival Trap ensnares leaders who fail to understand the inherent connections between these elements.

Let's apply the action framework to business. To measure results, executives rely on a variety of metrics to ascertain business performance in a comprehensive manner. These metrics evaluate organizational performance across five drivers: customers, costs, capabilities, competition, and context.

MineGroup, described above, is in a difficult position. Mining companies face tremendous pressure from a host of stakeholders with different agendas all accusing the mining company of wrongdoing. In the spirit of fairness, the track record of mining companies has been questionable.

Yet, in this specific case, stakeholders are already protesting Mine-Group operations while the company has not had a chance to deploy its business model. This has translated into vandalism, a high rate of theft on the mine property, union issues, and massive demonstrations.

The wave of leftist government that has swept through Central and South America has made matters worse. MineGroup personifies the North American giant coming to the region to exploit and extract resources with limited benefits to the local population. This is resource nationalism at its best. It does not seem to matter that the firm is investing billions and creating thousands of jobs.

Executives must consider the specific implications of their actions. Organizational success resides in a firm's ability to serve customers. The organization's business model encapsulates this ability, and is made of four dimensions: strategy, operations, assets, and reality. The choices executives make on these four dimensions define success.

MineGroup's business model relies heavily on acquisition to consolidate its operations globally and mobilize required resources to invest in the capital-intensive mining industry. The company's global value chain focuses on extractions in developing nations and value addition in a few global locations.

Things become less obvious when we get to underlying mindsets. While the role of culture in organizations is known, most executives struggle to influence or shape organizational culture. Mindsets affect both the four dimensions and the five drivers of performance.

In the case of MineGroup, a useful way to examine mindsets is to analyze stakeholder groups. For instance, workers and the community feel that wealth is a fixed pie (an example of zero-sum thinking). Their perception is that MineGroup must be exploiting them given the return it delivers for its shareholders. Suspicion against international investors is particularly high.

The operating reality is the silent influencer that often closes doors or creates opportunities for entrepreneurs. Three interrelated parts make up the context in which organizations operate: the organizational context, the national environment, and the international community. As noted before, the context is also informed by the results of previous actions.

Jaime operates in a difficult operating reality at MineGroup. A host of activists have taken MineGroup under their microscope, attacking its every move around the globe. Their main complaint stems from the environmental practices the firm had in the past. While it has begun changing things, the activists believe it is too little too late.

Strategic Approaches to Integrate Mindset Change to Business Models

The Survival Trap affects myriad stakeholders in BoP markets. Any strategy to break out of the trap must recognize this variety and address two imperatives. A successful strategy must encompass core mindsets that either block or favor superior performance, and offer a clear process to integrate mindsets with business performance. Solutions must provide tangible benefits to the organization, equipping executives to improve their five drivers of performance.

Assessing prevailing mindsets and their subsequent economic impacts provides guidance for selecting one of four approaches available for changing mindsets. Mindsets are ranked according to the degree they influence economic performance, and if they help or hinder an organization's overall objectives. Figure 4.1 offers a choice matrix, grouping options into four categories: defeat, alter, redirect, and emphasize (DARE).

- **Defeat**   Neutralize mindsets that undermine economic performance.
- **Alter**   Change unfavorable mindsets that are not critical to performance.
- **Redirect**   Redirect favorable, but noncritical mindsets, toward achieving high priority economic objectives.
- **Emphasize**   Stimulate, stress, and support favorable, high economic impact mindsets.

Choosing wisely among these four strategic approaches depends on clearly articulated strategic and performance objectives. This requires assessing both the nature of prevailing mindsets at an organization and understanding their impact on economic performance.

Courage, or the ability to dare to bring about the required change, is important in the process to transform a market. Executives must demonstrate courage in their ability to confront the mindsets at play in a productive way, and DARE to make the changes required to their business models.

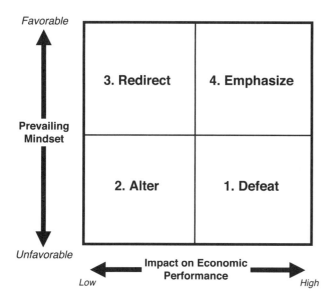

Figure 4.1   The DARE strategic approach to harnessing the opportunities

Defeat

Defeating unfavorable mindsets that highly impact economic performance requires executives to remember that mindset change, especially for large groups, is at best a medium term endeavor. With this in mind, executives must also assemble the right team to lead the campaign required to attain the result.

Building a team or critical mass of stakeholders willing to participate in the campaign is crucial to the effort's success. Opinion leaders should be selected based on their credibility as ambassadors, their communication ability, and their execution capacity in implementing new actions.

Alter

Using an "alter" strategy is often a way to deal with unfavorable mindsets before they mature into major threats to bottom line performance. Both mindsets and economic performance are dynamic. Executives must therefore be prescient in identifying those mindsets that have the potential to evolve into real barriers in the future.

On a cautionary note, altering unfavorable mindsets with low economic impact is still mindset change with all its imbedded challenges. Rather than trying to address all mindsets at once with a risk of diluting their focus, executives must avoid being distracted. Mindsets to alter should be lower priority than the ones previously discussed.

Redirect

A favorable mindset is too precious to waste, often hiding great strategic opportunity. Favorable mindsets can be refocused to help a firm or an institution reach its objectives.

Creativity is required in identifying these mindsets, which can be overlooked if they are not of immediate and obvious strategic importance. Adjustment is required in finding ways to take advantage of such mindsets. Such mindsets can be reinforced in the company's values to gain greater adherence toward the firm's overarching objectives, or to address other existing mindsets that are less favorable.

Emphasize

Executives should emphasize favorable mindsets with high economic impact to advance the firm's objective and its impact. This process involves both recognition and hardwiring.

Incentives must be created for key stakeholders to recognize, champion, and perpetuate positive mindsets. Simple practices such as recognizing stakeholders that best exemplify the mindsets and its associated behaviors are critical. Clear practices are needed to hardwire these mindsets in their business culture and the way their firms operate.

Leveraging the DARE Strategic Approaches

Mindsets require different treatments depending on their impact on economic performance. To be effective in escaping The Survival Trap, executives must use the right combination of DARE strategic approaches depending on the situation.

Prioritization is a vital step. Trying to change the wrong mindsets is not only inefficient but also counterproductive. It can give stakeholders the experience of being looked down upon instead of being treated as partners.

The process requires going beyond a one-time response toward an enduring discipline. Such a shift in perspective requires a clear demonstration of the benefits that thinking and acting differently can bring to businesses and the nations in which they operate.

A successful change process must integrate the two dimensions of thinking and acting differently. While the DARE strategic approaches provide some guidance on mindsets, that guidance must be complemented with a change process to upgrade the business model.

The DARE Process

This process is a systematic approach that that can be leveraged to bring change in their businesses. Figure 4.2 provides a description of this change model:

The DARE process comprises two distinct yet complementary parts: mindset change and business strategy. The analytical component forces executives to make informed choices. The process facilitates timely action. Both dimensions are important to escape The Survival Trap.

This process is structured to offer a combination of short- and long-term results. Escaping The Survival Trap takes time, but sustaining the momentum of the change process requires delivering quick wins.

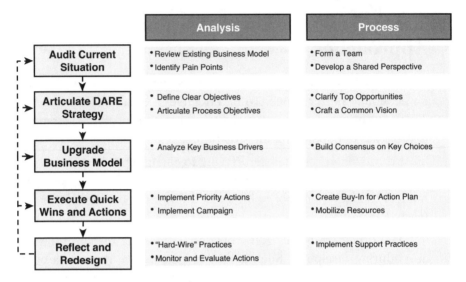

Figure 4.2   The DARE process

To achieve this, the process combines three important dimensions: essences, principles, and practices. We discuss these in Chapter 2. Building on clear essences related to specific opportunities, the process provides clear principles and target practices. This combination helps leaders retake control. Each stage requires rationale, outcomes, and elements of process. The following section provides a detailed overview of each stage as a guideline.

Stage 1: Audit Current Situation

The purpose of Stage 1, *Audit Current Situation,* is to build consensus at the start of the process on both opportunities and challenges, and the contextual dynamics inherent to the business. The analysis must first include a review of the business model combined with an analysis of key performance drivers.

Key mindsets at play must be identified, and their impact on the business model and key performance drivers assessed. For instance, MineGroup has high security costs because of a high rate of theft and break-ins from the local community. This is clearly an issue related to lack of trust.

On the process side, executives need to form a team that will lead the change process. Small organizations or individual entrepreneurs can choose external partners to collaborate with during the process. Larger organizations can build dedicated teams empowered to drive the change process.

When this stage is well implemented, executives move away with a desire for change. Specific outcomes include a common understanding of the current situation, the establishment of a clear baseline on the firm's performance, and a willingness to challenge mindsets to escape The Survival Trap.

> ### Key questions to focus the investigation at this stage include
>
> - What is our business model (strategy, operations, assets, people, and society)?
> - How are we performing across customers, costs, competition, capabilities, and context?
> - Who are the key stakeholders for our business (i.e., customers, investors, community, and workers)?
> - How do the key mindsets our stakeholders hold impact on our business?

Stage 2: Articulate DARE Strategy

This stage discusses how to get the team to agree on objectives of the change process using the DARE matrix in specific ways that create a clear sense of purpose. At this stage, the most important aspect is to hold open discussions about mindsets and their impact. Open and willing inquiry is essential as discussions about mindsets can be uncomfortable.

Inquiry sets the stage for change. Executives must begin by questioning their own assumptions and mindsets. Such candid assessment goes a long way toward building the trust required for other stakeholders to accept being challenged, and helps build a discipline of mastering mental models.

Executives may consider interviewing key stakeholders to test their approach. In the case of large organizations dealing with complex issues, a survey of key stakeholders can be useful, providing insights to inform the DARE strategy.

> ### Key questions to focus the investigation at Stage 2 include
>
> - What is our overall objective?
> - Which mindsets should we seek to defeat? Why and how?
> - Which mindsets should we seek to alter? Why and how?
> - Which mindsets should we seek to redirect? Why and how?
> - Which mindsets should we seek to emphasize? Why and how?

Stage 3: Upgrade Business Model

Stage 3, *Upgrade Business Model*, is the most critical stage of the transformation process. After auditing the current situation and agreeing on objectives, this stage brings focus on specific changes the firm must make to its business model to escape The Survival Trap.

Such changes must seek to upgrade the firm's strategy, operations, assets, people, and relations with society. A good place to start finding solutions is by using the Seven Opportunities outlined in this book. These opportunities were highlighted based on their prevalence and potential impact in BoP nations.

When upgrading the business model, it is important to focus on opportunities with a high business impact. Having a clear sense of the benefits keeps the process on track while facing difficulties. The motivation and sense of possibility are critical to escape The Survival Trap.

Executives must also implement a campaign where relevant messages and initiatives target specific stakeholders to not only change mindsets but also promote the associated behavior. This critical aspect is often overlooked in the change process with dire consequences for the overall process.

> ### Key questions for Stage 3 are as follows:
>
> - What improvements must we make to our strategy?
> - What upgrades are required on our operations to support our new strategy?
> - What are implications for our assets and people?
> - How do we overhaul our relations with the community?
> - What is our upgraded business model?

Stage 4: Execute Quick Wins and Actions

The momentum created throughout the process creates the conditions for Stage 4, *Execute Quick Wins and Actions*. The upgraded business model is only a good intention until it is translated into action. Ultimately, this stage delivers the results expected from the process.

In Stage 4, specific changes are linked to the appropriate performance metrics. If an upgrade is going to be successful it is paramount that the impact on customers, costs, capabilities, competition, and context be very clear. Without such clarity, monitoring and evaluation become difficult.

Here actions must be grouped under two categories: quick wins and actions. Quick wins refer to initiatives that can be implemented quickly as a way to sustain momentum and deliver quick results.

Actions form the backbone of the turnaround or business upgrade process. These are changes of a more fundamental nature. As such, most actions require more resources, skills, and time. This often means that actions are medium- to long-term initiatives.

Key questions for Stage 4 are as follows:

- What high-impact initiatives can we implement next week?
- What are elements of a business upgrade plan that would improve our business model?
- Who is better placed to lead each initiative under consideration?
- What investments in skills, time, or money do we need to make to upgrade our business?
- What specific improvements to the business drivers do we expect from each action?

Stage 5: Reflect and Redesign

Stage 5, *Reflect and Redesign* is about ongoing evaluation and improvement to assess whether their initiatives are effective. At the end of this stage, executives will have identified key improvements to make to achieve their stated objectives and embed changes in the firm's culture.

By way of analysis, this stage builds on the performance indicators identified in Stage 4. The analysis combines financial performance and business drivers. Results must be shared across the team to enable an open discussion that identifies areas for further improvements.

This process is an iterative one. Executives must develop the discipline to revisit previous stages continuously and create the habit of periodic evaluation to account for the reality that mindsets, business models, and context are all dynamic.

Ultimately, the process is continuous. It is necessary to develop an introspective and disciplined culture to leverage subsequent opportunities for improvement. Such a culture rests on executives embracing the discipline to change prevailing mindsets.

Key questions for Stage 5 are as follows:

- What results have we generated from this process?
- What actions have created those results?
- What are we learning from this process?
- What are the implications for our culture?
- What other mindsets or challenges do we want to take on?

Some Practical Considerations on the DARE Process

Engaging the DARE process for maximum benefit requires keeping some practical considerations in mind.

First, most organizations' needs are unique: firms gain the most from prioritizing main pain points or areas for concern, rather than looking for generic approaches. Having clear incentives for change and success is critical. Needs prioritization aligns incentives and ensures ultimate impact.

Building on the need for prioritization, it is important to note that no single business will struggle with all of the Seven opportunities. Otherwise, these organizations would have already imploded as a result of too many strategic and operational pressures. Instead, organizations must leverage existing strengths to address their weaknesses in an iterative fashion.

While the DARE process can be used throughout the life cycle of any organization, it works best when there is a specific challenge or an opportunity being examined and addressed. Clear focus provides the sense of urgency required to overcome the inertia that any situation represents.

The DARE Process in Action

Espousing this process is hard work. Leaders looking to effect sustainable change have to be willing to commit to a discipline that takes time to develop.

To sustain this commitment, it helps to be clear about the value that accrues to different types of organizations through this process. Stakeholders respond to incentives. What specific benefits are available for specific groups?

At the individual level, the DARE process offers three benefits:

- Reduces the feelings of loss of control that characterizes The Survival Trap
- Puts executives back in the driver's seat
- Gives everyone a chance to be part of the solution

At the organizational level, the process does the following:

- Gives executives the confidence that they will be able to make plans work
- Affords a chance to change their own and stakeholders' mindsets
- Improves performance through a more sustainable organization

At the cluster or industry level, the process

- Increases collaboration and competitiveness
- Clarifies barriers to building trust within clusters
- Supports drives for continuous improvements in the cluster business model

At the national level, the process creates a way to

- Make issues of mindset change explicit
- Drive public-private consensus on a prosperity agenda
- Lift segments of the population from the bottom of the pyramid

At the global level, the process helps to

- Analyze why some of the solutions advocated are failing
- Give an opportunity to chart a different and more sustainable path
- Create homegrown solutions

While it is far from a panacea and requires diligence, the DARE process provides a unique framework for BoP nations to graduate out of The Survival Trap.

Reconciliation and Prosperity

Mindsets are the heart of business operations. Despite their great importance for business success, mindsets are rarely explicitly discussable in management in developing nations, especially Africa, because of poor understanding, deference toward authority, and the absence of a clear linkage to economic performance.

The DARE process provides practical tools for identifying specific mindsets to change to upgrade business models. Its collaborative nature builds consensus and coalitions, and finally, it helps these leaders hardwire these changes through the DNA of their organizations.

To reconcile MineGroup to its stakeholders, Jaime and his team must not only improve mining practices but also develop a sustainable development strategy. This requires changing mindsets at the corporate level, a process that Jaime must lead. It also requires significant investments.

While this process takes time, Jaime and his team are more comfortable about their ability to build trust, improve their solutions, and bridge the leadership gap. Moreover, the MineGroup team is now clearer about the challenges their team faces on the ground. For the first time, Jaime has a distinct feeling of having a team.

Through this model, executives can change specific mindsets that prevent their businesses from thriving. The next seven chapters describe Seven Opportunities for BoP nations that are available through mindset change. These chapters help executives diagnose the underlying mindsets and apply the DARE process.

Vignette 2—Made in Africa: Manu Chandaria and Comcraft Group

A key challenge facing family businesses the world over is the struggle to outlive their founders. Nowhere is this struggle more pronounced than in BoP markets. Since 1929, the Chandaria family has built the Comcraft Group of companies, a diversified conglomerate operating in more than 50 countries around the world, from humble beginnings in Kenya.

That most people have never heard of Comcraft is by design. Inspired by their Indian roots and Jain principles, the Chandaria family espouses the values of humility, humanity, and integrity. These values inspired Comcraft to transform the BoP markets they serve while keeping a low profile.

Entrepreneurial Epic

It all started with one man's dream to escape poverty. In early 1916, Premchandbhai Chandaria moved to Kenya, with the goal of making 4,000 rupees—enough capital for him to set up a shop in his native state of Gujarat, India, and take care of his family. As fate would have it, things were more complicated than Chandaria envisioned.

After six months of working 18 hour days and sleeping on a shop floor, Chandaria senior received 120 rupees. He realized his dreams of making 4,000 rupees would take many years to achieve. Instead, he pooled resources with his extended family and began a shop in Kenya, which formed the foundation of the empire.

A determining factor was Chandaria senior's foresight in investing in his family's children. Dr. Manu Chandaria and his brother Keshav studied engineering and food technology in the US. Two other cousins—Kanti, a civil engineer, and Kapoor, with a commerce degree—joined them. Within the framework of the joint Indian family and with the guidance of the two elder brothers Devchand and Ratilal, the family business within five years had grown from 40 to over 800 employees; subsequently more members of the family with various qualifications from the US and UK joined, and by 1980 the business expanded to operations on almost all continents.

An unimposing man in his early eighties, Dr. Manu Chandaria, senior's son, shares this entrepreneurial epic in his talks as a testimony that success is possible. Voted East Africa's most trusted CEO three times, Manu Chandaria embodies principled leadership and compassion on a continent where business is often associated with corruption and greed.

Deeply rooted in his family history and Gandhi's philosophy, Dr. Manu Chandaria is a simple man with a self-deprecating sense of humor and an amazing intellect. Dr. Chandaria keeps a punishing schedule with the energy level of a man half his age. Being fully engaged with his family, business, and community sums up who this man is.

Ensuring maximum congruency between one's business and cardinal values is one of the lessons businesses aiming to build sustainability in BoP markets can learn from Chandaria. Comcraft has come to embody the values that the Chandaria family stands for in a way that is apparent from the success and operating practice of individual businesses in the conglomerate to the day-to-day the lives of its leaders.

Shaping to One's Operating Reality

When asked about their experience in BoP markets, many entrepreneurs initially note the difficult business environment. In sum, everything takes longer than expected, and whatever a business needs the most is scarce. In BoP nations especially Africa, the operating realities are highly unpredictable.

Comcraft is the story of a business that has leveraged its often-harsh operating environment. Where other businesses would see limited growth potential, Comcraft envisioned fast-growing markets. Where the context threatened to kill the business, Comcraft saw a rationale for regional diversification.

When asked to speak about entrepreneurship, Dr. Chandaria replies: "I did not even know what the word entrepreneurship means." He adds: "When put in a challenging spot, you can either sleep or you can act. Action is really nothing but a step towards entrepreneurship." In a nutshell, Dr. Chandaria defines entrepreneurship as one's attitude toward the operating reality.

To prevail despite challenges in one's operating reality, Dr. Chandaria offers simple advice: "The essence of entrepreneurship is 'the fire in the belly,' that drive. That is the key to open the constraints that are in your way. That's the key to open the doors that keep you inside instead of going out. You've got to walk to any destination."

Comcraft is the archetype of a business that has built itself while serving the bottom of the pyramid. Today, Comcraft still manufactures the pots and pans Chandaria senior started with more than 80 years ago. One of the group's main interest remains metallurgy, which serves to provide affordable roofing.

In their quest for growth, the Chandarias have sought to diversify their offering while remaining true to the markets where they are based. The group has spread throughout the world, but it has not forgotten its roots in developing products to serve the often-overlooked BoP segment so prevalent in these countries. In the process, it has invested greatly and provided jobs in BoP markets.

But achieving this feat did not happen overnight, or without major obstacles. Several changes in government resulted in difficult business operations at the best of times and complete loss of business at the worst. Over five generations, the Chandarias' epic included nationalization during Idi Amin, near bankruptcies, and political instability.

Reflecting on Idi Amin's nationalization, which caused the loss of all their Ugandan assets, Dr. Chandaria talks about how the experience was a blessing in disguise by inspiring the group to diversify and begin its international expansion. Rather than complaining about issues, Comcraft is a story of trying to shape the operating environment through resilience.

Entrepreneurial Solutions for Prosperity

The "fire in the belly" metaphor also captures a unique mindset where entrepreneurs begin to own the challenges in the operating environment. "You cannot grow otherwise" says Dr. Chandaria.

Such ownership is the precondition for an opportunity mindset, which is critical in devising homegrown solutions to the challenges they face, rather than let the operating reality get the best of them.

Comcraft under the leadership of Dr. Chandaria and his family offers a compelling example of how businesses operating in BoP markets can leverage the Seven Opportunities in this book to prosper and transform the markets in which they operate:

1. *Foster an Archimedean mindset.* The Chandaria family made its values of humanity, humility, and integrity a core part of the DNA of its operations around the world. This culture fostered a sense of ownership in their professional managers.

   Sharing an anecdote, Dr. Chandaria recalls. "In 1953, I went to my dad: 'Papa you should set up Chandaria Foundation.' He said: 'Are you stupid? You have lived too long in the US. We are not Rockefeller or Ford. We don't have enough to eat!'" A few months later, Chandaria Foundation was born, making it one of the oldest foundations in East Africa.

2. *Build trust.* Comcraft operates mostly in BoP markets where trust is scarce. This is particularly true in East Africa, where Indian business minority is often suspected to grow rich at the expense of the general population.

   Yet Dr. Manu Chandaria has managed to earn widespread respect and trust throughout society. When Dr. Chandaria speaks of building trusts he says, "It is not a one way game. For people to trust you, you first have to believe in them. Then a bond of trust is created."

3. *Focus on solutions.* Comcraft's evolving offering balances two factors: the core needs of communities as well as an appreciation of the pace of change in the world. Dr. Chandaria simply remarks: "We must continuously update our mindsets to remain economically relevant."

   As a matter of practice, the Chandaria family members live in their main markets. This proximity combined with the close links to all stakeholders has helped the Comcraft Group draw inspiration from its customers' operating reality in both its product offering and expansion plans.

4. **Operate efficiently and sustainably.** As a conglomerate with roots firmly in manufacturing, efficiency has always been a core part of the Comcraft philosophy. The firm applied the Kaizen process to all its plants.

This has resulted not only in lean manufacturing but also reduced waste and improved efficiency. The Comcraft Group realizes that the battle for sustainability is a never-ending race. The business does not left anything to chance, relying instead on proven methods.

5. **Enable prosperity ecosystems.** Comcraft recently established a one-hundred-million-dollar steel factory in South Africa. Comcraft pitched major competitors and engineered a partnership with a Japan-based steel producer to ensure it stood a chance to win in the middle market.

Enabling a prosperity ecosystem also means influencing the business environment. As chairman of KEPSA (Kenya Private Sector Alliance) Dr. Manu Chandaria has help in enabling key reforms for economic and societal progress.

6. **Seek intelligent capital.** A key growth factor has been the firm's willingness to reinvest profits. When presented with an opportunity, Comcraft takes a medium- to long-term view harvesting opportunities that it believes will yield profitability over time.

One of Comcraft's portfolio companies, UST Global, is a leader in India's fast growing BPO industry, and a testimony to smartly invested patient capital can yield impressive results. As the UST vignette demonstrates, Comcraft has also been able to instill its values to professional managers.

7. **Bridge the leadership gap.** Chandaria senior set a powerful example by sending his two sons and family's children to study in the US and India despite his limited means. His foresight inspired generations of Chandaria to seek education and avail education to others.

When reflecting upon the next generation, Dr. Manu Chandaria says: "We must ensure everyone that works with us has dignity. We want our children to remain on the ground so that they can understand the pain and become more generous than we are."

From Success to Significance

An opportunity mindset captures the approach that Dr. Manu Chandaria and the Comcraft Group have built their success on. This mindset formed the essence of the challenge Dr. Chandaria gave to the audience addressing the Wharton Global Alumni Forum in June 2009: "Success is not enough. We must strive for significance."

Dr. Chandaria defines significance as ensuring that business transforms the lives of people. The Comcraft Group illustrates how entrepreneurs in BoP markets can build an enduring legacy with the right mindset and a focus on values. Comcraft has moved from survival, past success, to significance. In the process, it has become an inspiration to other BoP firms.

Endnotes

[1] Chris Argyris explicits his action science theory in his book *Action Science, Concepts, Methods, and Skills for Research and Intervention* (San Francisco: Jossey-Bass, 1985). These concepts are further applied to organizations in his bestseller *Knowledge for Action: A Guide to Overcoming Barriers to Organizational Change* (San Francisco: Jossey-Bass, 1993). Michael Fairbanks and Stace Lindsay applied this model to developing countries in *Plowing the Sea* (Cambridge: Harvard Business School Press, 1997).

5

Foster an Archimedean Mindset

Connecting the Neighborhood

Remember Mariam, the cell phone unit retailer from Kibera, Nairobi, Kenya? Mariam's business grew out of a desire to help her neighbors.

Twelve years ago, Mariam's husband, a trucker, came back home with a mobile phone. Mariam had a complaint. One time their first son had been sick, and it had taken two weeks for her to notify her husband. She had no way of keeping in touch with him when he traveled. Her husband figured this device would bring peace to their household.

It brought peace and a lot more. Soon, Mariam realized that other women in the neighborhood had similar issues. Like her, some belonged to the club of distraught wives of migrant workers. Others wanted to speak to husbands and relatives throughout the country. A few even had relatives in the West sending remittances from time to time.

Soon, Mariam had a constant stream of visitors needing her cell phone. She turned this device into a business. Rather than have loads of visitors, Mariam invested her savings into two stands at strategic corners in the neighborhood. She also hired two students who became mobile cell phone booth operators.

Closed Doors

Today, something is keeping Mariam up at night. After more than a decade connecting the neighborhood, Mariam has a dream. Now at university, her first son has suggested that Mariam open an Internet café where people in the neighborhood could come to send emails, play computer games, and print documents.

Mariam loves the idea. It is a good complement to her cell phone business. She also reckons her son can help her manage the venture and stay out of trouble. She has estimated that she needs $10,000 to open her first center. After visiting similar cafés in town, she believes she can recoup her investment in a little over a year.

However, she is stuck. While she has some savings, Mariam has not been able to get a loan for the balance of the startup capital. Bankers keep telling her that she needs to give assets to the bank as collateral for the loan. "Why would I go to them if I had the money in the first place?" asks Mariam. This frustrates her to no end.

When asked about her ambition, Mariam talks about wanting to open her own doors. "Everyone keeps doors closed to businesspeople! That is unless you have a bribe. Otherwise, they force you to go under the door, around the door, or even create your own. Why have doors if we cannot go through them?"

Microentrepreneurs such as Mariam are not the only ones to face closed doors. Larger business entities—medium size businesses and multinational companies—face closed doors as well. While specific challenges may differ, the operating reality of BoP markets affects all businesses that operate in these markets.

Closed doors are a reality for all businesses that operate in BoP markets. The Doing Business Survey and the Global Competitiveness Report are but two empirical surveys that provide ample evidence of this challenge. For instance, 48 out of 50 bottom countries in both surveys hail from Africa.

Survival Business

Such closed doors keep businesspeople including entrepreneurs stuck in The Survival Trap. Beyond microentrepreneurs such as Mariam, leaders in larger business entities, such as Themba the CEO of a medium size IT firm and Jaime the country director of a mining corporation, share the same experience while stuck in The Survival Trap.

While the personal impact on these leaders and their businesses is tremendous, it is important to note that closed doors go so far as affecting the way they do business. Instead of focusing on opportunities, such leaders fight challenges. Instead of aiming for reward, such leaders seek to avoid risk.

In the face of closed doors, some businesspeople operating in BoP markets resort to "survival business." Four main characteristics define survival business:

First, it is replicative as opposed to innovative. In their drive to avoid risk, businesspeople start with what already works. For entrepreneurs, this means engaging in copycat behavior to minimize risks. For corporations, this means copying and pasting a business model that has worked in another market or part of the world to the BoP markets.

In both cases, replicative businesses can backfire. Copycat entrepreneurs in turn expose themselves to being copied by new entrants. Copying and pasting the wrong business model to the BoP simply limits growth opportunities. While entrepreneurs remain stuck in The Survival Trap, larger firms miss opportunities at the BoP.

In Chapter 11, "Bridge the Leadership Gap," Alexandre de Carvalho illustrates how a global pharma company faced a similar situation in its Africa business. Alexandre inherits a situation where his management has a limited vision of the growth potential in Africa because it insists on selling name brand medicines as opposed to generics.

Second, survival business often relies on pure opportunism. Opportunism is rooted in the desire for arbitrage in specific circumstances; for instance, an entrepreneur enters industry to take advantage of a specific relationship they have. In this case, the source of the advantage can be access to a specific leader or customers.

While the pursuit of opportunity is a core tenet in business, opportunism cannot become the sole raison d'être of a specific firm. The major risk with such opportunism is that it can become responsible for the fact that businesses in BoP seldom survive their founders.

Rather what is important is that the business is able to get past the initial opportunity to systematize its approach and begin delivering consistent solutions. Such businesses must develop what Allon Raiz,[1] the CEO of Raizcorp, calls an "economic reason for being." Allon is profiled later in the book. Without this economic reason for being business sustainability is very difficult.

Third, survival business tends to focus on short-cycle activities. Short-cycle activities tend to be those requiring neither sophisticated forms of capital (such as institutions, skills, etc.) nor a long-term perspective. Short-term activities limit exposure to the various risks inherent to the operating reality of BoP markets.

The best illustration is trading where profits are realized within months. While the closed doors make logistics in BoP markets a real challenge, trading offers lower risks than manufacturing and other activities with a longer term. Many fortunes in BoP markets originate from trading.

Mariam's current activity of retailing cell phone units is a good example of a short-cycle activity. While the margins are relatively small, Mariam can often recoup an initial investment of 1,000 shillings of airtime in a maximum of two days. It is also a replicative business inasmuch as all it takes is a cell phone and 1,000 shillings.

Finally, survival business tends to be factor based. The main objective of factor-based business is to extract a particular resource for which a global market exists, often in developed nations. Historically, foreign investments in BoP markets are largely driven by large resource firms such as those in mining and oil.

Resource firms have developed expertise in managing risks and global supply chains. While extraction happens in BoP markets, value-addition is performed in a more stable developed nation. Such business models generate limited impact in BoP markets. Thus, BoP markets remains stuck in The Survival Trap.

Remember Jaime, the mining executive working in Chile? Mine-Group is the archetype of a factor-based business. Even with healthy profit margins, such businesses can become stuck in The Survival Trap when they fail to properly appreciate the needs of the various stakeholders in their operating reality.

The point here is not that survival business is necessarily wrong. In fact, one could argue that it is the only pragmatic option given the closed doors in BoP markets. Businesspeople are rational and must let the operating reality of BoP markets inform what decisions provide the highest return on investments.

Rather, the point is that survival business leaves money on the table. By engaging in survival business, businesspeople ultimately fail to capture opportunities locally, regionally, and internationally. In the process, such firms fail to have maximum economic impact.

Keeping the Doors Shut

Beyond leaving money on the table, survival business can contribute to keeping the doors shut. Instead of blaming everyone else, businesspeople must face the inconvenient truth that they bear some responsibility for the status quo. Businesspeople miss opportunities to reshape their operating reality.

An important way by which businesspeople engaging in survival business keep the doors shut is by fueling two opposite misconceptions about business in BoP markets and its role in fostering prosperity. In ways that most fail to understand, these misconceptions set most businesspeople up to fail.

The first misconception is that the local private sector is weak. A World Bank survey suggests that informal SMEs account for 29 percent of jobs in low-income nations.[2] In Africa, most microenterprises and SMEs—and in particular, most small scale agricultural enterprises—are run by women.[3]

While the facts are correct, their interpretation can be problematic. The belief that the local private sector is weak can breed paternalism. Such paternalism can lead policy makers to design interventions that stifle innovations. Fairbanks and Lindsay identified paternalism as a major source of the lack of competitiveness.[4]

Furthermore, the belief that the local private sector is weak costs business to local players. It transforms BoP markets, especially countries in Africa, into distribution outlets. Eventually this can become self-fulfilling prophecy as it gives foreign firms the scale, knowledge, and reputation to win even more deals.

The second misconception is that supporting business is tantamount to making the rich richer. The reasoning goes that while a few businesspeople, and the elites who patronize them, have become rich, the vast majority of people have remained poor. The prevailing belief is that supporting business would make the income disparities worse.

Again the statistics for Africa are chilling. One in two people in sub-Saharan Africa survives on less than one dollar per day. A third of the African population suffers from malnutrition. One in six children dies before the age of five. This number is 25 times higher in sub-Saharan Africa than in the Organization for Economic Cooperation and Development (OECD) countries.

This last misconception does more harm than all others combined. It is one of the factors making poverty alleviation the number one objective for the international community. It is the mindset that has informed the debate around aid versus trade. While trade is gaining in prominence, the challenge persists.

Recognizing the Archimedean Mindset

Harvard's working definition of what makes an entrepreneur is the "pursuit of opportunity beyond the resources you currently control." In her bid to open an Internet café, Mariam is demonstrating textbook entrepreneurship. She is pursuing an opportunity beyond her current means.

Around 200 BC, Archimedes made a formidable dare: "Give me a lever long enough and a fulcrum on which to place it and I shall move the world." Two thousand years later, an end to poverty has become the world's most formidable dare. The world still is searching for the lever and the fulcrum to lift BoP markets out of poverty.

The fulcrum to lift the BoP out of poverty, however, may already exist. A new breed of businesspeople is emerging. This book illustrates their impact on the ground. These leaders epitomize the role of business in the BoP markets of tomorrow. To maximize their impact, businesspeople must understand what an Archimedean mindset is.

The ultimate key to open the doors in BoP markets is to have an Archimedean mindset.[5] To better understand this mindset it helps to emphasize similarities and highlight differences between business as usual and an Archimedean mindset. In other words, what ways is an Archimedean mindset similar or dissimilar to how people are currently doing business?

The core distinction that forms the essence of this mindset is a strong moral purpose. While they seek healthy profits, Archimedean businesspeople do not compromise on human values. Archimedean mindset acts from a strong desire to address needs—their own and others.

Such moral purpose often stems from the inside out. Archimedean businesspeople have a clear sense for why specific endeavors matter to them. Motivations may be financial, status or recognition, cause-driven, or as specific as providing jobs or solving an environmental issue.

An Archimedean mindset is truly distinctive, exhibiting a number of unique attributes making sustainable value creation possible. Innovation is central to the Archimedean requiring superior understanding of the operating reality that leads to stronger business models, two ingredients often missing in survival business.

True Archimedean businesspeople see opportunity where others see only risk. This ability makes them more likely to pursue unconventional solutions. They evaluate risk differently and are able to focus on solutions. This relationship to risk is an important tenet of this mindset.

An Archimedean mindset often translates into a human-centric approach to business. Such a human-centric approach begins with the recognition that every business has four sets of stakeholders. Michael Fairbanks calls this the COW-F model: customers, owners, workers, and future.

This new breed of businesspeople has mastered making the right trade-offs in serving customers, owners, and workers while respecting our future.[6]

Customers: Archimedean businesspeople strive to create sophisticated products for high paying and demanding customers. These business leaders innovate by embedding customer knowledge into their products. In doing so, they innovate and transform natural resources in BoP markets into competitive products.

Such businesspeople are able to answer the integrative question: "What am I selling to whom and why are they buying from me and not anyone else?" Beyond this question, they can also answer the question: "How is my business benefiting each one of its stakeholders?" which is helpful in ascertaining their impact.

The sense of purpose of Archimedean businesspeople expresses itself in an adulterated drive to provide real solutions to customer challenges as well as a desire to alter the operating reality in BoP markets. This explains the focus on solutions that we develop in Chapter 7, "Focus on Solutions."

Owners: The primary motive of business is to create shareholder value. Archimedean entrepreneurs are economically motivated. Often, they open their circle of shareholders to include their workers and community. This explains why some of them choose to operate within specific communities.

Most importantly, Archimedean businesspeople are rooted firmly in the pursuit of opportunity. Where most BoP citizens often choose to work cheaper and harder, Archimedean entrepreneurs understand that the world provides sustainable economic rewards only for smart work.

They not only want to make profits but also are unapologetic about their drive to make profits. What distinguishes them is that they define success beyond profits. This stance makes them willing to seek intelligent capital and take a long-term view on issues each time such a stance is required. We discuss this in Chapter 10, "Seek Intelligent Capital."

Workers: Archimedean businesspeople have graduated from the paradigm where workers are considered to be operating costs and have embraced the one where workers are the company's foremost

assets. They understand that the key to continuous innovation is paying high and rising wages, and training their workers.

Delivering an effective solution requires the integration of different disciplines. While they are often comfortable with their strengths,
businesspeople must have an acute sense of what they don't know.
This sense helps them bridge the leadership gap developing shared
ownership for all their stakeholders starting with workers.

This pragmatic sense of possibilities leads them to be collaborative when it makes sense for the advancement of their venture, and to
assemble teams with complementary strengths. This sense of collaboration makes it highly likely that Archimedean businesspeople will
enable a prosperity mindset.

The future: The concern of Archimedean businesspeople for the
future begins with their community. They are often contributors to
the social well-being of their employees and the wider communities
in which they are situated. This concern goes beyond their immediate
communities.

Archimedean businesspeople intuitively grasp an important reality. Traditional firms often make the wrong trade-offs, which disad-
vantage the weak or the silent, namely workers or the unborn
generations. Archimedean businesspeople adopt a different stance
that is informed by their moral purpose.

These business leaders adopt business practices, which leverage
our common natural capital endowment such as the environment,
responsibly. Archimedean businesspeople see themselves as stewards
of the natural resources we have and the community they operate in.
This makes them seek to operate sustainably and efficiently.

Fostering an Archimedean Mindset

Fostering an Archimedean mindset requires a combination of
two complementary approaches: introspective and environmental.
The self-reflective introspective perspective requires the business
leader to create one's own luck by putting oneself in the right
environment.

This book offers several examples of Archimedean businesspeople through the vignettes and selected chapters. It serves as a testament that such businesspeople exist at all levels in business and in different environments. Although many Archimedean businesspeople exist in BoP markets, they remain the exception rather than the norm.

Unfortunately, no obvious traits, physical or otherwise, distinguish them from the masses. It is more an art than a science to identify these business leaders. The best way to foster an Archimedean mindset is to equip businesspeople to see how they can upgrade their choices to espouse a COW-F business model.

This level of self-reflection is important as espousing and living an Archimedean mindset means being able to bring moral purpose, strong values, and a human-centric approach to one's unique set of circumstances (see Figure 5.1). Mariam's case illustrates how businesspeople can ensure they have the Archimedean mindset.

Essence	• Moral purpose			
	Strategy	**Operations**	**Assets**	**Reality**
Principles	• Vision	• Leapfrog	• Focus on Intangible Assets	• Ownership
Practices	• Confronting Current Reality	• Experimenting Continuously	• Building Intangibles	• Nurturing Relationships

Figure 5.1   Transforming your business through an entrepreneurial mindset

The first core principle is *vision*. Vision shapes business strategy. Stephen R. Covey, author of *The 7 Habits of Highly Effective People*, defines vision in his book *First Things First Every Day*. He says,

"Vision is the best manifestation of creative imagination and the primary motivation of human action. It's ability to see beyond our present reality, to create, to invent what does not yet exist, to become what we not yet are. It gives us capacity to live out of our imagination instead of our memory."[7]

Vision matters in BoP markets because it helps businesses move beyond the immediate concerns of their operating reality. The Survival Trap kills leaders' ability to dream and see beyond existing challenges. Vision allows businesspeople to move beyond the short-term orientation identified in Chapter 2, "Rwanda's Metamorphosis."

Mariam has the embryo of a vision for her business. Her Internet café will contribute to establishing her as someone providing full IT-based communication solutions for her community. Building on her desire to see her student son work at her business, she could add an educational component to her vision.

The practice that supports articulating a vision is the ability to confront reality. This begins with the businessperson being very clear about the opportunities and challenges that are present in the operating reality. Rather than becoming a source of disempowerment, such clarity is critical to developing the right strategy.

Mariam sees the opportunities and challenges in her environment clearly. Her experience as a cell phone unit retailer has shown her that addressing the telecommunication needs of her community can be a lucrative opportunity. She is also clear about the closed doors she faces.

What she must now do is articulate how her Internet café will be different from the other ones offering similar services in the community. Mariam has noted that most adults of her generation with basic reading skills have no experience with computers. She could consider offering tutorials to address this challenge.

The second core principle is *leapfrogging*. This principle is about making sure Archimedean entrepreneurs establish the required systems to achieve their vision. Leapfrogging is the notion that radically different approaches to operational issues, which may be more appropriate to the BoP, can enable unique competitive advantage.

To espouse leapfrogging, businesspeople must become adept at experimenting. Such experimentation gives them the chance to adopt new operation systems while reducing risks to the business. Experimentation requires that business leaders be open to new technologies but also empower their teams to take risks and pioneer new ways.

Mariam is clearly leapfrogging by moving toward an Internet café with computers while her current business model relies on the much simpler phone technology. She must make a number of choices on how she will operate her Internet café in terms of opening hours, services offered, and so on.

The third core principle is *focus on intangible assets*. A focus on intangible assets translates into a focus on relationships with COW-F stakeholders. Each stakeholder must see her role and ownership of the work at hand, creating loyalty, trust, and connections.

Focusing on intangible assets translates into ownership at two levels. First, leaders must find a way for stakeholders to own the firm's vision so that it becomes their own. It is about stakeholders feeling understood and cared for. Second, ownership is about the business feeling responsible for some of the conditions within its operating reality.

The practice that supports this focus on intangible assets is nurturing relationships. Archimedean businesspeople spend a lot of time investing in the relationship with their employees, investors, customers, and the community. The larger the business, the more time the leader must spend in nurturing these relationships.

Mariam's intuition is to have her son involved in the Internet café. However, upon reflection she realizes that this responsibility will conflict with his studies. Furthermore, he lacks the IT skills required to ensure the machine works properly. Rather than save the money for a salary, she decides to hire a young IT graduate with the right skills.

Enabling Archimedean Businesspeople

A specific challenge that BoP nations face, especially in Africa, is how to foster an Archimedean mindset in their business communities. For a host of reasons described previously, a significant proportion of businesses end up being survival businesses. This is a challenge worth addressing as it translates into missed opportunities for society.

Beyond the introspective approach, the environmental approach is about enabling Archimedean businesspeople to flourish. While most successful businesspeople are action oriented and self-starting problem solvers, too many closed doors can undermine anyone. It is therefore critical that the rest of society configure to enable them.

The environmental approach is about making sure other stakeholders have an incentive to open doors and enable businesspeople to espouse and practice an Archimedean mindset. These perspectives represent the tension between the business leader holding the locus of responsibility and the role of the enabling environment.

Before the rest of society can enable Archimedean businesspeople, it is critical that people in BoP markets see business as a potential solution to poverty. This goes against the prevailing paradigm in BoP nations, especially Africa, that continue to see government or development partners as the solution.

Enabling businesspeople begins with addressing the misconception that business is only interested in profits. While profits remain a powerful driver of business, Archimedeans show that some businesspeople can widen their definition of success to include the impact of their ventures on their stakeholders.

BoP markets must achieve what Clayton Christianson describes as "a discontinuous leap in productivity."[8] BoP's new economic agenda should focus on finding and unleashing these forces for creating prosperity. Archimedean entrepreneurs can be powerful actors in achieving this leap, a leap that benefits society.

Archimedean businesspeople can help create prosperity in BoP markets for one major reason. They offer solutions for all key stakeholders specifically their customers, their owners, their workers, and the community. In so doing, they can align incentives for all to collaborate toward prosperity creation.

Attempts of fostering Archimedean mindsets or other entrepreneurship related drives in a systemic and systematic way are met with skepticism. People debate whether entrepreneurs are born or made. They argue about how corporate environment shapes the mindsets of its staff.

While both are valid concerns, they are also beside the point. What we must all recognize is that it is possible with the right approach to increase receptiveness to an Archimedean mindset. What is important is for us to realize that businesspeople operating in BoP markets may not have been exposed to different business models.

The approach to enable an entrepreneurial mindset must combine a push and a pull strategy. While the push is about creating the right mindset within the businessperson, the pull is about creating the conditions for business to develop and enable entrepreneurial solutions for prosperity.

When people decide to launch or get into a business, they are often inspired by role models in their environment. A demonstration effect[9] is important in creating a stronger sense of possibility in a future entrepreneur. Prize and media activities can help foster such demonstration effects because it is societal validation of success.

The anchor of the push strategy is about harnessing the power of the demonstration effect. McKinsey just completed a study on philanthropic prizes that demonstrated that competitions could have a positive impact in stimulating different behavior.[10] Such prizes and competitions are beginning to be implemented generally in BoP markets.

At a specific community level, it is possible to have dedicated initiatives such as the Become Entrepreneur (BE) campaign from Color Creations that Eva Muraya is implementing in Kenya. These initiatives offer entrepreneurs a way to develop their business appropriately. Eva Muraya is profiled later in the book.

In creating the conditions for entrepreneurs to benefit from mentorship or training, efforts such as the BE campaign are critical for entrepreneurs to gain some of the basic skills to run a business. This is a particularly notable gap in Africa where tremendous entrepreneurs see their firms crumble for lack of basic business skills.

The pull is about removing the constraints for businesspeople to be able to develop an Archimedean mindset. An important drive here is to ensure that BoP markets reform their business environment. That alone can create the conditions for the mainstreaming of Archimedean mindsets.

Cash and Credit

Remember in Chapter 1, "Identifying the Problem—And the Solution," Mariam faced a difficult decision between choosing to buy credit and keeping her cash. But Mariam made the bold decision to further her business. Mariam saw a specific opportunity that she sought to address by investing in her business in the face of risks. It is critical that BoP markets, especially in Africa, foster the type of environment where Archimedean businesspeople thrive.

Archimedean businesspeople have a strong moral purpose. While they seek healthy profits, Archimedean businesspeople also adopt a human-centric approach to business. Such a human-centric approach begins with the recognition that every business has four sets of stakeholders.

As discussed in this chapter, businesspeople, when equipped with an Archimedean mindset, can become the vector of their nations' escape from The Survival Trap. While business is often a personal experience, several interventions can be employed to support entrepreneurs and shape the next generation of business leaders. Such interventions must build trust.

Vignette 3—Tokunbo Talabi and Superflux Ltd.

Christopher Columbus once remarked that: "by prevailing over all obstacles and distractions, one may unfailingly arrive at his chosen goal or destination." Talabi has made great strides toward his chosen goal to build a successful business that represents a beacon of integrity in Nigeria.

The soft-spoken and dynamic entrepreneur has built Superflux Limited into a diversified group anchored on its unique offering of security printing. Transcending beyond the perception of Nigeria, Tokunbo has managed to thrive in a business where trust and integrity are the key differentiators.

Trial by Fire

The son of a middle class family, Tokunbo fell on hard times in university. Struggling to pay for his school fees, he lived on one meal a day, usually a simple plate of pounded yams. To his amused classmates who did not know his plight, Tokunbo was nicknamed "Fufu man" after his frugal diet.

Tokunbo also credits these hardships with building his faith and character. Tokunbo credits his faith with giving him the values that permeate throughout everything he does. Tokunbo decided very early, "My purpose is more than what I amass for myself. This has helped me deal with everything that has come my way."

It was during this time that Tokunbo discovered the power of enterprise. His first business was to organize viewings of videos rented from the cinema board. This first venture allowed Tokunbo to support himself and his younger brother. It would not be the last time he puts into practice his philosophy of "taking my destiny in my hands."

Building a Foundation

Tokunbo's experience with Nigeria's Guaranty Trust Bank completed his formative years. First, Tokunbo learned that one could make money without sacrificing one's values. Tokunbo noted that integrity was critical in an environment fraught with ethical shortcuts: "There must be integrity of purpose. As an entrepreneur, there must be no variance between your talk and action."

Tokunbo also gained a great deal of experience and exposure. His intimate understanding of the needs of financial services firms enabled him to provide targeted solutions and a strong reputation. Finally, his own training and exposure also helped plant the seeds for a deep appreciation for investing in one's employees.

Most importantly, Tokunbo noticed something: "It used to take a long time to get checks in this country," Tokunbo recalls quite simply. Where other people saw a nuisance, Tokunbo sensed a business opportunity. In 1998, Tokunbo resigned as senior manager in the prestigious bank, in order to pursue the less-certain world of entrepreneurship.

The Paradox of Trust

Tokunbo's intuition soon developed into business. Security printing deals with the printing of items such as checks, banknotes, passports, stock certificates, postage stamps, and identity cards. A key objective in security printing is to prevent forgery, tampering, or counterfeiting.

Tokunbo leveraged his network to supply checks to the fast-growing Nigerian banking sector. At first, Superflux partnered with Kalamazoo, a well-known UK-based security printing company. As the firm's track record and reputation grew, it established its own factory in Nigeria. Today, Superflux has expanded beyond Nigeria.

In an environment where kickbacks are the norm, Tokunbo decided to take the road less traveled: the one paved with integrity and zero-tolerance to corruption. With this choice came great pressure: The firm has lost potentially lucrative opportunities along the way. This choice also meant Tokunbo needed to develop a strong personality.

Nonetheless, this choice is now paying off. First, not paying kickbacks means that dollar for dollar Superflux can deliver a much better quality product. The firm is also able to perform costly reruns, invest in training, and upgrade its equipment. The firm has developed a penchant for unmatched quality and superior customer service.

Second, senior executives now trust any quotes from Superflux thanks to its clean record. These executives reason that if Superflux did not pay kickbacks when they were at a junior level, they are certainly not going to find staff that will collude to load up invoices now. Paradoxically, this as reputation is now winning business for Superflux.

An Archimedean Entrepreneur

A careful analysis of the Superflux business model suggests a firm that has fostered an Archimedean mindset while building trust with his core stakeholders.

Tokunbo is a prime example of an Archimedean entrepreneur. His ability to see an opportunity to solve a problem and to turn that solution into profits is the essence of an entrepreneur. But, it is his commitment to varied stakeholder groups that make him the kind of innovator that unleashes prosperity for all those around him.

First, Tokunbo says: "We do not take our customers for granted. Customers are our partners." This spirit of trusted partnership has won 17 out of 24 Nigerian banks for Superflux. A large driver of Superflux's fast growth is the fast growth of Nigerian's banks. Superflux's partnership with its customers is paying off.

Second, Tokunbo nurtures the entrepreneur in each of his employees: "If you can't make money for yourself, you can't make money for others," Tokunbo remarks. Not only does he provide stretch assignments for his employees, he also ensures they get exposed through international training.

Finally, bridge the leadership gap. Tokunbo has also extended this trust to his team. "One of the challenges African entrepreneurs have is that they do not trust their staff. This forces them to run their business in a non-professional way and keep everything to themselves," Tokunbo remarks.

As a result, the Superflux team as has bridged the leadership gap, preparing to run the firm while Tokunbo, the founding CEO, takes a back seat.

Africa's Pioneer of Prosperity

The world is starting to take notice of Tokunbo's remarkable journey with Superflux. In 2008, Tokunbo was recognized when he won the Grand Prize for the Pioneers of Prosperity Africa Awards, an initiative created by the SEVEN Fund[11] to recognize entrepreneurs with a truly sustainable business model.

Entrepreneurs such as Tokunbo are the catalysts for change that will certainly lead Africa and other BoP markets toward prosperity. Superflux is getting ready for the test of a truly sustainable business: running without its founder at the helm. The next phase of Tokunbo's journey is surely one that should inspire other BoP entrepreneurs.

Endnotes

[1] Profiled later in the book, Allon Raiz expands on the concept of "economic reason of being for a business."

[2] Meghana Ayyagari, Asli Demirguc-Kunt, and Thorsten Beck, "SMEs Across the Globe" (Washington, DC: World Bank, 2003).

[3] The World Economic Forum on Africa, Briefing material, Pricewaterhouse Coopers, 2010.

[4] Michael Fairbanks and Stace Lindsay, *Plowing the Sea: Nurturing the Hidden Sources of Growth in the Developing World* (Cambridge, MA: Harvard Business School Press, 1997), p. 103–121.

[5] This concept of Archimedean mindset was first introduced by Eric Kacou in an article for the *Africa Policy Journal* at Harvard; it was then further developed in the book of essays *In the River They Swim*, edited by Fairbanks, Fal, Escobari, and Hooper (West Conshohocken, PA: Templeton Press, April 2009).

[6] The model was first developed and written about by Michael Fairbanks in *The Natural Advantage of Nations*.

[7] S. R. Covey, *First Things First Every Day: Daily Reflections—Because Where You're Headed Is More Important Than How Fast You Get There* (Chargrin Falls, Ohio: Fireside, 1997).

[8] C. M. Christensen, "Assessing Your Organization's Innovation Capabilities," *Leader to Leader Journal*, 21 (Summer 2001): 27–37.

[9] Demonstration effects are effects on the behavior of individuals caused by observation of the actions of others and their consequences. The term is particularly used in political science and sociology to describe the fact that developments in one place will often act as a catalyst in another place.

[10] McKinsey & Company, "And the winner is...: Capturing the Promise of Philanthropic Prizes," 2009. http://www.mckinsey.com/App_Media/Reports/SSO/And_the_winner_is.pdf.

[11] SEVEN (Social Equity Venture Fund) is a virtual nonprofit entity run by entrepreneurs whose strategy is to markedly increase the rate of innovation and diffusion of enterprise-based solutions to poverty.

6

Build Trust

Against the Odds

Trust matters in business especially in financial services. Skeptics should look no further than the 2008 global recession. Issues with selected global banks almost sent the world economy on a downward spiral. The world is yet to recover from this trust-induced crisis.

Late 2008 is the time Emerging Capital Partners (ECP), an Africa focused private equity firm, chose to purchase a significant minority stake in la Nouvelle Societé Interafricaine d'Assurance Participations SA (NSIA), the leading insurance group in French-speaking West and Central Africa.[1]

While global insurance giants such as AIG were receiving bailout money to survive, NSIA attracted the US$47.7 million (€35 million) private investment in a show of trust. With a turnover of more than 150 million euros, the firm averaged an impressive 20 percent year-on-year uninterrupted growth for five years running.

"This partnership aims to help us accelerate our regional development," justifies founder and group chairman Jean Kacou Diagou. The ECP investment provided NSIA with resources for organic and external growth as well as the equity strengthening of the company's banking affiliate, Banque Internationale d'Afrique Occidentale (BIAO).

A Late Bloomer

NSIA was founded in 1995 by 20-year insurance industry veteran Jean Kacou Diagou. A published composer of religious songs, the Ivorian entrepreneur has built a great business anchored on trust. ECP's investment was an additional vote of confidence on his achievements.

Yet, very few people would have bet on Jean Kacou Diagou, when at the beginning of the 1990s, he was dreaming about building an insurance company with African ambition. The married father was then a 48-year-old executive who had spent his career as senior manager for a major French insurance company.

Diagou's first move was to improve the operating reality for insurance in Africa. At the time, the market was very small and dominated by French firms. Elected President of Fanaf (Fédération des sociétés d'assurances de droit national africaines) in February 1990, Kacou Diagou launched a sectoral reform.

Diagou recalls: "A small committee proposed against the consensus back then that there was a common regulation for all countries in the franc zone." Two years later, the ministers signed on July 10, 1992. In January 1995, right before the treaty was launched, Kacou Diagou founded NSIA.

"Some French insurers were unhappy. They gave me two years to fail!" remembers the businessman. Patiently, NSIA developed its philosophy: ally itself to national insurers to increase its scope of activities. Since, the company has launched activities in a new country every other year. The group has grown to a staff of 1,000.[2]

Fifteen years later, Jean Kacou Diagou's bet is paying off. NSIA is maturing into an African insurance giant thanks to its long-term view. Furthermore, Diagou has gained trust not only in his community but also for international investors. Somehow the Ivorian entrepreneur is trading in trust, this scarcest of business capital.

Broken Bridges

Reflecting on the level of trust in his country, a leading Haitian businessman observed: "Our small island is full of broken bridges." He continued: "Somehow, people believe they are islands unto themselves. As a result, you cannot trust anyone!"

Yet, trust is central to our modern way of life. In his book *Trust: the Social Virtues and the Creation of Prosperity*,[3] Fukuyama defines trust as "the expectation that arises within a community of regular, honest, and cooperative behavior, based on commonly shared norms, on the part of other members of that community."

In other words, trust is the currency that enables society to work. Fukuyama argues that prosperous countries tend to be those where business relations between people can be conducted informally and flexibly on the basis of trust. He also notes the contribution of strong institutions in building trust.

The recognition of this importance of trust in prosperity creation has led social scientists to develop a segmentation of nations between high-trust societies—where trust is extended beyond close networks—and low-trust societies where trust ends at the border of the family or a close community.

The broken bridges metaphor does not apply only to Haiti or developing nations. In the tenth year of its global trust barometer, Edelman, the world leading PR firm, remarked: "In the past decade, both business and government have violated stakeholder trust—and demonstrated how plainly its loss can corrode reputation."[4]

The firm continues: "Trust has emerged as a new line of business—one to be developed and delivered. Companies that embrace the new reality, where the interests of all stakeholders must be considered equally, will see their credibility rise accordingly." In short, trust has become a preeminent issue in global business.

While trust has emerged as a global business issue, broken bridges take a special significance in BoP markets because of their contribution to keeping stakeholders stuck in The Survival Trap. As discussed in Chapter 3, "Why Mindsets Matter," trust is one of the gaps that perpetuate The Survival Trap.

Anyone who looks specifically at Africa would doubtless conclude that lack of governance undermines the flourishing of enterprise on the continent. Global indexes including the Global Competitiveness Index, the Doing Business Survey, and the Opacity Index provide ample evidence.

While the focus seems to be on governance as failure to respect the rule of law and corruption, there is little recognition of how mindsets affect governance. From the perspective of how businesspeople are impacted every day, corruption and governance issues are clearly linked to mindsets.

Corruption begins with the attitude that it is acceptable to appropriate resources for one's own use. As this mental model becomes entrenched at the firm (i.e., a practice of paying/accepting bribes) and industry/cluster level (i.e., seeking government intervention or favors), it comes to affect the whole nation and the international landscape by crystallizing into a mindset where good governance is optional.

Beyond being a social issue, trust is a business concern for those operating in BoP markets. While they may easily identify BoP markets as low-trust environments, most businesspeople are likely to underestimate the impact broken bridges have on their top and bottom lines.

For the top line, businesspeople may struggle to close deals regardless of their competency in environments where the level of trust toward outsiders is very low. This can be a major challenge as it creates conditions for cronyism and corruption. It also means that customers and society may get suboptimal solutions.

The corollary is true. Like Diagou, building trust has been a key success factor for most leaders profiled in this book. Nigerian entrepreneur Tokunbo Talabi has built a security printing business in a country known for financial frauds. Dr. Manu Chandaria has been elected East Africa's most trusted CEO three times.

For the bottom line, while trust is often considered soft-infrastructure, its impact on transaction costs can be felt in hard dollars and cents. Lack of trust erodes profitability in the same way that limited power supply and poor roads affect the bottom line.

The World Bank Doing Business Survey offers some interesting illustrations. On average, it takes 660 days in Africa to a resolve a business dispute, versus 300 in the United States.[5] Assuming a mere $200 dollars per day per lawyer, this translates into $70,000 dollars more. This is cost alone represents 60 times the average yearly income in sub-Saharan Africa.

Understanding the overarching impact of low levels of trust on stakeholders, especially the ones stuck in The Survival Trap, is an important prerequisite for attempts to build trust. In low-trust environments, The Survival Trap's effects can be seen at the levels of various stakeholders.

Individuals perceive a lack of moral purpose and poor leadership. Businesspeople are believed to cut corners and participate in corruption. Local entrepreneurs are said to lack standards. Government plays the blame game and exhibits defensiveness to criticism. Development partners are seen feeding into the corruption system.

In BoP markets, lower levels of trust impact business performance. We now look at specific mindsets that broken bridges have on performance.

Fixing Broken Bridges

To understand how to repair broken bridges, we must understand how trust develops. Naturally, trust develops through direct experience of someone's behavior over time. The importance of direct experience cannot be overstated. Direct experience provides the most immediate way to shape mindsets across stakeholder groups.

Here businesspeople themselves have an important role to play in restoring trust in BoP markets. In many cases, direct experience with business practices suggests a lack of ethics and an absence of concern for the public good. This is the reason why fostering an Archimedean mindset is so important in BoP markets.

Fixing broken bridges requires that we understand the mindsets that undermine moral purpose in business. Three core mindsets outlined in Chapter 3 explain why moral purpose is often missing in BoP markets. These three mindsets are a short-term orientation, zero-sum thinking, and connectocracy.

Businesspeople with short-term orientations seek to extract maximum benefit from every transaction *now*. Political instability and poor governance mechanisms create an incentive for unethical businesspeople to focus on maximizing their gains immediately. In short, they cut corners.

Short-term orientations can be exacerbated by The Survival Trap. In situations where businesses are struggling, it takes bravery to focus on the long term. The universe of possibility is therefore reduced to the immediate future. Being stuck in The Survival Trap often contributes to a second mindset called zero-sum thinking.

In economics, a zero-sum game is a situation in which a stakeholder's gain or loss is exactly balanced by the losses or gains of other participants. Cutting a cake is zero- or constant-sum, because taking a larger piece reduces the amount of available for others. Yet, businesspeople with zero-sum mindsets see others strictly as competitors or even predators.

While zero-sum situations exist in business, relationships with core stakeholders seldom follow a zero-sum game structure. Assuming the counterparts are acting rationally, most commercial exchanges are non-zero-sum activities. Very few businesses can succeed in the long run based on zero-sum thinking.

Literally, connectocracy refers to the rule, government or business by connections. It refers to a mindset that divides the world into *us* versus *them*. In such cases, most connections tend to be inherited either through family, ethnic, or social links. Nonetheless, networking with the right people becomes a core skill.

In a conversation, Evelyn Lewis, one of Sierra Leone's leading entrepreneurs, offered the term "connectocracy" as a way to describe this situation. Connectocracy refers to people's unwillingness to trust stakeholders outside their families, ethnic group, or close affiliated network. Connectocracy dictates that collaboration is limited to a small group excluding a large share of stakeholders due to lack of trust.

In *low-trust societies*, connectocracy becomes the way of business. It often implies that businesspeople only trust or deal fairly with people within their close circles. While such mindsets provide great benefits for those within these circles, it destroys trust beyond.

Ultimately, connectocracy often creates small groups of elites that collectively possess zero-sum thinking and short-term orientation. Combined with The Survival Trap, these three mindsets explain why businesses operating in BoP markets often start with a trust deficit that they must climb out of to achieve their aspirations.

An illustration of connectocracy driven collaboration is within certain ethnic affiliated communities. In most African countries, Lebanese entrepreneurs have built a powerful network that controls entire sectors. Within the communities, credit is extended, purchases are grouped, and information is shared. The Fulani in Nigeria and the Bamileke in Cameroon provide similar examples.

In her book *The World on Fire*,[6] Yale Law School professor Amy Chua studies the impact such powerful economic minorities can have on political stability.

The Trust Ladder

In BoP markets, businesspeople must recognize trust as a foundational mindset. Climbing the trust ladder starts with seeing its dual essence—integrity and empathy (see Figure 6.1). Jean Kacou Diagou and NSIA offer practical ways to climb the trust ladder.

Integrity is about a business honoring its commitments to stakeholders. Establishing a foundation of integrity, which fundamentally means delivering on what one promises, matters because stakeholders can take our words to the bank. Stakeholders will honor our commitments.

This integrity must be balanced with empathy. This is important as empathy shows stakeholders that beyond delivering on what we promised, the business will also strive to do what is right or even what is best for stakeholders. Empathy is also essential to a human-centric approach to business.

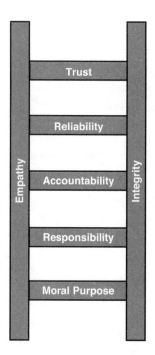

Figure 6.1   The trust ladder

For trust to be present, integrity and empathy both matter. These are two pillars upon which businesspeople can put the rungs that complement the trust ladder. To achieve trust, businesspeople also need moral purpose, responsibility, accountability, and reliability. These are the steps that help businesses climb the trust ladder.

Integrity and empathy are central to NSIA's success. Through its motto, "The true face of insurance," NSIA strives to not only meet its commitment to subscribers in times of need. The company has made integrity and solidarity two of its four core values. Diagou's focus has been to ensure these values are lived through the group.

The first step in the trust ladder is moral purpose. To climb the trust ladder, businesspeople operating in BoP markets must embrace the principle that business must be conducted for both profits and purpose. As discussed in Chapter 5, "Foster an Archimedean Mindset," this moral purpose is also the essence of an Archimedean mindset.

NSIA's main markets display a large population at the BoP. With an insurance penetration at 1 percent, NSIA realizes it has a big role to play in providing insurance. Innovations such as the concept of "bancassurance," which refers to insurance being sold through banks help in realizing this moral purpose.

The second step in the trust ladder is responsibility. Building on moral purpose, responsibility is about striving to follow-through on various commitments the business has toward its key stakeholders. Beyond being a vague concept, responsibility must be anchored on skills.

Again, NSIA takes his responsibilities toward its customers and stakeholders seriously. The company seeks to demonstrate its loyalty to its customers by fulfilling its commitments. Such loyalty has also inspired the company to take a long-term view on issues in an operating reality where most focus on the short term.

The third step is accountability. Accountability is about a business creating mechanisms and incentives for stakeholders to monitor and evaluate the business performance on its core promises. This is especially important in BoP markets where the overall legal framework tends to be weaker.

Step 4—reliability—is the last rung before trust is achieved. It's one thing to be accountable, but people have to feel like they can rely on us to do what we are supposed to do. Once the first two pillars are there and the first four rungs we have described are put in place, trust flourishes.

To institutionalize reliability, NSIA has embraced the value of professionalism. Jean Kacou Diagou strives to recruit competent and qualified talent. Furthermore, he has instituted a meritocratic system that forces its team to deliver and reinforces reliability throughout the group.

Climbing the Trust Ladder

Recognizing the trust ladder is only the beginning to climbing the trust ladder. Businesspeople must also embrace specific practices that help them institutionalize the trust. These practices are specific interventions tailored to meet the demands of the operating reality in BoP markets.

Standards play a big role in making accountability real in a business. By implementing standards, companies are compelled to put in place specific steps to live their promises to clients. In the case of NSIA, the company was the first insurance company in Africa to receive the coveted ISO 2001 certification in April 2009.

The next practice is openness. This practice translates into communication. A clear distinction must be made between communication and public relations. It is about building trust through disclosure. NSIA adopted a stance toward transparency, which has translated into the company being open about its financial performance.

The last practice is about effective governance. Improved governance is essential to building trust. NSIA's partnership with ECP will also help the firm improve its structure and financial transparency through more rigorous management methods. This will be essential to the future success of the firm.

Building a Mosaic of Trust

In its trust barometer, Edelman made an interesting discovery. Globally, when asked which stakeholder should be most important to a CEO's business decisions, 52 percent said that all stakeholders are equally important, underscoring that this is no longer a shareholder but a stakeholder world.

In summary, Edelman suggested that companies build a mosaic of trust. Such a mosaic of trust is paramount to businesspeople serious about building trust in BoP markets. Having an Archimedean mindset rooted in strong moral purpose is a key element in building such a mosaic of trust.

Through its human-centric approach to business, Jean Kacou Diagou offers a prime example of how businesses in BoP markets can leverage the trust ladder to build a mosaic of trust. Michael Fairbanks' COW-F model offers a good framework to think about this mosaic:

Customers: NSIA has built trust with its customers through superior service delivery, solid financial performance, and transparency. Furthermore, the company's strategy to enter new markets through acquisition has helped in preserving trust with customers.

Archimedean businesspeople are able to foster solutions that meet the intrinsic needs of their customers. By launching bancassurance, Jean Kacou Diagou is experimenting with a powerful innovation that could well represent a breakthrough for his group.

Owners: NSIA and its leaders make no excuses of their desire to be leaders in terms of growth and profitability. The company has also taken a long-term approach, which has helped with its growth trajectory.

NSIA has delivered solid shareholder value consistently since its inception. This solid performance and solid prospects have been recognized through the ECP acquisition that sends a signal to the market that NSIA is a top performer.

Workers: NSIA makes no mystery about its focus on recruiting and building a talented team. The group has structured itself in a way that has allowed its founder to focus on the vision and culture while the insurance and banking groups were led by seasoned professionals. In reflecting on his experience, Mr. Bene Lawson, the managing director of NSIA Insurance, notes: "I joined NSIA from a position in industry because of the stature of Mr. Jean Kacou Diagou and the firm's values."

NSIA has also established itself as a leader in an important yet often ignored area especially in BoP markets: the promotion of women professionals. NSIA has not only ensured that several of its senior most leaders are female but also has created a work environment where these leaders can contribute at a maximum.

The future: The concern of Archimedean businesspeople for the future begins with their community. They are often contributors to the social well-being of their employees and the wider communities in which they are situated. This concern goes beyond their immediate communities.

Jean Kacou Diagou has been a tremendous contributor to the leadership agenda of Cote d'Ivoire. Through its leadership of the private sector apex organization, this executive has been one of the key leaders behind Cote d'Ivoire 2040 a visioning exercise aiming to design a future scenario for his country.[7] He also became chairperson of the business association in West Africa in September 2010.

Dealing in Trust

Trust is an important currency for business the world over. Yet, businesspeople often underestimate the impact trust can have on their success especially in BoP markets. To build trust, businesspeople must consider that profits and purpose need to be integrated in their business model.

Insurance veteran Jean Kacou Diagou offers a great example of ways in which businesspeople operating in BoP markets can leverage trust to their advantage. This entrepreneur has built one of Africa's top insurance companies through a balance of integrity and empathy.

A foundational mindset, trust creates the conditions for businesspeople operating in BoP markets to establish strong relationships with key stakeholders. These relationships give these businesspeople a unique opportunity to understand customer needs and articulate superior solutions.

Vignette 4—Kaelo Taking on the Silent Killers

A successful financial director and his wife are seated across from the Kaelo counselor; they are reluctant to take antiretrovirals (ARV) after hearing Thabo Mbeki, the former president of South Africa, say that ARVs are toxic. "What do you want most in life for your family?" she asks. A timid reply comes: "We would like to see our two sons grow into men." Holding onto this thread, the counselor offers a solution: "Your boys deserve to grow up with their parents. Unless you start antiretroviral therapy (ART), you won't make it to their 16th birthdays!"

Such interactions give meaning to Kaelo Consulting, the South African holistic healthcare firm that Justin Savage, Thabang Skwambane, John Jutzen, and Tony Karpelowsky have built since 2004. Offering solutions for HIV/AIDS and other chronic diseases, Kaelo has grown into a profitable business helping companies care for employees and their families.

Embracing the Healthcare Challenge

Most households in BoP markets rely on one breadwinner. When chronic diseases such as HIV/AIDS, diabetes, and hypertension affect a breadwinner, they rob millions of families of their quality of life. As a result, families are left without a stable source of income, which precipitates them into The Survival Trap.

The impact of chronic diseases in BoP markets is not limited to families. Employers are also affected. Companies and institutions face significant productivity and talent losses. Governments face growing healthcare costs while their tax bases shrink significantly. Chronic diseases contribute to making The Survival Trap systemic.

Through its impact on households and enterprises, AIDS has played a more significant role in the reversal of human development than any other single factor.[8] In sub-Saharan Africa, 1.4 million adults and children died as a result of AIDS in 2008 alone. There are an estimated 18 million AIDS orphans in Africa.

For businesses, HIV/AIDS squeeze productivity by adding costs and depleting skills. In Southern Africa, the combined impact of AIDS-related productivity declines, healthcare bills, and recruitment and training expenses cut profits by at least 6 percent to 8 percent. In East Africa, absenteeism accounted for between a quarter and half of business costs.[9]

In the most affected countries, AIDS creates a loss of around 1.5 percent per year on the gross domestic product (GDP).[10]

In the face of the "silent killers," such as HIV/AIDS and other chronic diseases, companies and governments in BoP markets must keep breadwinners alive and productive.

Taking on the "Silent Killers"

Keeping breadwinners alive and productive help ensure families, companies, and countries have a fighting chance to escape The Survival Trap. This has proven a challenge because silent killers have undermined the ability of the public sector in developing countries to mount an effective response.

While businesses often have financial resources and an economic incentive to keep their employees alive and productive, very few tailor-made and efficient solutions exist. Furthermore, the inability to track the progress and financial impact of their healthcare investments against has been a hindrance.

Enter Kaelo Consulting. Thabang says: "An entrepreneur is someone who sees opportunity where others see challenge." Where others saw a challenge, Justin, Thabang, John, and Tony saw an opportunity in the fight against Africa's silent killers.

The company first realized it needed to know the enemy. A serial entrepreneur with experience in healthcare, Justin saw an important gap in existing healthcare offerings. HIV/AIDS and other chronic diseases had completely reshaped the operating reality in South African healthcare. Yet, the local healthcare market had not yet reconfigured to meet all the challenges. An opportunity existed for impact and profit.

Regulations such as the King II Report on Corporate Governance, as well as the Johannesburg Stock Exchange (JSE)/Global Reporting and Employment Equity Reporting, demanded that companies take appropriate steps to mitigate the HIV risk within their businesses. Yet, no provider offered a solution that helped companies manage this risk.

Thabang saw the impact of chronic diseases through the eyes of orphans and vulnerable children (OVC). One day, while visiting a rural community in South Africa, a two-year old girl was scraping her plate against the door. The young child was carrying a plate of chicken feet and maize meal (called Nshima, Pap). As if the image of this lonely child was not enough, a caregiver in the room suggested that "it is good she is learning to be self-sufficient!"

Shaken, Thabang left his merchant banker career to join the fight. "The work has only just begun. My journey is only the beginning of an even harder challenge, a war against an enemy we cannot see and who has already struck leaving us with millions of casualties of war!" Thabang explains passionately.

Integrating Risk Management and Compassion

Armed with their respective experiences, Justin, Thabang, John, and Tony joined forces through Kaelo Consulting. Kaelo's model recognizes both patients and executives as key customers. This dual focus required the firm to develop proprietary tools and approaches that meet the needs of both groups.

This dual focus called for a delicate balance. In essence, it became clear to Kaelo that the solution called for a holistic approach that balanced the need for companies to manage business risks and cost associated with chronic diseases, and the need for compassion and effective preventative and curative health solutions for employees and their families.

From the employee perspective, Kaelo's initiatives integrate workplace health and wellness programs that focus on the overall health and well-being. As a result, employees access a one-stop healthcare shop that covers everything from mental and emotional well-being to prevention to diagnostics to ongoing chronic management and care.

Patients are able to receive the best possible treatments from qualified professionals that understand the impact of poor health on their work productivity and family life. Through task-shifting, Kaelo has managed to address the high costs associated with providing such high-quality healthcare in an environment where skilled resources and talent are scarce.

From the perspective of the business executive, Kaelo provides tailored programs for their employees that span the range of prevention, treatment, and ongoing patient management. These programs are delivered by experienced healthcare providers and coordinated by a business-savvy customer relationship manager.

Beyond these services, Kaelo helps the business executives by offering a data-driven and continuous assessment of return on investments on healthcare spending. Through proprietary tools and surveys such as AIDSrating®, Kaelo helps corporate clients make informed choices and comply with regulations.

Entrepreneurial Solutions for Healthcare

Understanding how Kaelo has managed to generate profits while balancing risk management and compassion is beneficial for businesspeople serving BoP markets.

The first insight is the opportunity mindset that characterizes Kaelo Consulting. Armed with their passion to keep breadwinners alive and productive, the Kaelo team has been able to articulate a holistic solution that encompasses prevention, treatment, and management. This opportunity helped Kaelo leverage three entrepreneurial solutions in particular.

Build trust: Trust is central to Kaelo's success. When the financial director and his wife met with the Kaelo professional, they had recently been diagnosed with HIV. This life-changing diagnosis happened at a time when there was much general skepticism around antiretrovirals (ARVs), which resulted in a number of patients refusing treatment.

Kaelo has worked tirelessly to build trust with its patients, corporate clients, and the regulating bodies. The firm has progressed through its leaders becoming outspoken ambassadors for health and wellness in South Africa. Here the charisma and passion of Thabang have been powerful factors in making Kaelo's voice heard.

To achieve this, Kaelo combines contracting and task shifting, a system whereby all tasks that do not require specialized healthcare training are shifted downward to semiskilled, non-healthcare qualified personnel. Contracting allows Kaelo to use health practitioners as contractors as opposed to full-time staff. Task shifting allows Kaelo to train community health workers to provide services that do not require a high level of expertise. This has helped in bridging the leadership and talent gaps.

Focus on solutions: The secret to Kaelo's success lies in the firm's innovativeness, which originates from its founders' ability to see the many layers of chronic diseases, especially HIV/AIDS, in South Africa. Kaelo's recognition of chronic diseases as more than medical issues has been crucial.

Clearly seeing other effects such as education, stigma, business costs, and compliance issues has pushed Kaelo to develop solutions to these often neglected layers of the problem. This ability to embrace complexity while offering simple tools has allowed Kaelo to succeed.

Operate efficiently and sustainably: Kaelo has grown to more than 72 full-time staff and a network of 800 healthcare professionals. In an industry where talent is critical, scarce, and costly, Kaelo has managed growth through its ability to operate efficiently and sustainably.

I Live

Every year for the past six years, that couple has come to Kaelo at the same time of year they started treatment to update the team on their progress. They have seen both their boys graduate from high school and begin university. Most importantly, they are recognizing their dream of seeing their sons grow into men.

Kaelo was appointed by a donor-funded agency to launch the I Live campaign to encourage people to identify what they live for: "I live for my family, for my community, for World Cup 2010, etc." As the developing world looks for breakthroughs in healthcare, innovative approaches such as the one embodied by Kaelo are the only real option for scalable breakthroughs.

Endnotes

[1] Emerging Capital Partners website: http://www.ecpinvestments.com/news/1686.xml.

[2] Groupe NSIA website, http://www.groupensia.com/; NSIA accelere son developpment (NSIA is accelerating its development), *Jeune Afrique*, 02/18/2009, http://www.jeuneafrique.com/Article/ARTJAJA2510p064-065.xml0/assurance-jean-kacou-diagou-nsiansia-accelere-son-developpement.html.

[3] Francis Fukuyama, *Trust: The Social Virtues and The Creation of Prosperity* (New York: Free Press, 1995).

[4] Edelman is the leading independent global PR firm. More information about Edelman's Global Trust barometer is available at: http://www.edelman.com/trust/2010.

[5] The World Bank Group "Doing Business: Measuring Business Regulations," http://www.doingbusiness.org/ExploreTopics/EnforcingContracts/2010

[6] Amy Chua, *World on Fire: How Exporting Free Market Democracy Breeds Ethnic Hatred and Global Instability.* (New York: Doubleday, 2002).

[7] Interview with Jean Kacou Diagou, *Jeune Afrique*, 01/09/2009, http://www.jeuneafrique.com/Articles/Dossier/ARTJAJA2536-37p110-111.xml0/interview-jean-kacou-diagou-cgeci-crise-mondialejean-kacou-diagou-le-plus-difficile-est-derriere-nous.html.

[8] United Nations Development Program, Human Development Report 2005, overview, http://hdr.undp.org/en/reports/global/hdr2005/.

[9] "HIV/AIDS: It's Your Business," UNAIDS, 2003, http://data.unaids.org/publications/irc-pub06/jc1008-business_en.pdf.

[10] Robert Greener "The Impact of HIV/AIDS on Poverty and Inequality" in *The Macroeconomics of AIDS*, ed. Markus Haacker (Washington, DC: International Monetary Fund, 2004).

7

Focus on Solutions

Diop, Zero...

It was my first time in Rome. My tour of Vatican City had just ended. As I stepped out of the square, a young man closed in with a grin.

"This is an original Louis Vuitton bag. I will give it to you for 200 euros!" The look on my face was unequivocal. "Okay! Because you are my brother, give me 100 euros *only*!" Diop pronounced my wife needed a Louis Vuitton handbag—a fake one at that. The only detail to square away was price.

Senegalese traders are very persistent. In less than two minutes, Diop gave me a litany of reasons why my wife needed the bag. When he realized I was not yet married, Diop decided my sister needed the bag even more. Within five minutes, a mob of traders was fighting to offer me the exact same bag. The price was now at 30 euros.

The offering is different, the strategy familiar. Senegalese traders are to customers what packs of wolves are to their prey. They overwhelm lonesome, unsuspecting customers and do not give up until the prey succumbs. Like most survival businesspeople, their main weapon remains price.

Persisting in Supplying the Survival Products

One of the greatest tragedies in BoP nations, especially Africa, is the fact that stories like Diop are not isolated. While the specifics may be different, hardworking individuals, businesses, industries, and even countries persist in supplying the *survival products*. While this may seem an unfair pronouncement, the evidence is unmistakable.

Seeing this evidence requires that businesspeople consider the impact of their offering on key stakeholders. As useful framework to unveil this evidence is the COW-F model that we introduced in Chapter 5, "Foster an Archimedean Mindset." Such *survival* products can be identified through a fourfold impact on stakeholders.

First, survival products fail to meet the intrinsic customer needs. In the age of the experience economy, customers at all levels of the economic pyramid are looking for offerings that give great value for the money while respecting their dignity. This is one of the key failings of survival products.

Practically, such survival products translate into easily replicable, below standards offerings that are often stuck in unattractive market segments. Such products weaken businesses by forcing them to compete on price. As such, survival products are often a key factor in the perpetuation of survival business.

Diop's counterfeit bags are the archetype of the survival products. Mass tourism is an example of such an offering that applies to a whole industry. For instance, Kenya and Mauritius's tourism receipts amounted to US $500 million in 1995. However, Kenya had 844,000 visitors while Mauritius had only 80,000.

Second, survival products fail to meet the basic needs of workers. The key selling point for survival products is often price. The elusive quest for the lowest price often means that businesspeople must keep their costs as low as possible. Given a difficult operating reality in BoP markets, this often translates into a reduction in wages.

Observably, workers who produce survival products often end up at the economic BoP. In Africa and the rest of the developing world, subsistence farmers often make up the bulk of this category. Most remain price takers in markets that they do not understand or control. This also means they receive low wages.

Again, Diop's great bags went from 200 to 30 euros in five minutes. This challenge also plays out nationally. While the emergence of China and India has fuelled a commodity boom, the long-term trend in commodity prices has been down. This is yet another pointer to the impact that survival products can have on BoP markets.

Next, survival products prevent businesspeople and their shareholders from building sustainable organizations and sustainable wealth. In most cases, survival products translate into companies with lower profitability or hand-to-mouth operations. This often means that the risk adjusted returns are below par.

Observably, the structure of the private sector in most BoP markets is a testimony to this challenge. On the one hand, most private entities are micro and small-scale firms revolving around one person. Second, a very small number of entities survives their owners. Both aspects contribute to perpetuating The Survival Trap.

Finally, survival products represent missed opportunities for the community. This is arguably one of C. K. Prahalad's greatest contributions. In *Fortune at the Bottom of the Pyramid*, Prahalad unveiled the vast market at the economic BoP. As discussed in Chapter 1, "Identifying the Problem—And the Solution," four billion BoP citizens represent a market of $5 trillion.

An often overlooked yet important drawback of survival products is their negative impact on the environment. One of the trade-offs that businesspeople engaged in survival business often make is with the environment. We discuss this issue in Chapter 13, "Societal Innovations Through Mindset Change."

The observation that most businesspeople in BoP markets, especially Africa, supply survival products could seem unfair; the vast majority of businesspeople strive to improve their lot under a stifling operating reality. Furthermore, BoP markets are increasingly home to the world's greatest fortunes.

The issue with survival products is not that they do not profit firms. Rather, survival products keep BoP markets, especially Africa, stuck in The Survival Trap.

Why Do Businesses Persist in Supplying Survival Products?

It is important to unveil why businesspeople and sometimes country leaders persist in supplying survival products. Many businesspeople continue to focus on the *wrong* products because these operators hold beliefs and mindsets that undermine their ability to seize attractive opportunities in BoP markets and beyond.

While every businessperson faces a unique set of challenges, three main mindsets undermine their efforts.

The first mindset is that price is the main determinant of value. The traditional approach to price is flawed. While price often serves a good *proxy* for value, price is not value. The standard response to competition is often to drop prices. Yet, a lower price does not always translate into more value for customers.

The culprit here is a lack of understanding of customer needs. In the absence of an actionable understanding of what customers really want, most businesspeople use price as a shortcut. This mindset results from a poor understanding of customer needs and applies equally to indigenous and international managers.

As discussed above, an unbridled focus on price can result in hand-to-mouth operations. Businesses will lack resources to train workers, innovate on offerings, and grow the business. In a global world where the movement of goods and services is facilitated, a failure to train, innovate, or grow often means total business failure.

Next is the assumption that money is the main driver of innovation. Instead, knowledge in the form of qualified staff is the main driver of innovation. A good example is Nuru Energy, which has managed with limited capital to create one of the most innovative portfolio of energy solutions for the BoP markets.

Failure to recognize the primacy of staff in driving innovation leads to missed opportunities for customer retention and diversification of offerings. It also prevents businesses from learning about relative position in the market. Businesses must realize that quality staff trumps money when it comes to innovation.

Finally, leaders often mistakenly equate a low income with lack of opportunity. International managers are more likely to fall prey to this misconception. Such managers often come with preconceived notions about the structure of markets, business models, and opportunities in Africa.

Vijay Mahajan seeks to debunk this belief in *Africa Rising*. Mahajan makes a strong case for businesspeople to change the way they think about Africa, from a collection of countries with varying agendas and conflicts, to a unified pan-African consumer base of one billion people with tremendous purchasing power.

The three misconceptions outlined above derive from mindsets induced by The Survival Trap. The second way in which this vicious cycle contributes to businesses focusing on the wrong product is by perpetuating an operating reality that makes innovation and creativity costly and difficult.

...Mo, One!

Remember Diop? My escape came when my phone rang. A client managed to track me down all the way to Rome on my international number. As I responded to the call, Diop and his crew zeroed in on another target. Thirty minutes later, the cell phone company had just made the thirty euros Diop and his crew wanted so badly.

Sudanese telecom entrepreneur Mo Ibrahim has become one of Africa's most celebrated business success stories. Not only did Mo succeed in building one of Africa's leading cell phone companies but also he did it with flair. In 2005, the $3.4 billion Zain's acquisition of Celtel was the capstone of his business career.

Building in the footsteps of entrepreneurs such as Mo Ibrahim, cell phone companies have made headway. Africa is the fastest growing mobile market in the world with mobile penetration in the region ranging from 30 percent to 100 percent and in most countries exceeding the fixed line penetration.[1]

A key factor in that success has been the ability of mobile operators to leverage technology to address real needs, especially at the economic BoP. Kenya's Safaricom has become the archetype of this trend through its flagship M-Pesa, mobile banking platform. In the process, Safaricom has slowly emerged as arguably Kenya's biggest bank.

As survival entrepreneurs such as Diop continue to struggle to make ends meet, a new generation of businesspeople is creatively tapping into the vast potential of BoP markets. Instead of focusing on price, these businesspeople focus on value instead. Their offering is different and so is their strategy.

Redefining Value Through Design Thinking

To bring the right focus on solutions, businesspeople must revisit their mindsets. This begins with recognizing that good businesses generate profits and great businesses create value for their customers and stakeholders. The quest to create customer and stakeholder enduring value must top the business agenda.

Within the operating reality of BoP markets, this quest to create enduring customer and stakeholder value is hardened by at least three challenges. First, markets and distribution are not clearly defined. This often expands the scope of activities that businesspeople must perform well to be successful.

Second, basic inputs such as skills, infrastructure, and even security are often missing especially in BoP communities. While we highlighted this reality as one of the greatest opportunities in BoP markets, it is important to recognize this opportunity as a formidable challenge for businesspeople as they try to create value.

Finally, the previous two challenges combine to create a third one. Ill-defined markets and lack of basic inputs mean that businesspeople must often rely on a host of stakeholders in the community to be effective. This challenge also translates into the needs for prosperity ecosystems as discussed in Chapter 9, "Enable Prosperity Ecosystems."

What is required to go beyond products toward solutions? Innovation. Businesspeople need to be truly innovative if they are going to articulate and offer solutions. The brand of innovation required does not necessarily require years of fundamental research. Instead, it is a brand of innovation grounded in the reality.

The three challenges outlined above means that businesspeople operating in BoP markets must rely on innovation more than any other location. This innovation must be rooted in a quest to provide enduring customer and stakeholder value. This innovation must go beyond existing products and offerings into a quest for solutions.

In BoP markets, the ability to ground innovation in reality is particularly important. As discussed extensively throughout this book, The Survival Trap creates significant operating constraints for businesses. Copycats that focus on replicating models from other geographies to BoP markets often fail.

The best thinking on how businesspeople can increase their focus on solutions comes from an annex field to business that has been marginalized of recent. While most businesspeople perceive design as an odd combination of art and aesthetics, its essence offers the key to help businesspeople migrate from mere products to solutions.

In his landmark *Harvard Business Review* article, Tim Brown CEO of IDEO introduces the idea of design thinking. Brown asserts that thinking like a designer can transform the way you develop products, services, processes—and even strategy. In short, design thinking not only offers solutions but also upgrades business models.

Brown defines design thinking as a methodology that imbues the full spectrum of innovation activities with a human-centered design ethos. Building on the systemic view that design thinking entails, Brown then proceeds to outline three core interrelated aspects of this process: inspiration, ideation, and implementation.

Brown invites businesspeople to go below the surface and draw their inspiration from the reality that customers or stakeholders are facing. Nowhere is this reality richer than in BoP markets. As a result, businesspeople that adopt design thinking will be able to seize great opportunities in BoP markets.

The key contribution of design thinking for BoP markets is that it is a "people first" approach; design thinkers can imagine solutions that are inherently desirable and meet explicit or latent needs. Great design thinkers observe the world in minute detail. They notice things that others do not and use their insights to inspire innovation.

Building on this idea, Rwandan designer Amin Gafaranga suggests that Human Centered Mean goes beyond traditional marketing. It is people-centered solutions, participatory approach, and collective solutions, which require a unique understanding of culture and context. Such an understanding must come from businesspeople's ability to embed themselves in the reality of BoP markets.

Furthermore, the unique understanding means looking at people's values and way of life as a means and fuel for inspiration for innovative solutions to their challenges. This is an important distinction as the ability to look at people's values and integrate them into solutions is critical in restoring dignity to customers especially the ones at the BoP. As illustrated in Figure 7.1, the SOAR framework can be a powerful mechanism for developing innovative solutions for customers at the BoP.

Essence	• Design thinking			
	Strategy	**Operations**	**Assets**	**Reality**
Principles	• People-Centered	• Collective Actions	• People Focus	• Holistic Innovation
Practices	• Deriving Inspiration from People Experience	• Delivering the Solution Together	• Listening for Breakthrough	• Experimenting for Discovery

Figure 7.1　Transforming your business through solutions

Focusing on Solutions

The good news is that applying design thinking to BoP markets does not require artistic flair or deep functional expertise. Instead it requires embracing some key principles and practices that have the potential to revolutionize a company's offering by changing its strategy, operations, assets, and operating reality.

This undoubtedly requires hard work. While some may be skeptical and question the return of their investments, the various entrepreneurs and managers discussed throughout this book suggest this is not only possible but also profitable. Furthermore, it is significant by way of impact on parts of the world that need it the most.

Building on some of these success stories we illustrate how businesses can focus on solutions by embedding design thinking into their business model. These illustrations cover a range of opportunities in various industries highlighting the relevance of solutions for BoP markets.

The first core principle is being people centered. A strategy that is people centered begins with a clear identification of the customers or stakeholders being served. After this identification, businesspeople must realize that their offerings must address prevailing needs in a comprehensive way.

Here, the businesses operating in BoP markets must go beyond traditional segmentations to understand the variety of customers involved in the usage of any products and purchase decisions. Identifying the needs of customers and that of key influencers is important.

To become people centered, businesspeople must learn to derive their inspiration from people experiences. Such experiences must be rooted in the operating reality of the stakeholders targeted. As noted by Tim Brown, design thinkers have a keen sense of observation noting minute details that hold the key to truly innovative solutions.

A good example for a design thinking inspired solution is Nuru Energy. Nuru's CEO Sameer Hajee says: "When developing products for base of pyramid markets, many companies (and leaders) unfortunately make some terrible assumptions about what customers need and would be willing to pay for."

He continues: "Typically, these assumptions are drawn out of their own reality and not from having spent any significant time with the customer. It is no wonder why products that have tried to displace kerosene (solar lamps, home solar lighting systems) for years haven't made any significant headway in rural Africa."

In the context of BoP markets, the most practical way to derive such inspiration is to look for opportunities to interact with customers in their own environments as they use a business's offering. Such direct observation when complemented with conversations with stakeholders is often paramount in identifying real constraints.

Beyond surveys, the Nuru Energy team led a discovery process that involved a combination of visits and observations. This helped them understand life according to kerosene users. The two-year process helped eventually to inform the work of Nuru's industrial design team.

The second principle is collective action. This principle must inform the operations of businesses operating in BoP markets that are seeking to focus on solutions. Collective action is about designing business operations is such a way that customers and other key stakeholders are empowered to deliver the solution with the business.

A good example of such collective action comes from Eva Muraya, the CEO of Color Creations. Through its BE (or Becoming Entrepreneur) campaign, Color Creation Trust aims to help 22,000 unemployed young Kenyans establish merchandising firms selling and distributing branded products.

In a nutshell, Color Creation is co-creating these businesses with the young entrepreneurs. By leveraging technology, Color Creations is empowering these young entrepreneurs to develop their own business and create an offering of branded merchandise for the communities where they live.

As it relates to assets, businesspeople must realize focus on people. That is the third principle. In the developed world, customer-centered or people-centered approaches have become somewhat of a fad. While everyone professes to put employees and customer first, most businesses have not necessarily developed the appropriate mindsets.

Archimedean businesspeople are the archetype of business leaders with a clear focus on people. As previously discussed, this focus is informed by moral purpose that places stakeholder needs at the center of the entrepreneurial pursuit while creating the conditions for economic profitability.

A people focus is even more difficult to come within businesses operating in BoP markets. On the customer side, this can be blamed partly on the lack of formal mechanisms and tools to ascertain customer needs. On a stakeholder side, this can be blamed on bigger needs in the community that no businesses have resources to address.

Kaelo Consulting, the South African holistic healthcare business profiled in Chapter 6, "Build Trust," offers a good example of a people-focused business. Beyond their people-focused mission, this firm has built people-centered assets through its vast network of qualified professionals who provide services thanks to its task-shifting model.

Alexandre de-Carvalho provides another example of a corporate leader who has built a people-centered business model. As discussed in detail in Chapter 11, "Bridge the Leadership Gap," Alexandre manages to build a strong national team that eventually replaces all expatriates and starts sending professionals back to his headquarters in France.

Last but not least, operating reality in BoP markets is characterized with many constraints that require that businesspeople innovate holistically. This last principle must be grounded in the business's capacity to integrate across domains to provide a holistic solution that is aligned with the true constraints customer are facing.

The practice that supports such holistic solutions is experimentation. Rather than waiting to roll out the perfect solution, it is important that businesses be willing to run experiments. Such experiments accelerate learning especially when the businesses can fail fast and as a result migrate toward a sustainable solution.

Recognized for its innovation process, UST Global offers a good example of a business that is big on looking for ways to integrate across domains. One of UST's strong points is the IT solution firm's ability to network with best-of-class solutions providers from the industry. This has helped the firm remain ahead of the competition.

It is also a great strength as the company seeks to develop ever more innovative solutions in the very competitive IT services space. The firm has leveraged specific technology tools to sustain such innovations. Last but not least, the firm has embedded such holistic experimentation in its culture.

Virtuous Cycle of Innovative Solutions

Why should businesses invest in upgrading their products? Because businesses that succeed in upgrading their products graduate out of The Survival Trap. These firms see their position improve greatly thanks to a virtuous cycle of innovative solutions. It helps to articulate clearly how the virtuous cycle of innovative solutions works.

Customer- and stakeholder-centered solutions are likely to attract the right channel partners and help in fostering a prosperity ecosystem. Eventually such an ecosystem will help with sales and distribution. Intrinsic product quality coupled with great marketing improves customer and stakeholder experience.

Satisfied customers and stakeholders are more likely to pay a higher price that provides the business with the capital required to reinvest in its people and technology. Sufficient capital drives product innovation, which eventually kick starts, the process anew. While this virtuous cycle goes on, the business and its solutions build a great brand.

This virtuous cycle provides a couple of specific benefits that should be discussed. First, limited employee skills: Offering sophisticated products often calls for skilled workers who by virtue of their training command higher wages thanks to the superior offerings they create. Eventually, this is an important key in helping BoP markets graduate from The Survival Trap.

Workers also start deriving enormous pride from solutions that translate into customer service. Pride also creates a sense of ownership of the firm's problems and opportunities. As a result, business strengthens, workers are motivated, and satisfaction increases. This satisfaction matters a great deal for it helps innovation.

Next, greater profits mean shareholders have a better chance at realizing a higher return. Continuous innovation often means consistent profit. A virtuous cycle of innovative solutions provides sustainable and attractive returns. In time, high returns create incentives to brave the difficult operating reality.

This virtuous cycle of innovative solutions can help transform the bottom of the pyramid. As discussed earlier, higher wages mean such employees have a chance to escape The Survival Trap themselves. Higher skills translate into employees having the knowledge and resources to invest in the skills of their own children.

Being at the bottom of the pyramid, employees have first-hand knowledge of the challenges facing the average citizen. More skilled and resourced employees often have a better chance at articulating better business solutions for these challenges. Eventually, some will graduate as entrepreneurs offering homegrown solutions.

Communities need entrepreneurs to develop products that address some of the societal needs in an affordable and sustainable fashion. In Chapter 13, we outline critical areas where BoP markets, especially Africa, need novel entrepreneurial solutions that must be rooted in design thinking.

Toward a Solution Paradigm

This chapter suggests strongly that businesspeople must be proactive when it relates to focusing on solutions. While they have a clear responsibility, it is important to recognize that the operating reality is a major challenge to this responsibility.

As discussed throughout the book, businesspeople operate in a context that makes innovation difficult. For instance, soft infrastructure (i.e., standards, corruption, etc.) and hard infrastructure (i.e., power, electricity, roads, etc.) matter a great deal in fostering innovative solutions. Yet both are often unreliable when operating at the BoP.

Addressing constraints related to the operating reality matters a great deal to businesspeople in focusing on solutions. It is important to recognize that upgrading this operating reality cannot be the sole responsibility of businesses. Governments also share the responsibility to create the conditions for businesses to thrive.

The success or failure of products or services is often viewed as a private problem. Adopting a solution paradigm requires BoP markets to create the conditions for their firms to develop innovative solutions. But before BoP markets, especially Africa, can embrace these new ways, leaders must be committed to supporting entrepreneurs.

To adopt a solution paradigm, BoP nations, especially Africa, must go beyond the rhetoric that government responsibility is to create an environment for business to thrive. Instead, nations must invest in specialized infrastructure, business development services, and knowledge that support business.

Targeted at the operating reality, specialized infrastructure refers to investments such as cold chains or targeted guarantee funds. Such specialized infrastructure must target a set of firms operating in entire industries. We examine how businesses can induce such efforts in Chapter 9.

Business development services refer to targeted capacity building interventions aiming to reinforce the ability of businesses to upgrade their operations. Such services are considered a public service in most developed nations. In Africa, these offerings are still rare, making it difficult even for willing businesspeople to upgrade their products.

A Fighting Chance for Diop

Businesspeople such as Diop contribute a great deal to BoP markets, especially Africa. Such businesspeople create the conditions for the continent to begin addressing its own problems and escape The Survival Trap. It is critical for such entrepreneurs to have a fighting chance at winning globally.

This fighting chance begins with the recognition that such entrepreneurs must upgrade their products. The new approach has to begin with entrepreneurs themselves engaging with the mindsets about customer and stakeholder value. It also requires government leaders to create the conditions for innovation.

Embracing design thinking or people-centered innovation is the essence of focusing on solutions. Eventually, this innovation must be hardwired throughout the company's business model and form an integral part of the contract between businesspeople and their stakeholders.

As the various vignettes of entrepreneurs throughout this book suggest, it is possible for leaders operating at all levels of business in BoP markets especially Africa to embrace solutions. Such embracing holds a twofold benefit that translates into economic success and transformed communities. It also leads to a desire to operate effectively and sustainably.

Vignette 5—Nuru, an Alternative to Dark Light

Laurent Hakizimana owns a business in a small community in rural Rwanda. Laurent operates a small shop like many microentrepreneurs in developing countries. As a retailer of necessity goods, Laurent plays an active role in the Mayange district, one of the poorest areas in Rwanda due to its arid lands.

Recently, Laurent's fortunes started improving. His newest product, a small LED lamp ably named Nuru or literally "light" in the local language, is leading to a dramatic increase in sales. Since he started retailing and recharging these lamps, Laurent Hakizimana sees a bright future not only for his community but also his business.

Kerosene: The Dark Light

Access to light is a cross cutting challenge for development. Children struggle to study after sundown. Businesses face high operating costs when resorting to alternative sources of power. Overall, a lack of access to light reduces productivity dramatically by forcing people to adjust their activity to sunlit hours. It is estimated that the African BoP spends $10 billion annually on lighting.[2]

In the absence of alternatives, rural communities in Africa have resorted to kerosene lamps. Since their inception in 1853, kerosene lamps have used a petroleum derivative in a rudimentary device to produce concentrated light around the device. Today, an estimated two billion people use kerosene lamps in communities living at the bottom of the pyramid. In Africa alone, these people spend $4 billion annually on kerosene lighting.[3]

Yet, the empirical evidence on the drawbacks associated with kerosene lamps is sobering. The World Bank estimates that 780 million women and children breathing kerosene fumes inhale the equivalent of smoke from two packs of cigarettes per day. This exposure results in more than one million deaths annually, more than 60 percent of which are of children under age 14.

Kerosene lamps further cause countless deaths by burns, fires, and suffocation. Recent studies suggest that as many as 4 percent of deaths are caused by indoor pollution linked to kerosene fumes and fires.

To make matter worse, kerosene is a significant cost to most families at the BoP. Families spend 10 percent to 40 percent of their income on kerosene-based lighting. When coupled with the evidence on toxicity, this statistic suggests too high a cost.

Kerosene also has significant adverse impact on the environment. Kerosene emits nitrogen oxides and sulfur oxides, which contribute to acid rain and ozone depletion. This situation ultimately undermines the very ecosystems these communities depend on. Climate change has been described by the UN Secretary General Ban Ki-moon as the "greatest collective challenge we face as a human family."

Out of the Darkness

The kerosene example illustrates an important dynamic that keeps entire communities in BoP markets stuck in The Survival Trap. Poor access to basic infrastructure such as electricity, water, and roads keeps individuals focused on basic survival and increases the cost of doing business. In short, lack of access to basic infrastructure negatively impacts productivity.

Such situations become so overwhelming that a frantic search for solutions ensues. For example, people resort to kerosene lamps, a familiar alternative. The good news is that it palliates the immediate need for light. As this solution goes wholesale, significant drawbacks emerge that people must live with for lack of alternatives.

Similar cases exist for other issues not only around infrastructure, but also in healthcare, education, and access to finance.

When considering available technology, this vicious cycle presents leaders with a major moral challenge. This challenge is best framed as a question: Why do these leaders and businesspeople insist on distributing products that keep them stuck in The Survival Trap instead of finding efficient and sustainable solutions?

Customer-Centric Approach to Innovation

A duo of young entrepreneurs, Sameer Hajee and Julio de Souza, has elected to answer the call. In their mid-thirties, the pair met while working at the United Nations in Nairobi. After they uncovered the kerosene story, it became a fixation that they could not just sweep under the rug. They decided to take on the challenge.

Sameer and Julio chose Mayange as the first battlefield in their war on kerosene. With family roots in East Africa, Sameer, the CEO, aims to change mindsets around sustainable energy. "When developing products for base of pyramid markets, many companies (and leaders) unfortunately make some terrible assumptions about what customers need and would be willing to pay for. Typically, these assumptions are drawn out of their own reality and not from having spent any significant time with the customer. It is no wonder why products that have tried to displace kerosene (solar lamps, home solar lighting systems) for years haven't made any significant headway in rural Africa," the soft-spoken Sameer says. An athletic Brazilian with an infectious laugh, Julio moved his wife and two children to Rwanda three years ago.

Julio's first mission was to help the firm understand the perspective of kerosene users. Beyond surveys, the Nuru Energy team led a discovery process that involved a combination of surveys, visits, and observations. This helped them understand life according to kerosene users. The two-year process helped them draw inspiration from the reality of their future customers to refine their products and the system in place to deliver them. This data informed the work of Nuru's industrial design team under the leadership of Barry Whitmill and Simon Tremeer, two South African industrial designers.

The result was a brilliantly simple yet powerful idea: Produce a rechargeable light whose characteristics mimicked those of kerosene—extremely portable, reliable, and could be purchased in increments. This posed a design challenge for both the light and its accompanying battery. "After many tries, we came up with a unique pedal generator that can charge the lamps and other appliances quickly," recounts Julio.

But the solution for Nuru did not stop with its patent-pending LED lamp design and chargers. The firm realized that traditional distribution would not work. Nuru Energy's team elected to build a dedicated distribution model that invests in local entrepreneurs to expand their activities by including Nuru Energy.

Local entrepreneurs like Laurent Hakizimana act as a critical link in selling, educating, and servicing the lights in their communities. With a penetration of 20 percent in Mayange in 18 months, Nuru Energy is doing something right. Julio has now shifted his attention to recruiting, training, and retaining this growing network of Nuru Energy entrepreneurs.

In Rwanda alone, Nuru Energy aims to distribute 100,000 lights over a two-year period and to abate on average 30,000 tonnes of carbon dioxide equivalent per year. Carbon credits revenue will help Nuru make its products affordable and accessible to rural households in Rwanda. It also creates an incentive for the firm to remain sustainable.

Keeping the Commitment

Despite its patented product, tremendous progress, and fast growth, the young company has faced customary challenges for firms operating in BoP markets. Access to intelligent capital to scale up the solutions has been lacking. While the team is truly innovative, it readily admits the need for strategic support to scale their solution.

"The biggest challenge we have faced is support to our entrepreneurs from microfinance institutions," Sameer remarks. At a cost of around $200, the generators are beyond the reach of most microentrepreneurs. Averse to risk, microfinance institutions have been unreliable partners in financing Nuru Energy entrepreneurs.

Nuru performs its design in South Africa, and then manufactures in China to distribute its products in Africa. Given its low price, managing such a global supply chain has been challenging. The second challenge is how to grow a viable business while operating a global supply chain.

Reflecting on this challenge, Julio suggests: "Our objective is providing Nuru light at an affordable cost while making it attractive for our customers. Growth is critical." In addressing this second challenge, Nuru Energy needs to build trust and enable a prosperity ecosystem at a global scale.

Nuru Energy: Value-Added Design

Nuru offers unique insights for businesses operating in BoP markets around three specific entrepreneurial opportunities for prosperity:

Archimedean mindset: Sameer and Julio are entrepreneurs who are unapologetic about making money while making a difference. The desire to leverage an entrepreneurial solution for prosperity is at the heart of Nuru's business model. The firm offers a great example of a business model seeking to serve all stakeholders.

Focus on solutions: Nuru Energy is the archetype of a firm applying design thinking to BoP challenges. Nuru's team led a discovery process that helped the firm articulate the right solutions both from a technological, as well as a distribution, perspective. This focus on solutions is critical for societal innovations to escape The Survival Trap.

Operate efficiently and sustainably: Nuru has resolved the tension between environmental sustainability and low costs. Nuru's patented design allows the firm to create a state-of-the-art LED light at a very small cost. At the same time, the firm is driving toward sustainability by creating a business model where it generates carbon credits and revenues.

Lighting Africa

The world is beginning to believe that Nuru is on to something. The firm has won a number of prestigious prizes including recently being named one of the "Top 10 Ideas to Change the World" by CNBC, winner of the 2010 UNEP Sasakawa Prize, and Grand Prize winner of the Global Social Entrepreneurship Competition.

The biggest recognition for Nuru's efforts comes from microentrepreneurs such as Laurent Hakizimana. Laurent says: "I make money and I am now part of making sure our children can study." An example to businesses operating in BoP markets, Nuru Energy offers a key to changing the lives of millions not only in Rwanda, but throughout the developing world.

Endnotes

[1] African Mobile Factbook 2008, Blycroft Publishing http://www.w3.org/2008/MW4D/wiki/images/9/9c/FrontPage%24Africa_Mobile_Fact_Book_2008.pdf, p.4.

[2] Dalberg Global Development Advisors, "Lighting Africa," May 2010, p.4.

[3] Dalberg Global Development Advisors, "Lighting Africa," May 2010, p.6.

8

Operate Efficiently and Sustainably

Changing Colors

After 20 years of dedicated struggle, Haile's family has reached the pinnacle. Today the family business is one of the top finished leather goods manufacturers in Ethiopia. Haile wishes his dad could be here to see EDL's success; unfortunately, his father passed away from an undiagnosed respiratory disease.

From its humble beginning in the handicraft sector, Ethiopian Distinguished Leathers (EDL) has forward-integrated into the manufacturing of high quality branded leather goods that are now distributed in Europe's fashion capitals. The company has been recognized as one of Africa's best leather exporters to Europe.

Yet, the situation is far from perfect. With only $5 million in revenue, the firm remains a small drop in the $40 billion global finished leather goods market. EDL is losing market share to competition from China and India. Furthermore, the firm is not competing in the newer, fast-growing sustainable leather segments.

What really worries Haile is a tradition that could prove to be EDL's undoing. Since its inception, EDL has relied on the wet blue process for tanning. Chromium, a little known heavy metal, is responsible for the blue color in "wet blue." Chromium is also a carcinogen. Haile feels stuck with EDL's manufacturing process.

Standing on Quicksand

Haile's fears are common to many businesspeople operating in BoP markets. Market shares are decreasing, margins are dwindling, and new markets seem out of reach. For these businesspeople, the experience they have is not unlike standing on quicksand: They feel pulled down by forces beyond their control.

This pressure stems from a fundamental change in the world economy that is pressuring businesses to change and improve productivity. The change is globalization, the accelerating integration of the world's economies. While globalization offers opportunity for the prepared, it is a formidable challenge for the rest.

Rapidly declining costs of communication and transportation translate into easier and less costly access to an ever-increasing variety of new products and services. The globalizing environment helps customers become more sophisticated and creates more competition among suppliers, from more nations, to provide better value.

Their initial reaction is to look for ways to maintain their cost competitiveness. This often means stepping on the cost-reduction treadmill. Nowhere is the reaction to globalization stronger than in manufacturing. Manufacturers from BoP markets, such as Haile, face a tough operating reality where basic infrastructure is not only unreliable but also more costly than in the rest of the world. As a result, the only cost they think they can control is labor costs.

The rise of China in Africa is a good illustration of this reality. China's top 20 exports to Africa are mostly in light manufacturing goods. The World Bank estimates that the cost of doing business in Africa is 20 to 40 percent above that for other developing regions.[1]

It comes as no surprises that most businesspeople are ambivalent about globalization. Yet, they must embrace globalization, not resist it, and this embrace must include a commitment to continually improve productivity. What businesspeople working in BoP markets really need is to operate efficiently and sustainably.

The lack of sustainable practices creates more difficult environmental situations for customers and businesses alike. The bottom of the pyramid is the first victim of environmental degradation. Pollution, disease, and climate change impact this vulnerable part of the population greatly.

International Panel on Climate Change (IPCC) Chairman Rejendra Pachauri told journalists at the recent release of the UN Climate Change Report: "It is the poorest of the poor in the world, and this includes poor people even in prosperous societies, who are going to be worst hit. This does become a global responsibility in my view."[2]

This initial reaction only reinforces the experience of standing on quicksand. Indeed, it keeps such businesses in The Survival Trap. When the focus remains on indiscriminate cost reduction, businesses operating in BoP markets and BoP citizens fail to benefit from globalization. Instead, they become victims.

A Difficult Operating Reality

To understand why businesspeople operating in BoP markets experience standing on quicksand, we must unveil specific challenges in the operating reality that give rise to this experience. Given the difficult context, these business leaders must only bear part of the blame.

Ironically, the operating reality provides a strong rationale for seeking to operate efficiently and sustainably. As previously illustrated, logistics costs are high, delays abound, and critical inputs such as water, power, and skills are scarce. Such a difficult environment favors the leanest companies.

Operations are shaped by the context in which an organization exists. In reality, businesspeople quickly realize that their margin of maneuver to address these contextual challenges is limited. Most give up after several failed attempts. Rather than fight gravity, they elect to focus on what they can control.

In thinking about efficient and sustainable operations, it helps to distinguish between constraints that are within a business and those that are outside the firm. Addressing constraints that are outside the firm often requires collaboration. We address this issue fully in Chapter 9, "Enable Prosperity Ecosystems."

This distinction is even more important because a weak legal system, the lack of trust, the prevalence of zero-sum thinking, and defensiveness contribute to fostering an environment in BoP markets that is not conducive to collaboration. It also creates a situation that makes the internal mobilization required to upgrade costs difficult.

Lack of proper skills is often a potent contextual barrier to efficient and sustainable operations. The dearth of appropriate technology is also another challenge. Engineering expertise is relatively scarce and costly. Again, certain BoP nations especially in Africa lag behind in operational research or sustainable processes and technology.

Scarce capital is another constraint that impacts to operate sustainably and efficiently. Whether in skills, machinery, or learning, upgrading to efficient and sustainable operations requires capital. Businesspeople stuck in The Survival Trap do not always have the resources to make this transition.

The next element that contributes to resistance is poor understanding of relative cost position, which handicaps them as they seek to select areas where to improve their operational efficiency and sustainability.

Regional economic integration and the fall of international trade barriers mean that businesspeople today have an even more limited understanding of relative cost position. As a result, efforts to build efficient and sustainable operations often focus on cost-related dimensions where firms should seek to invest such as labor and quality.

Keeping the Eyes on the Wrong Prize

In BoP markets, businesspeople put considerable effort into operations. Nonetheless, most see their efforts wasted. Exploring the constraints they face is important in rectifying this situation. We must identify those mindsets that these businesspeople hold that stand in the way.

Overresponsiveness to customers' price concerns is the first challenge. Businesspeople learn quickly and, sometimes the hard way, that customers must be the priority. Yet, focusing too much on prices can detract from efficient and sustainable operations when it creates a mindset that as long as customers get a discount, everything is fine.

The BoP context increases this particular challenge. Price competition can become an incentive to cut corners. When combined with survival business, this mindset becomes a formidable challenge: Standards are dropped, investment into equipment upgrades is delayed, and training is abandoned.

A closely related mindset is the delinking of strategy and operations, customers and costs, offerings and processes. Originally, this mindset was formed when operations played a smaller role in the overall customer experience. Traditional commodities such as minerals or perennial crops offer a good example of this situation.

Globalization and the information age have resulted in a convergence between strategy and operations. Specifically, the simplest products have now matured into experiences that require entrepreneurs and managers to carefully integrate strategy and operations. A growing share of customer value is closely related to operations.

In BoP markets, this translates into customers who are not only interested in price but also want convenience. At the bottom of the pyramid, it means customers who want products packaged, priced, or distributed in a way that gives them dignity, choice, and value for their money.

The Wrong Thinking

Attitudes toward sustainability are often fuelled by a different set of underlying mindsets. The first of such mindsets is the perception that shifting toward sustainable operations is both risky and expensive. This mindset originates from the reality that often the technologies associated with sustainable operations are new and unfamiliar.

Businesspeople reason that their current operations are complicated enough as is. Operating in BoP markets often means that firms face power cuts, water shortages, and significant delays. As a result, they want to avoid potentially costly disruptions to their tenuous operations by experimenting with unproven technology.

Leaders reason "why mess with a complicated process that barely keeps us going?" The risk and pain of change can be overwhelming. Instead, many determine it is better to leave things as they are. This mindset explains in part why Haile had to wait this long to consider changing his process even when he suspected chromium to be lethal.

A complementary mindset at play here is that BoP businesspeople's contribution to sustainability is marginal when compared to larger firms in other parts of the world. Those holding this mindset want to see change on the other side of the table first. While grounded in reality, both mindsets prevent efficient and sustainable operations.

A second mindset specifically related to sustainability is the perception that resources are free and limitless. This belief prevents businesspeople from making careful choices based on a rigorous assessment of the human and economic costs of depleting and degrading natural resources.

The last two mindsets find their roots in a series of national and global mindsets that must also be considered. One perspective is that the biggest polluters should bear most of the costs. While sensible and fair, this attitude does little to address the environmental degradation that is likely to have its largest impact on those at the bottom of the pyramid.

Developing nations want to see the West alter its behavior toward the environment and provide financial assistance to support their migration toward sustainable operations. The outcome of the Copenhagen talks provides a clear example of how such mindsets can undermine progress toward sustainability.

Deming Meet Hardin

Operating efficiently and sustainably is about ensuring that a firm delivers solutions in the most resource efficient and environmentally friendly way possible. If strategy focuses on solutions, then efficient and sustainable operations is about how to ensure the best possible process, systems, and activities according to this strategy.

More than any other thought leader, Dr. William Edwards Deming has influenced the modern understanding of operational effectiveness the most. He is widely credited with improving production in the United States during the Cold War, although Deming is perhaps best known for his work in Japan.

Dr. Deming made a significant contribution to Japan's later reputation for innovative high-quality products. He is regarded as having had more impact upon Japanese manufacturing and business than any other individual not of Japanese heritage. More than ever, Deming's insights are relevant for firms in BoP markets. Operational efficiency has a direct impact on environmental sustainability. Figure 8.1 illustrates this very important business relationship.

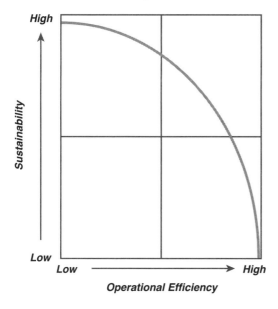

Figure 8.1   Operating efficiently and sustainably

He suggested that when organizations focus primarily on quality, defined by the result of work efforts over total costs, quality tends to increase and costs fall over time. However, when people and organizations focus primarily on *costs*, costs tend to rise and quality declines over time.

Deming also proposed that by adopting a different management philosophy, organizations can increase quality while reducing costs (by reducing waste, rework, staff attrition while increasing customer loyalty). The key is to practice continual improvement and think of manufacturing as a system, not as bits and pieces.[3]

The major insight Deming provided is the linkage between mindsets and the results a firm gets in its operations as defined by costs. What Deming offered was a way for organizations to escape The Survival Trap by changing their mindsets around costs and operations. In a nutshell, mindset change is the solution.

While environmental sustainability was not as much of a concern in Deming's time, it is easy to see how closely linked sustainability is to his work. In fact, the continual improvement way of thinking and acting aims to reduce waste. What is more wasteful than depleting our resources in a way that endangers the present and future generations? Figure 8.2 outlines how the SOAR framework can be applied to ensure resource stewardship and overall efficiency.

Essence	• Stewardship			
	Strategy	**Operations**	**Assets**	**Reality**
Principles	• Holistic	• Balance	• Discipline	• Systems Thinking
Practices	• Articulating Choices	• Making Trade-Offs	• Providing Incentives	• Ascertaining Impact of Choices on Other Stakeholders

Figure 8.2   Operating sustainably and efficiently

For efficient and sustainable operations, the essence is stewardship. The real tension that organizations face around operations is that profits can be generated immediately for costs that are delayed and paid by the whole community later. Since the community does not often perceive these externalized costs, massive action to force stewardship is lacking.

Stewardship is a corollary to resource-oriented thinking. While resource-oriented thinking is about unleashing all the forms of capital available to address business challenges, stewardship is about the recognition that a business must be responsible in the way it leverages all resources at its disposal.

Stewardship offers a way of resolving what economists call the tragedy of the commons. In his seminal article, Garrett Hardin[4] describes a dilemma in which multiple individuals, acting independently, and rationally consulting only their own self-interest, will ultimately deplete a shared limited resource.

The tragedy of the commons points to an interesting dilemma because it shows that such depletion will occur even when it is clear that it is not in anyone's long-term interest for this to happen. Stewardship offers business in BoP markets a high road when facing the tragedy of the commons all while meeting business objectives.

While one of the major benefits of the first aspect of stewardship is cost control, it goes beyond just cost control. Stewardship translates into a sense in employees, customers, and the community that the business is responsible. A second and important aspect of stewardship is environmental responsibility.

As a value, stewardship plays out in two ways. First, stewardship naturally leads to operational effectiveness inasmuch as businesses realize that they must avoid wasting resources. Beyond cost controls, stewardship inspires businesses to deliver solutions in the most effective way possible.

A second and often neglected aspect of stewardship is about environmental responsibility. Despite increased media coverage, most businesses do not know in practice how to upgrade their operations so that they are environmentally sustainable. What happens instead is a proclamation of sustainability that is divorced from reality.

Climbing Out of Quicksand

Strategy must be the starting point. To operate efficiently and sustainably, businesspeople must begin with the solutions they are seeking to provide customers. This often identifies ways to improve operations while increasing customer satisfaction. We revisit Haile to see how he may climb out of the quicksand.

EDL starts in a much better position than most firms facing similar challenges. Haile and his team have built a diversified customer base including sophisticated buyers from Europe. Haile can benefit from leveraging existing relationships with these buyers in his bid to climb out of the quicksand.

The first core principle is articulating holistic and inclusive strategies. To embrace stewardship, businesses must articulate strategies that are holistic and inclusive of a variety of stakeholders, including "silent" ones such as the community and future generations.

Such holistic and inclusive strategies matter because they help businesspeople redefine targets and objectives away from short-term profitability. In turn this helps them avoid focusing too much on short-term cost pressure at the expense of long-term trade-offs. Ultimately a holistic strategy is the way out of quicksand.

Now that he has learned more about chromium, Haile realizes that the business may have had something to do with his father's early demise. Chromium has been linked to respiratory diseases and cancers. Rather than relating to holistic strategies at a philosophical level, Haile sees this challenge as a real and personal one.

In practice, a holistic and inclusive strategy must be supported by the discipline to clearly articulate the various choices that the business faces to fulfill its vision. Articulating choices is about identifying the many options possible to achieve the stated vision, while making the cost-benefit trade-offs for all stakeholders clear.

EDL faces at least two critical choices. First, he can decide what market to serve. While it has traditionally focused on finished leather goods, newer segments such as environmental friendly leather are emerging. For instance, wet white now represents a $400 million market growing at 35 percent per annum.[5]

The second choice that EDL faces is a choice of technology. Wet blue processing offers the benefit of a faster tanning cycle. This is an important advantage for a producer focused on short-term cost gains. However, new tanning processes such as wet white are evolving that offer competitive options to wet blue.

Choice of market and technology is particularly important in BoP markets where businesspeople often have the experience of being reactive as opposed to proactive. Escaping The Survival Trap requires this important shift in perspective. Articulating choices is an important key in addressing this challenge.

The second core principle is balance. It is about resolving the tension that both Deming and Hardin saw. Balance ensures that the activities, processes, and systems of the firm address the two aspects of stewardship—effectiveness and sustainability.

To espouse balance, businesspeople must become adept at making trade-offs. Once strategic choices are made, organizations can begin thinking about ways to make the right trade-offs in their operations. Such trade-offs may require some experimentation to move the process forward.

After defining the solution, selecting the right operational improvements becomes easier. While collaboration is effective for addressing context-related costs, the focus here must be on costs that are related to specific activities. This creates a concrete yardstick for entrepreneurs and managers to improve progress.

A good place to begin is a detailed cost analysis between existing processes and the new processes being considered. In the case of Haile, a cost comparison between wet blue and wet white shows potential savings in wet white by eliminating the need for treatment of contaminated wastes from the plant.

To complete the picture, Haile can also begin to think about the types of production equipment and skills required if EDL is to upgrade. These considerations inform the ways in which EDL can stagger its operational trade-offs over time and offer a roadmap to facilitate a transition toward balance.

Third, discipline supports efforts to ensure that assets operate sustainably and efficiently. Once decisions have been made to embrace efficiency and sustainability, more than any manual or charters, businesses require the discipline to relate to their assets and deploy in a different, more balanced way.

What is often required is a clear choice to embrace a different culture. Shaking operational traditions does not happen by accident. In the case of EDL, Haile could consider seeking manufacturing certifications such as ISO or Kaizen. He could also consider embracing the type of continual improvements described by Dr. Deming.

Such processes work in making discipline around assets a reality because they help in providing clear incentives for the business to progress toward a holistic vision of efficient and sustainable operations. It helps businesspeople keep their eyes on the prize as they help their organizations improve their performance.

To sustain the commitment, it helps to make the choices measurable and public, thus increasing accountability, transparency, and the likelihood that balance is achieved. Here businesspeople benefit from making their commitment explicit to their customers, owners, workers, and the community.

This is particularly important in BoP markets where, as we discussed, the operating reality is fraught with challenges and businesses face many internal constraints especially around skills. Such processes offer a proven way to provide critical skills that can help businesses make the transition to operating sustainably and efficiently.

Contrary to Haile's apprehension, the EDL team may welcome the change. Employees could feel more valued as they are trained. The process could also help identify new leaders that Haile empowers to drive innovations and process improvements. A new energy may well be ignited that EDL has not seen since its inception days.

EDL could consider making its choice to move away from the toxic wet blue process explicit in the industry. This would not only make sure that the company becomes differentiated in the eyes of its customers, it would also provide an opportunity for the firm to influence the whole Ethiopian leather sector.

Considerations linked to the operating reality in BoP markets are important for operating efficiently and sustainably. The essence of sustainable operations is to make choices that prioritize the welfare of the community and future generations. Opportunities can often emerge to serve the bottom of the pyramid.

To seek ways to influence their operating reality, businesspeople must employ systems thinking. To understand complex trade-offs in sophisticated decisions where both delaying profit and choosing operating processes with potential costs later may impact the community, systems thinking helps make the underlying patterns explicit.

As discussed in previous chapters, systems thinking is the process of understanding how things influence one another within a whole. Operating efficiently and sustainably requires businesspeople to think of their impact both on their organizations, communities, and the world as a whole.

Adopting systems thinking as an approach to achieving sustainable and efficient operations helps businesspeople in BoP markets view their activities as parts of an overall system. This is paramount in helping them develop the appropriate set of habits that are informed by the right mindsets.

The higher price of wet white leather translates into higher margins for EDL. To sustain these margins, the firm must pick the best hides and skins. It therefore introduces a differentiated pricing model that benefits cattle owners at the bottom of the pyramid. A better product influences the whole value chain.

Efficient and Sustainable Operations in Practice

As discussed, reaching efficient and sustainable operations is more of a journey than a destination. It is therefore important for businesspeople to develop the pattern recognition required to know whether they are yielding results in their attempts to upgrade. How do we recognize efficient and sustainable operations in practice?

At the individual level, efficient and sustainable operations provide peace of mind and satisfaction—peace of mind in helping individuals identify solutions to today's challenges and satisfaction from the sense of doing the right thing while ultimately doing well. Both mind and heart are engaged in this case.

Firms that operate efficiently and sustainably gain the ability to constantly reinvent themselves as their environment changes. New technologies are integrated into processes; new processes and activities are always aligned to the business model. Such a culture also creates a positive working environment for employees.

At the cluster, or industry level, a culture of operating efficiently and sustainably translates into stakeholders working together to innovate on products. Such clusters also identify ways to work together to achieve operational efficiency and sustainability. Customers and markets reward such clusters with greater market shares.

At the national level, efficient operations provide the opportunity for higher wages. This in turn translates into better living conditions especially at the bottom of the pyramid. Sustainable operations mean conserving scarce resources. Communities benefit greatly from this, and living conditions improve throughout all levels.

A Comforting Outlook

In BoP markets, especially Africa, firms have traditionally overemphasized markets. In many industries, not just manufacturing, globalization, information technology, and the environmental crisis dictate that this mindset, and practical change is not optional. Operating sustainably and efficiently provides a way to address this challenge.

Businesspeople must truly embrace efficient and sustainable operations as an imperative. Proven processes reduce the business risks associated with operational upgrade. The key is for entrepreneurs and managers to choose instead of letting the market choose for them.

Efficient and sustainable operations represent an opportunity not only to increase profits but also serve more attractive customers. This opportunity helps discerning entrepreneurs and managers lead their organization out of The Survival Trap on the path to prosperity. It will also help build livable communities and nations for present and future generations.

Considering his new wet white process, Haile feels confident that he will be leaving his children and grandchildren a really healthy business. He also sees a way to make his firm the undisputed leader in Ethiopia's competitive leather sector—a business that is healthy, not only in terms of profit, but also in terms of environmental impact and sustainability.

This comforting secret gives Haile confidence for the future. His secret hope is that his sons also join the business. Thus, this would help Ethiopian Distinguished Leathers (EDL) become one of Ethiopia's first generation of entrepreneurs to have emerged from within the country from humble beginnings during the communist era.

Vignette 6—Offering Unique Experiences: Rwanda's Tourism Industry

On June 6, 2010, more than 300 international guests joined tens of thousands of Rwandans in celebrating Kwita Izina. In a ceremony like no other, eighteen baby gorillas and two gorilla families were named.

Rwanda's mountain gorillas are heralded as one of Africa's great conservation success stories. Rwandans have worked with international partners to preserve one of mankind's closest relatives. These magnificent primates symbolize tourism's transformative impact on Rwanda's economy since 2001.

A Struggling Industry

In 2001, the Rwanda tourism industry was in shambles. The country's national parks received a paltry 2,000 visitors annually compared to a peak of 39,000 in 1984. The 1994 genocide left a major scar on Rwanda and its tourism industry.

International perception existed that Rwanda was not a safe destination. Tour operators resisted the idea of sending travelers to the country. At the country's first participation in International Turismus Borse (ITB) in Berlin in 2002, one honest tour operator put it bluntly: "Most of us remember 1994. There is no way people are going to Rwanda!"

Domestically, local communities were at odds with the parks. Rwanda has one of the highest population densities in the world. With the high influx of refugees following 1994, the population routinely encroached on parks such as the Volcanoes National Park putting endangered species, including the mountain gorillas, at risk.

The predicament of Rwanda's tourism industry was not unlike that of other industries stuck in The Survival Trap. Receipts were decreasing, infrastructure was lacking, human resources were limited, financial capital was scarce, and the overall perception of the industry was poor both within and outside the country.

When facing a decline, most industries in BoP markets do more of the same traditional strategies. Agricultural industries offer a good illustration of this sad reality. As revenues decline, producers seek to increase supply to compensate for their loss. An increase in supply without a surge in demand only depresses prices. This phenomenon has been at play in the global tea industry and others.

Furthermore, competition within the industry increases as everyone seeks to secure scarce clients. Trust is reduced and collaboration decreases. In countries with a challenging operating reality, this lack of collaboration results in a loss of competitive advantage for all. This situation further perpetuates The Survival Trap.

Inception of a Turnaround

The perception of Rwanda tourism was bleak. The almost perfect consensus was that a tiny African nation, scarred by genocide and located in the tumultuous Great Lakes region, could not possibly build a vibrant tourism industry. The evidence made this story seem not only the most plausible, but the only possible outcome.

Yet in truth, the consensus was not perfect because a small group of Rwandans refused to accept that story. While the desolation angle captured the operating reality of tourism in Rwanda, it did not capture the vision these Rwandans had for their industry. This group saw potential where the world saw hopelessness.

Under the leadership of the late Florence Nkera, a group of leaders from government, business, and conservation groups formed Rwanda's Tourism Working Group. Facilitated by OTF Group, this stakeholder group decided to articulate a vision to turn around the Rwandan tourism industry.

In June 2002, after working together for eight months, Rwanda's Tourism Working Group articulated a bold vision: "Generate $100 million in tourism receipts in 2010 by focusing on creating high value and low environmental impact experiences for Eco-travelers, Explorers, and Individual Business Travelers." In 2001, receipts were estimated at only $8 million.

The group realized it faced a significant challenge in realizing this vision. It identified three conditions as paramount to the realization of new approach—a culture of execution, the coordination of public and private sector investments, and the endorsement of the tourism vision by the Government of Rwanda.

Rwandan tourism got the highest endorsement in the form of President Paul Kagame as a champion. This patronage was important because it kept the industry focused on its objectives when the situation became difficult. It also ensured that the government of Rwanda recognized tourism as a priority and took the necessary steps to support the sector's growth at critical junctions such as conservation policy and budget allocation.

Enabling a Prosperity Ecosystem

In 2009, tourism generated an estimated $168 million in receipts, becoming the top foreign exchange earner for Rwanda. Furthermore, each international tourist in Rwanda spends more than $1,200, more than double the $500 that Africa's average tourist spends. Permits to visit the prized mountain gorillas are sold out in the high season.

The country's tourism industry is doing its part to help Rwandans escape The Survival Trap. Hotel rooms have topped 3,000 from a mere 600 in 2001. More than 100 firms have joined the tourism industry. Wages in tourism have increased at 20 per annum over the past eight years.

A major achievement for Rwanda tourism is its success in conservation. As the industry grows, communities surrounding the parks are beginning to reap some benefits through jobs, shared revenues, and investments. A good example is the Sabinyo Community Lodge, a high-end property owned and operated by the community.

Back in Berlin, the mood is festive. Rwanda has been named best African exhibitor at ITB for three years running, setting a record for this international tourism fair. This accolade gives a hint into the key to Rwanda's tourism metamorphosis. The country has built a vibrant prosperity ecosystem.

Informed by a spirit of interdependence, Rwanda tourism stakeholders have coalesced around a shared vision. At a recent tourism working group event, Ms. Rica Rwigamba, an entrepreneur who now heads the tourism board, remarked: "Our true competitive advantage is our ability to work together as business and government to realize our vision."

As healthy ecosystems do, the Rwanda tourism sector has enabled many new entrants to engage in the system; Marriott and Hilton have both announced their intentions to operate properties in Rwanda, joining Serena and Dubai World.

Starting with the Operating Reality

Rwanda's gorillas have become synonymous with high-end eco-tourism in Africa. Tourism has become Rwanda's pride. Rwanda's tourism industry is arguably the best illustration of the spirit of interdependence that has informed the country's amazing transformation since 1994.

This spirit of interdependence was present at the sixth Kwita Izina on June 6, 2010. As he received the Global Environment Award, President Paul Kagame presented it to the community, exhorting them to continue leading the world in the conservation of the prized mountain gorillas.

Endnotes

[1] G. Mutume, "Loss of Textile Market Costs African Jobs," *African Renewal*, 20, no.1 (2006), 18-28.

[2] B. E. Johansen, *The Encyclopedia of Global Warming Science and Technology.* (Santa Barbara, California: Greenwood Publishing, 2009).

[3] W. Edwards Deming, *The New Economics for Industry, Government, Education,* 1993.

[4] "The Tragedy of the Commons" was first published in the journal *Science* in 1968.

[5] "Aim and Focus on ITC's Export Development Assistance to the Leather Sector over the Next 5 Years," International Trade Center (ITC) position paper, 2005.

9 ⸻

Enable Prosperity Ecosystems

Miracle in Tunisia

Tunisia has succeeded where most African nations have failed. Fifty years after its independence, Tunisia has emerged as a beacon of prosperity and stability. This natural resource "poor" nation now boasts a per capita income of $7,100, one of the highest in Africa. In the Arab world, Tunisia also stands out for its openness and modernity.

Tunisia's biggest current challenge is to speed its economic growth rate. The country's leadership chose Information and Communication Technologies (ICT) as a key growth driver. Early results are encouraging: ICT's share of the nation's GDP has more than doubled from 4.5 percent in 2002 to 10 percent in 2008 and is poised to reach 13.5 percent in 2011.[1]

ICT entrepreneurs—or "technopreneurs"—have played a key role in this growth. Located in Africa's first technopark,[2] the Elgazala Incubator enables aspiring technopreneurs to bring Tunisia closer to its goal of becoming an ICT society. Business incubators accelerate the growth of entrepreneurial companies through a range of business support.

Nurturing the Fruit Flies

Reflecting on the fragility of startups, Wharton School entrepreneurship Professor Ian MacMillan once observed that "entrepreneurs are almost as fragile as fruit flies." In BoP markets, especially Africa, this insight takes on new significance given the myriad of challenges facing not only entrepreneurs but business in general.

This insight can also be extended to efforts aiming to support business in BoP markets especially Africa. These efforts share at least one characteristic with the businesses they work to support: Both need a favorable business environment to flourish. Both need a complex web of relationships or an ecosystem to flourish.

According to *Webster's*, a natural ecosystem is "the complex of a community of organisms and its environment functioning as an ecological unit in nature." Like their natural equivalent, prosperity ecosystems integrate both stakeholders and the operating reality prevailing in BoP markets.

Considering the pernicious effects of The Survival Trap, prosperity ecosystems are critical for businesses to innovate, flourish, and prosper in BoP markets. As noted by Dan Isenberg,[3] "these entrepreneurship ecosystems have become a kind of holy grail for governments around the world—in both emerging and developed countries."

In *Fortune at the Bottom of the Pyramid*, C. K. Prahalad advocates for the emergence of private sector-led market-based ecosystems for wealth creation. According to Prahalad, such ecosystems must include large businesses working with small and micro firms as well as selected NGOs with market-based models.

To illustrate this powerful concept, C. K. Prahalad provides the example of Hindustan Lever Ltd. (HLL) a fast-moving consumer goods company in India. This multibillion dollar company has an effective ecosystem including 80 in-house manufacturing units, 150 outsourced units, and a vast network of more than four million distributors.[4]

To complement such ecosystems, business, governments, civil society, and development partners must come together to create the conditions to transform the operating reality in BoP markets or transcend the many constraints inherent in trying to serve the bottom of the economic pyramid.

The Elgazala Incubator and its incubatees have reaped the benefits of such an ecosystem designed to promote innovation. Tunisia's leadership embrace of ICT as a growth driver has provided the political will required to alter the operating reality.

In Tunisia, the champion has been no one else but President Zine El Abidine Ben Ali. In his swearing in address on November 12, 2009, he said: "We have accorded a special place, in our program, to the building of the society of knowledge and technological innovation, based on our conviction that no progress can be achieved without modern technologies."

This political commitment to evolve Tunisia into an ICT society has materialized. The country has made massive investments in ICT infrastructure. In 2010, The World Economic Forum has ranked Tunisia for the third year in a row, first on the Maghreb and African levels, and 38th on the world scale, out a total of 134 countries.[5]

Another physical attribute of great importance is the country's connectivity to Europe and its openness to its northern neighbors. Daily flights and transshipment runs make it possible to serve the European market at a low cost. Combined with the ICT infrastructure, this comparative advantage has translated into a competitive one.

What is more difficult to see, however, are Tunisia's investments in the "softer" forms of innovation capital. The country is training a corps of young, highly qualified knowledge workers to fuel the ICT industry. The country has 13 universities and 24 Institutes for Higher Education in Technology.

Furthermore, the country ranked in the top third of countries evaluated by the World Economic Forum for their political and regulatory environment. In addition, ICT startups have growing access to financing through the RITI (System of Incentives for Innovation in the Field of Information Technologies) venture capital fund, the SME financing bank, a guarantee company, and a national network of business incubators.

What Mindsets Prevent the Emergence of Ecosystems?

Tunisia's example of Elgazala above is the exception rather than the rule. In BoP markets, collaborative efforts to create such prosperity ecosystems are rare. Outside stakeholders—business, government, or community—can be part of the problem. Even when they are not, business leaders often see them as part of the problem.

At the heart of the challenge lie specific mindsets that undermine collaboration and prevent the emergence of prosperity ecosystems. Again, low levels of trust and zero-sum thinking are the two main mindsets at fault.

Collaboration requires trust. As discussed throughout this book, leaders of firms operating in BoP markets especially the ones trapped in The Survival Trap are less likely to trust stakeholders whether internal or external. Such low level of trust translates into a formidable barrier to collaboration.

As discussed in Chapter 5, "Foster an Archimedean Mindset," the prevalence of survival business in BoP markets is a factor that can exacerbate lack of collaboration. The scarcity that characterizes The Survival Trap means that instead of collaboration, great energy must be spent trying to outsmart the competition or prevail in a difficult operating reality.

Zero-sum thinking is to ecosystems what rat poison is to rats. Zero-sum thinking reduces the likelihood that business, government, and civil society leaders pull resources together to address cross-cutting challenges impacting business or any other stakeholders for that matter.

An insidious way in which zero-sum thinking plays in business is when stakeholders are perceived as a cost factor or inconsequential. When perceived as a cost factor, businesses try to minimize the role of such stakeholders. When perceived as inconsequential, businesses ignore such stakeholders.

These two mindsets interact to create defensiveness as a third mindset and also prevents the emergence of ecosystems. Defensiveness fosters a blaming atmosphere where stakeholders—business, government, development partners, and the community—resort to finding a scapegoat as opposed to finding solutions.

A good illustration of this mindset is the blame that educational institutions often receive. In BoP markets especially Africa, a weak tradition of collaborating with universities or other educational institutions exists. Yet, such institutions not only train qualified staff but also serve as an important potential source of innovation.

These three mindsets prevent the emergence ecosystems by breeding actions or omissions. While dealing with nonproductive actions or constraints can be easier, the insidious nature of omissions makes them a lot more difficult to detect and therefore address in the quest to foster prosperity ecosystems.

One action that functions as a constraint is copycats. The easiest way to start a business is simply to copy a successful business. Replicating a winning formula is perceived as a sure way to do well. Copycats can often come from former employees or suppliers. Such actions increase reluctance to collaborate.

Another action is the focus on government as a customer. The small and informal nature of economies with a large BoP means that government emerges as a top customer. In an operating reality lacking governance, unscrupulous business leaders and their political associates engage in nontransparent transactions.

One clear example of an omission is the lack of staff training around collaboration. Many business leaders fail to train their staff on how to recognize opportunities for collaboration. Even when they recognize these opportunities the framework for collaboration may be nonexistent.

An omission from governments is the failure to provide well-functioning support institutions that business needs to flourish. Not only are dedicated ecosystems such as Elgazala rare but also basic services such as bureaus of standards, revenue authorities, and other regulatory bodies are bureaucratic.

The mindsets and their accompanying actions and omissions clearly represent a key barrier to the emergence of prosperity ecosystems. These constraints become stronger within the operating reality that is prevalent in BoP markets. Failing to recognize such challenges undermines any attempts to enable prosperity ecosystems.

A Stifling Operating Reality

As previously discussed, one of the key features of The Survival Trap is its self-perpetuating nature. The Survival Trap persists because it creates an operating reality that makes it more difficult for businesses to tap into the very opportunities that would help them escape this vicious cycle.

While a myriad of challenges exist, three critical elements in the operating reality of BoP markets appear as top barriers to any attempts at enabling prosperity ecosystems. These elements are a lack of well-functioning clusters, an absence of ecosystems, and a weak regulatory framework.

The concept of cluster has emerged as a preeminent item of the competitiveness agenda of countries the world over thanks to the work of Michael Porter. Clusters are defined as a series of interrelated firms and supporting institutions working in a given industry.

According to Porter,[6] clusters allow firms to collaborate and compete in at least three ways. First, clusters support innovation by pooling expertise and sharing best practices. Second, they help business and government come together to develop joint solutions. Finally, clusters reduce costs by allowing firms to share specialized resources.

Vibrant clusters are the exception in BoP markets especially Africa. This is not for lack of trying. Governments and development partners alike have invested vast sums of money in such initiatives. Unfortunately, such initiatives often have limited stakeholder ownership. This means that collaboration dries up with funding.

Tunisia has managed to develop a vibrant ICT sector. Tunisia now has more than 700 services and computer engineering companies, which employ some 7,200 engineers. The sector has now become one of the most important providers of high quality employment with starting salaries of 1000 TND (Tunisian dinar, the local currency), or US 750 per month.

The private sector-led market-based ecosystems C. K. Prahalad advocates are still few and far between in BoP markets. This is not because larger businesses do not work with smaller suppliers and distributors. Instead, these relationships are not construed as true, symbiotic partners that would help everyone escape The Survival Trap.

Businesses leaders, especially managers of large multinational corporations (MNCs), have a critical role to play in fostering the development of such ecosystems to unleash the economic potential of BoP markets. However, to play this role, such leaders must begin with diagnosing the mindsets that prevent them from delivering such ecosystems in the first place.

The Elgazala Technopark has benefited from the presence of anchor technology firms such as Alcatel, Ericsson, and Huawei Technologies. Such firms not only provide sophisticated demands for startups within the park but also these firms contribute to reinforcing skills available in the technopark.

Finally, a weak regulatory framework is a barrier to the emergence of prosperity ecosystems. Collaboration often requires information sharing. In the absence of strong intellectual property or competition laws, the only way firms know to protect their innovations is to limit disclosure.

Limiting disclosure can be a factor in perpetuating The Survival Trap inasmuch as it prevents business leaders from working with other stakeholders to articulate and implement joint solutions to their challenges. Improving the regulatory framework must be a priority.

Again, the Tunisian legal and regulatory framework has been a strength. Over the last decade, the country developed legislation to protect both consumers and businesses, including the Electronic Business and Signature Law (2000), the Telecommunications Code (2001), and the Personal Data Protection act (2004).

As discussed earlier, barriers to the emergence of prosperity ecosystems exist in both the mindsets and the prevailing operating reality. Addressing these constraints requires business leaders and their counterparts in government and civil society to find a cross-cutting solution.

Interconnectedness as the Essence of Prosperity Ecosystems

Enabling prosperity ecosystems requires a dual shift in mindset. On the one hand, firms must begin to see outside stakeholders in a different light. Rather than being constraints, such outside stakeholders including competitors can help in harnessing opportunities and prevailing over the operating reality.

On the other hand, outside stakeholders especially government must take a different stance toward business. Such a stance must go beyond speeches and public declarations and include some specific actions that can address the challenges that prevent the emergence of prosperity ecosystems.

The core distinction that forms the essence to enable a prosperity ecosystem is interconnectedness. As noted by Rev. Martin Luther King Jr.: "In a real sense all life is inter-related. All persons are caught in an inescapable network of mutuality, tied in a single garment of destiny. Whatever affects one directly affects all indirectly."

"The inter-related structure of reality" described by Martin Luther King Jr. has tremendous impact on business. The concept of interconnectedness forms the central idea behind a host of approaches that have been developed to apprehend economic relationships such as value chain, clusters, and co-opetition (that is, collaboration and competition at the same time).

Interconnectedness begins with the realization that businesses and their stakeholders are mutually joined in the same operating reality. This realization creates the conditions for collaboration. It provides the base for businesspeople and other stakeholders to articulate and align incentives to collaboration.

Practically, interconnectedness helps businesspeople begin to seek specific ways in which stakeholders through collaboration and a prosperity ecosystem can impact their business model. They begin to look at tangible implications for their Strategy, Operations, Assets, and Operating Reality.

This essence is useful in helping businesses shift their perspective to stakeholders outside their customers. While most businesspeople understand that customers are the raison d'être of their firms, they do not have such a clear stance on other stakeholders. Yet, businesses cannot be islands.

Soon, such businesspeople see how interconnectedness enables ecosystems. Customer needs can be fulfilled when ecosystems work. New market niches at the BoP can be tapped into when ecosystems flourish. Costs can be reduced and operating reality challenges such as infrastructure and skills can be solved through ecosystems.

Interconnectedness is also an essence that is likely to reinforce moral purpose in a business person. By making the symbiotic relationship with key stakeholders explicit, interconnectedness allows businesspeople to embrace an Archimedean mindset that looks for concrete ways to create value for key stakeholders.

Enabling Prosperity Ecosystems

Enabling prosperity ecosystems must happen at least at two interrelated levels: businesses and operating reality. Regardless of firm size, opportunities for collaboration exist. Yet, such business-led initiatives can benefit a great deal for more systemic efforts to enable prosperity ecosystems where government leaders must play a big role.

As suggested above, enabling prosperity ecosystems must be accomplished in a way that outlines clearly how the business model of the firm is going to be impacted by collaboration. The greater the understanding, the more leverage business and government leaders will have in enabling a prosperity ecosystem. Figure 9.1 provides a framework to enable prosperity ecosystems.

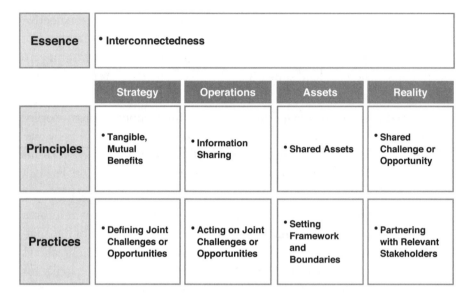

	Strategy	Operations	Assets	Reality
Essence	• Interconnectedness			
Principles	• Tangible, Mutual Benefits	• Information Sharing	• Shared Assets	• Shared Challenge or Opportunity
Practices	• Defining Joint Challenges or Opportunities	• Acting on Joint Challenges or Opportunities	• Setting Framework and Boundaries	• Partnering with Relevant Stakeholders

Figure 9.1   Enabling prosperity ecosystems

The first core principle is defining tangible mutual benefits. As noted by Morten Hansen in his book *Collaboration*:[7] "The key point in disciplined collaboration is to start with the end in mind. The goal of collaboration is not collaboration but better results! This means you should only collaborate when it is the best way to improve results."

Many attempts fail for lack of tangible mutual benefits. Clear benefits enhance collaboration. Businesses either stuck in The Survival Trap or dealing with a difficult operating reality in BoP markets will only sustain a collaboration drive if this one can deliver tangible mutual benefits.

Defining tangible mutual benefits also helps stakeholders of a business understand why it makes sense for them to enable a prosperity ecosystem. This translates into government leaders that upgrade their mindsets to genuinely support business. It also turns into workers or customers who go beyond the call of duty.

The practice that supports articulating tangible benefits is defining joint opportunities and challenges. Such opportunities or challenges often serve as an anchor to the collaboration agenda that forms the basis for the prosperity ecosystem. Such clarity helps in leading business and government leaders to keep the commitment.

In the case of HLL described earlier in the chapter, members of the ecosystems get a clear chance to escape The Survival Trap and see their lives transform. In the case of Elgazala, government sees ICT as a key driver in its economic development while entrepreneurs welcome the great platform the technopark represents.

The second core principle is information sharing. Information is essential to collaboration and prosperity ecosystems. Yet as discussed, the operating reality of BoP markets often makes such information sharing unlikely. This principle is about disclosing the necessary information on the opportunities being pursued.

To espouse information sharing, business and government leaders must get into the habit of acting on joint challenges and opportunities. The basic idea here is that stakeholders must see the benefits of information sharing in a tangible way. Such benefits only become explicit once action is taken.

To share information, businesspeople must be comfortable that their core capabilities are enhanced yet secure. As discussed above, the various improvements to the legal environment in Tunisia have gone a long way toward making Tunisia's ICT sector a vibrant player.

The third core principle is shared assets. As discussed above, collaboration often creates shared assets for all stakeholders to enjoy. Furthermore, prosperity ecosystems are anchored on such shared assets whether in the form of joint relationships, knowledge, or intellectual property.

Shared assets can sometimes help in reducing costs. Costs often provide the most natural opportunity for collaboration. This opportunity is rooted in the powerful incentives that greater profits provide for businesses. This natural inclination can be leveraged to foster collaboration.

Embracing shared assets happens through the practice of setting clear frameworks and boundaries. These are often about reducing the risk of collaboration especially in an environment where the legal frameworks may not be strong. Furthermore, such frameworks and boundaries institutionalize the collaboration making it sustainable.

As it relates to the operating reality, the last principle is shared opportunity or challenges. In BoP markets, the challenging operating reality combined with the unmet customer needs of bottom of the economic pyramid provide a host of challenges and opportunities that can serve as anchor for collaboration.

Again, costs often provide a good starting point. For instance, it helps for entrepreneurs to see how such collaboration reduces direct and indirect costs. In the case of Elgazala, it helped a great deal that the technopark offers a reliable and cost-competitive infrastructure for ICT at a subsidized rate.

Revenues provide the second opportunity. Specifically, HLL sees a great opportunity to increase its sales through its ecosystems. This ecosystem has helped this multibillion dollar subsidiary of Procter & Gamble meet its financial objectives. In so doing, it has aligned incentives not only for HLL but also for its stakeholders.

Collaboration in Action

As previously discussed, entrepreneurs and managers fail to collaborate not because they cannot appreciate the importance of collaboration, but rather because their mindsets and the context in which they operate make such collaboration impractical.

Addressing this challenge in a practical fashion requires entrepreneurs and managers to experience the benefits of collaboration in a tangible way. The key to such first-hand experience is to have a demonstration effect. Rather than aiming quickly at grandiose, sweeping results, collaboration must begin with realistic, tangible goals.

To collaborate to compete, businesspeople must define their issues in a clear, actionable, and measurable fashion. Real issues around customers, capabilities, costs, and context provide opportunities. Once issues have been defined, actions must be taken around specific opportunities.

Collaboration must start at the periphery and gravitate toward the core of business. It is easiest for entrepreneurs and managers to begin collaborating to improve the context. As a firm's comfort with collaboration grows, it can tackle costs, capabilities, and customers in increasing order of strategic importance according to its business needs.

Beginning with the operating reality is sensible. BoP markets, especially Africa, is arguably the world's toughest business environment. The good news is that myriad challenges mean as many collaboration opportunities. Such challenges matter for collaboration for the benefits from solving them accrues to all stakeholders involved.

The first step is to select a common issue whose solution translates into greater profits for all. The second step often missed is to quantify the cost of inaction for all stakeholders. Next, stakeholders must research best practices and then agree on a common solution. Finally, they must engage relevant stakeholders to solve the problem.

Here are some practical considerations. On this issue, certain types of regulatory changes are good first-time candidates. The relevant stakeholder is known: government. The payoff accrues to all and can be big: reduced costs. The definition of success is clearly known: The law is changed starting on a given date in a specific direction.

In selecting the relevant costs, businesspeople must remember that a large proportion of costs are shared. Specifically, finance, power, water, transportation, and taxes are five cost drivers that impact all businesses operating in a given industry. There is therefore a clear incentive for entrepreneurs and managers to collaborate around these cost items.

The role of clusters could be revisited here. Clusters and private sector associations can be good platforms for collaboration on context-related challenges. Yet, their existence, while a good start, is not enough. Collaboration frameworks quickly lose steam, relevance, and focus.

Cluster workgroups and associations are as relevant as the last issues to be solved or the last place for opportunities to be created. Businesspeople seeking to leverage such efforts must insist that the groups be focused and practical. They must also involve themselves in leading the change process.

Businesspeople serious about collaboration must also seek opportunities to source supplies jointly. They must improve financing through guarantee funds. Last but not least, they must collaborate with government and development partners in making their needs known.

Another way to reduce risks in collaborating on costs is to engage in targeted initiatives with suppliers or customers. Under such scenarios, the limited number of actors involved means that incentives can be aligned and risks diminished. It also helps in forging the type of partnerships that can help fuel business growth.

Collaboration on capabilities faces similar challenges. For one, the fear is even greater: Capabilities are at the core of what makes a business unique and successful. Businesspeople rightfully feel uncomfortable divulging any sensitive information that would put competitors on the path of understanding how they win.

Rather than focusing on specificities, collaboration on capabilities must instead bridge gaps that undermine all competitors. In Africa, availability of qualified staff, consistent standards, and confusion around stakeholder roles and responsibilities are the biggest cross-cutting gaps that affect collaboration on capabilities that must be targeted.

Three specific opportunities can make a difference. First, training and capacity-building initiatives such as certifications and seminars, can bring tangible progress. Next, industry-inspired and self-monitored standards can also make a difference for firms. Finally, targeted initiatives to help support institutions can also make a tremendous difference.

Finally, businesspeople must seek ways to collaborate on customers. Collaboration on customers holds the greatest promise for business. Delivering a superior product or experience is the key to ultimate business success. When successful, collaboration on customers can lead to increased business and market share.

Widespread collaboration on customers tends to be limited except around branding and prospection issues. Whether in tourism, manufacturing, or agriculture, clusters can benefit greatly from a strong regional brand that is often grounded in collaborative efforts to promote the essence of a country's offering.

Prosperity Ecosystems in the Marketplace

As discussed above, tangible mutual benefits are helping in grounding collaboration at the core of individuals, firms, clusters, and nations.

At the individual level, collaboration translates into serenity in the face of challenges and confidence in one's ability to make plans work. Collaboration affords an opportunity to gain leverage and regain control. Regaining control creates the space to articulate and act upon a strategy to escape The Survival Trap.

At the firm level, collaboration creates clarity around business strategy and stability in a fast-paced world. Collaboration improves performance within and outside the firm. It also improves the ability to serve attractive customers in a cost-effective way thanks to distinct capabilities that differentiate the business in a difficult operating context.

At the cluster level, collaboration fosters a competitive spirit and camaraderie. When such camaraderie is present, innovation flourishes and the relative position of the cluster as a whole improves. Cluster stakeholders realize that someone's problems can be another one's business opportunity.

At the national level, collaboration creates a platform for dialogue and opportunity for a move beyond dialogue into concerted action. Prosperity ecosystems help firms, government, and development partners come together to execute a common agenda for prosperity. This is paramount to escaping The Survival Trap.

Miracles and Wonders

Many businesspeople struggle with the operating reality of BoP markets especially Africa. Enabling prosperity ecosystems is the key to miracles and wonders. Such ecosystems are paramount in gaining control over challenges and tapping into tremendous opportunities at the BoP.

Back in Tunisia, entrepreneurs hosted in the incubator of the Elgazala Technopark have reaped the benefits of a prosperity ecosystem designed to promote innovation. Not only are barriers to growth removed but also entrepreneurs feel like they operate in an environment where opportunity can be created not just inherited.

As Mohamed Mouha, Managing Director of Progress Engineering,[8] explains, "We used to believe we needed money, connections, or the right genes to start a business. The Elgazala incubator makes it possible for almost anybody to walk in with an idea and come out with a business."

By focusing on ICT startups, fostering collaboration within the Elgazala Technopark, and leveraging favorable conditions in the Tunisian business environment, Elgazala has largely succeeded in creating a sense of possibility for a new generation of Tunisian entrepreneurs.

Rather than embracing prosperity ecosystems and collaboration in a philosophical way, this case study demonstrates the clear payoffs that are available when government and business can collaborate to promote a specific sector such as ICT. Such a pragmatic approach aligns incentives and keeps all stakeholders honest.

It also demonstrates the unique brand of leadership that is required to escape The Survival Trap. Developing one's ability to collaborate is the foundation of this transformative leadership. Chapter 11, "Bridge the Leadership Gap," discusses how entrepreneurs and managers can bridge the leadership gap.

Vignette 7—The Business of Entrepreneurship: Allon Raiz

There is a unique glow in Allon's eyes when he talks about entrepreneurship. That glow is not unlike a groom talking about his bride or a priest speaking about his faith. It is the glow of pure unadulterated passion.

Anyone who meets Allon Raiz undoubtedly concludes that his passion is entrepreneurship. Everything about Allon speaks about entrepreneurship: Beyond the businesses he has run, he spends his life with entrepreneurs. What is more difficult to understand, but equally compelling, is the story of how Allon has been able to make a business out of entrepreneurship itself.

Defying Gravity

Allon Raiz has managed to do what many have said is impossible— to operate a private business incubator profitably. It took him five years and one month to achieve this goal. But eventually, Allon's incubator, Raizcorp, become profitable because he was unwilling to accept the prevailing mindset that incubators could not be profitable.

This is no small feat given that sub-Saharan Africa boasts several incubators. Most are government run, or donor-subsidized operations, or both. The global literature on incubators suggests that they do not make money. Most experts agree that money losing incubators help launch the next generation of profitable businesses. Allon disagrees.

In a way, Allon never chose to run a business incubator. Instead, the business chose him. Reflecting on his first business, a philosophical Allon says: "I had a big business, but I was not passionate about it. I pursued it for money but not anything else. As a young man, I learned the hard way that money alone does not make us happy."

Around the time when he fell out of love with his first business, Allon started advising entrepreneurs. Quickly his advisory role focused on two promising entrepreneurs. His first two clients worked in different industries at opposite ends of Johannesburg, forcing Allon to commute intellectually and physically.

Allon recalls with a smile: "I had a realization of what I was good at. I enjoyed it. I also realized that the two firms could pay me a quarter of my salary each. They agreed and the fee was introduced into the Raizcorp model. And then somebody else heard about it. At one point, we all moved in together. This is how Raizcorp was born."

This seems an unlikely path for someone helping entrepreneurs run better businesses. Not only did he not have a business plan, Raiz is unapologetic about it. He continues: "When I started Raizcorp, I never had a vision. I find MBA talk impractical. I started Raizcorp by mistake. I never started with a business plan, sold a vision, or got a team."

Yet, Allon managed to defy gravity. He broke the cardinal rule of business incubators, in that they are not to make a profit. The first thing that helped him achieve this feat is that Allon did not know for an entire year that what he was running was a business incubator; therefore he was not limited by conventional wisdom.

Allon recalls: "One year after starting Raizcorp, I was financing the overhead on a credit card. I was at a BBQ when somebody asked me what I did. I explained and he said: "Oh! You're an incubator!" I went home and downloaded a document called Best Practices on Business Incubation. Tick, tick, tick. I was an incubator. It said incubators did not make money. I was not making money. So they were correct."

Then came one of Allon's defining moments: "I had no intention to become an NGO or collect government funds. My crisis was around what do I do now? Do I close? Or do I carry on? It took me another four years and one month to make it work." In the darkest days of doubt, Allon became intimately familiar with The Survival Trap.

Opportunity Mindset

Allon gladly shares the struggles he had when he was starting his business. He explains how his main struggle was to remain motivated while the rest of the world thought he was a failure and should get a real job. He also volunteers some of the self-motivational tools he used to succeed.

Raiz does not forget to pay tribute to his wife. "If at any point in time, my wife had stopped believing in me, I would have probably gotten another job. However, she stood by my side all this time." Those around an entrepreneur play a key role in creating support networks and enabling their success.

Raiz prevailed over The Survival Trap thanks to an opportunity mindset that helped him identify practical insights to grow successful entrepreneurs. With their young and fast-growing populations, many BoP nations resort to entrepreneurship development schemes as a way to help their populations, especially young recent graduates, create jobs.

While he suggests that there is no universal description of an entrepreneur, Raiz draws a sharp distinction between necessity entrepreneur and growth entrepreneur. For him, the key characteristic that truly sets entrepreneurial businesspeople apart is their attitude toward growth.

Raiz continues to suggest that the one element that entrepreneurs must focus on if they are to transcend the myriad challenges they face is to clarify their "economic reason for being." He insists that customers are the best financing source, but customers will only buy if the business creates unique value and thus has a clear economic reason for being.

Raizcorp or Incubation 2.0 for BoP Nations

This opportunity mindset has translated to Raizcorp's offerings. The company offers unique solutions that combine coaching, courses, and facilitation to help entrepreneurs grow their businesses. For a fee, entrepreneurs hosted at the Raizcorp incubator have access to all these services provided by Allon Raiz and his trained facilitators.

Raizcorp works hard with its clients to ensure they not only clarify their economic reason for being, but also put in place the systems necessary to deliver on this promise. In Raizcorp's experience, this does not happen by accident. Rather it requires a careful set of experiences that are informed by coherent business logic.

The firm's proprietary method breaks down this process by saying: "The way that we work with our clients is that we build them. We ensure that all the fundamentals are in place by answering the following questions a) what is the value? b) what am I selling? c) who am I selling it to (and why do they buy from us)? d) Do I have ability to sell the value? e) If I sell it will I make money (this is the finance part)?"

Again, Allon goes back to passion as a key ingredient: "It all starts on the premise that I want to be doing this. When an entrepreneur reaches hard times, it is only her passion that will take her through. Once that's in place, we start working on the creativity. Everything has a different way to be looked at."

According to Allon, this creativity can be an avenue to free cash in business: "You can start looking at all your resources differently to start generating cash. If your challenge was a good thing, what would that mean? If I said that the fact that you could not access capital was a good thing, what that would happen? Would you find new sources to generate income, or find creative ways to cut your costs?"

By challenging his clients to think differently, he is able to encourage innovation and solutions that may have otherwise been missed. Recognizing, and acting on those potentially missed opportunities, are what have made Raiz and his clients so successful.

Opportunities for Incubation

To accomplish all that he has, Allon Raiz has leveraged many of the Seven Opportunities. But in particular two specific opportunities were critical to his success:

Archimedean mindset: Allon Raiz is a quintessential example of an Archimedean entrepreneur. He has been able to see opportunity where others saw impossibility. He saw a need and was able to meet it in a way that is sustainable. Furthermore, he has flirted with failure but managed to prevail through mindset change.

But beyond being an example of entrepreneurship, Raiz has made it is his business to develop and enable that entrepreneurial mindset to flourish in others. By supporting other entrepreneurs and challenging them to think differently about their businesses, he has been a part of the development of many BoP entrepreneurs.

Seeking intelligent capital: Raizcorp is the archetype of a firm providing intelligent capital to entrepreneurs operating in BoP markets. Rather than focus on injecting money, the firm ensures that the right insights are present. Raizcorp believes in intelligent capital so much, it attaches its profits to the success of their clients.

Nobel Prize Material?

Allon Raiz found an entrepreneurial solution to a societal challenge. Where the world believed business incubation must be subsidized, Raizcorp shows that it is possible to have profitable business incubation. Raizcorp is now equipping the entrepreneurs they incubate to relate to their challenges differently.

In its essence, what Allon Raiz has achieved is no different than what Mohammed Yunus did in minting the microfinance industry. By demonstrating the sustainability and the scalability of business incubation Allon Raiz may become a serious contender for the Nobel Peace Prize within a generation.

Endnotes

[1] *Investing in ICT in Tunisia*, Ministry of Communications Technology, Republic of Tunisia.

[2] Elgazala Communication Technopark was established in 1999 as the first in a program to establish ten technoparks over ten years.

[3] Dan Isenberg is a professor of management practice at Babson College and executive director of the Babson Entrepreneurship Ecosystem Project. He is the author of the article "The Big Idea: How to Start an Entrepreneurial Revolution," found in *Harvard Business Review*, June 2010.

[4] C. K. Prahalad, *The Fortune at the Bottom of the Pyramid* (Upper Saddle River, NJ: Wharton School Publishing, 2006), 93.

[5] Soumitra Dutta and Irene Mia, "The Global Information Technology Report 2009-2010," World Economic Forum. http://www.weforum.org/documents/GITR10/index.html.

[6] Michael Porter, *Competitive Advantage of Nations* (New York: The Free Press, 1990); and "Clusters and the New Economics of Competition," *Harvard Business Review*, 1998.

[7] Morten Hansen, *Collaboration: How Leaders Avoid the Traps, Create Unity and Reap Big Results*, (Boston: Harvard Business Press, 2009).

[8] Progress Engineering is the first company to graduate from the Elgazala Incubator.

10 ——————————————————

Seek Intelligent Capital

Jacob's Dilemma

A gentleman closed in on me quickly: "My name is Jacob. I have a great project to plant and process palm oil. How can you help me find money?" I had just spoken at an agribusiness forum in Amsterdam. While my speech dealt with investments in Africa, I started wondering how my words put me in this situation.

Over 20 years, Jacob had built an agro processing plant specializing in edible oils such as soy and peanut. What began as a small shop was now a major factory with 200 employees. Now, Jacob wanted to diversify into palm oil: 20,000 hectares and a state-of-the-art factory.

This is a big opportunity that requires big money: eight million euros. Putting my MBA cap on, I replied that a typical venture capitalist would seek at least a 30 percent return and equity. "But I thought there were loans at 3 percent in Europe. I have some documents I can give to the banks," he added.

When I suggested his venture was too risky for the average commercial bank, he replied: "My brother, this is what they keep saying: I am not giving them my business. The next thing you know, they will take everything. I will start small and do it on my own!" Jacob's disappointment was palpable.

Scarce All Around

Access to capital is one of the foremost business challenges in BoP markets. Small- and medium-sized enterprises (SMEs) suffer most acutely from a lack of access to finance. While larger firms access commercial banks, and individuals benefit from microfinance, SMEs form a "missing middle."

Overreliance on commercial banks contributes to worsening the missing middle. In BoP markets, most banks provide collateral backed loans with a maturity inferior to five years. Businesses often finance long-term assets with such short-term loans. This in turn can negatively impact the business model by creating an undue short-term focus.

With SMEs representing more than 95 percent of firms in some key markets, lack of financing can fundamentally bring progress in entire sectors grinding to a halt. Collectively, the SME finance gap comes at a great cost to BoP markets; constrained SMEs translate into higher unemployment levels, low capital formation, and limited tax revenues.

This scenario in turn creates the conditions for The Survival Trap to thrive. It keeps many firms on a hand-to-mouth routine. Furthermore, a mismatch between financing capital and business model puts strains on many firms. It also keeps financial capital scare and its cost unnecessarily high.

In BoP markets, some businesses fail or never realize their potential, not necessarily because they are inherently nonprofitable. Rather, such businesses run out of capital. As a result, businesspeople especially SME leaders find themselves engaging in survival business as described in Chapter 5, "Foster an Archimedean Mindset."

Venture capital and private equity are relatively new to these markets, small in scale, and not optimized to invest in indigenous firms. Intelligent capital has the potential to catalyze growth for SMEs, while providing the necessary resources for entrepreneurs to thrive in BoP markets.

While in BoP markets financial capital can be scarce, the current focus on money only tells part of the story. Instead, businesspeople must upgrade their mindsets around capital to find the right partners.

Rather than focus on raising large sums of money, businesspeople must seek intelligent capital.

Even when managers are convinced of the pertinence of finding local shareholders, larger firms often refrain from listing on national or regional stock exchanges. They are left handpicking individuals, which can be a hazardous task. Larger firms are often left with having to select politically connected individuals, which creates governance issues.

What Is Intelligent Capital?

Intelligent capital is financial capital delivered concomitantly with the right amount of insights. Most financiers—banks, venture capitalists—are single-mindedly focused on exits defined as reimbursement, or other liquidity events. Too great a focus on exits puts financiers on the side of the table opposite businesspeople.

Intelligent capital focuses on *solutions* as opposed to exits. Through this focus on solutions, intelligent capital sees itself as a partner to businesspeople in the fulfillment of their mission. This stance matters in BoP markets where the operating reality is difficult. This core distinction translates into five observable attributes:

- **Focus on *skills*** Intelligent capital focuses on skills while empowering businesspeople to drive their business. It sits beside businesspeople.

- **Strengthen the business *model*** Intelligent capital sits beside businesspeople to identify ways to strengthen the business model.

- **Foster a greater *action-orientation*** This focus on execution combined with skills and business model contributes to value creation.

- **Oriented toward *results*** Specifically, it seeks to see the business deliver great financial returns but also tremendous societal impact.

- **Appreciate the importance of *time*** Intelligent capital has a pragmatic relationship to *time*, which is critical in BoP markets. It knows how to be patient when necessary.

While businesspeople may have difficulty identifying such capital in the maze of options available, these five attributes make the search for intelligent capital worthwhile. Businesspeople must remember that true to its name intelligent capital is SMART.

As illustrated in Figure 10.1, lack of balance between money and insight can keep business stuck in The Survival Trap.

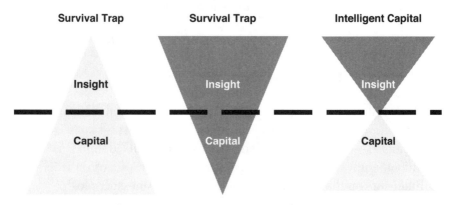

Figure 10.1   Intelligent capital—the right balance of money and insight

What Keeps Intelligent Capital Elusive?

Specific mindsets combine with the operating reality in BoP markets to keep intelligent capital elusive. It is important to diagnose both before attracting intelligent capital.

Three overarching mindsets are obstacles to intelligent capital— ambivalence about capital, lack of trust, and zero-sum game. First, businesspeople operating in BoP markets develop ambivalence about capital: While most want capital to grow, they fear surrendering any control in exchange of capital.

This ambivalence is heightened by the operating reality. In BoP markets, businesspeople see myriad opportunities that could be harnessed. As the most obvious constraint, capital becomes the scapegoat. Yet, even when it is there, businesspeople fear surrendering control because of weak legal framework and absence of a venture culture.

Closely related to this, the second mindset is that capital partners are not trustworthy. Not only do they charge too much but also they have complicated requirements. The reality of BoP markets makes this perception worse. Very few role models exist of businesspeople who have succeeded thanks to capital providers.

The next mindset is a zero-sum mindset. Businesspeople question the value created by capital partners. In a low-trust context such as BoP markets, businesspeople can resent seeing total strangers benefit from years of hard work. Instead, they prefer keeping 100 percent of a smaller pie.

Jacob offers a good example of an entrepreneur harboring these three mindsets. His complaint that "30 percent was too much" is typical yet unfounded. Return must be assessed in relationship to the risk incurred. Yet, these three mindsets combine to make him see the world differently than capital partners.

Within the operating reality of BoP markets, these three mindsets translate into a love-hate relationship between businesspeople and capital partners. To be fair, capital partners are also to blame for the love-hate relationship. Sometimes, the greed, arrogance, and inflexibility of certain capital providers are not matched by their talents.

The undue focus on aid as the main bottleneck to economic development makes matters worse. This prevailing mindset creates a resonance for the false beliefs and associations that businesspeople have about the importance of capital as a constraint to business. Businesspeople find solace in the fact that their sentiment is echoed.

All these mindsets combine to form a powerful barrier that prevents businesspeople from working in earnest with capital providers. This creates a situation where individuals, firms, clusters, and nations remain stuck in The Survival Trap when intelligent capital is available that could help them upgrade their business models.

Diagnose the Mindsets That Keep Intelligent Capital Elusive

As suggested above, intelligent capital blossoms at the intersection of three sets of stakeholders: businesspeople, capital providers, and the public sector. It is therefore on these three communities that the diagnostic of mindsets that keep intelligent capital elusive must focus.

The first level diagnostic for businesspeople begins with financials. Is the venture only financed by equity? Is the term of the financing aligned with the lifetime of the assets? Specifically, long-term assets financed by short-term debt should bring a concern that there is a mismatch of terms between assets and financing.

The second level diagnostic looks beyond the obvious. Are there opportunities where collaborating with a capital partner could be executed? Who would be ideal capital partners? Beyond money, how can a capital partner make my solution or venture better? "Nothing" as an answer should be a red flag that something is amiss.

Next, capital providers must also ascertain whether they are capital partners. Intrinsically, they realize that value creation should be the focus rather than value sharing. Capital providers should ask themselves: "How can we support the business leaders in upgrading its business model?"

Beyond these questions, capital providers must uncover any attitudes or practice that would trigger a defensive reaction from entrepreneurs and managers. Here it helps to be candid and seek feedback. Capital partners should ask: "How can we help you upgrade your business?"

Finally, leaders must grow skeptical when money becomes the scapegoat. This is often a sign of more fundamental problems being ignored. One simple question is to ask stakeholders: "If you had the resources today, how would you deploy them?" A good answer should explain how the additional capital will improve the business.

Having diagnosed the mindsets that keep intelligent capital elusive, leaders are now ready to embrace this powerful lever to allow them to succeed in BoP markets,

Resource-Oriented Thinking

The necessary mindset is resource-oriented thinking. It is an approach that helps leaders facing a challenge to begin solving it with the resources within their control. Rather than focusing on gaps, business leaders rethink their strategy to address the constraints by redeploying available resources to meet their vision.

Resource-oriented thinking allows for a breakthrough by allowing businesspeople to redeploy existing resources in a creative fashion to achieve their vision. It creates a focus on outcomes and a shift in perspective that is often the key to making plans work in BoP markets.

It builds on design thinking that is central to focusing on solutions. As Roger Martin notes, "the dominant attitude in traditional firms is to see constraints as the enemy. For design shops, constraints are never the enemy. On the contrary, they serve to increase the challenge and excitement-level of the task at hand. Instead, they are inclined to say: 'Bring it on!'"[1]

Businesspeople with resource-oriented thinking see lack of capital or any other constraints as an innovation challenge to be addressed. This in turn gives them the resource to solve their problems. Resource-oriented thinking plays out differently depending on the perspective: businesspeople, capital providers, and the public sector.

Businesspeople experience a shift in attitude from the mindset that money is the solution to all problems to one that recognizes that a successful business needs a lot more than just money. It allows businesspeople to put the proper emphasis on skills, planning, and innovative thinking.

Capital providers learn to match the capital extended to the type of opportunity at hand. Proper appreciation of resources is also about making sure not to overcapitalize or create a financing mismatch. It also identifies ways to bridge gaps that are nonfinancial in nature.

Public sector leaders begin to look for systemic solutions to improve the operating reality that go beyond responding to the call for more money. Specifically, public sector leaders begin thinking about ways to foster an entrepreneurial ecosystem that helps businesspeople implement entrepreneurial solutions for prosperity.

When all stakeholders embrace resource-oriented thinking, this creates conditions for businesspeople to adopt key principles and practices to transform their business model. Figure 10.2 demonstrates how resource-oriented thinking enables businesspeople to unleash the power of intelligent capital.

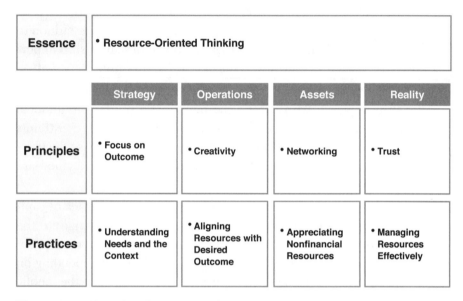

Figure 10.2   **Transforming your business through intelligent capital**

Building Solutions, Not Exits

As suggested above, resource-oriented thinking creates the conditions for businesspeople to begin leveraging intelligent capital to transform their firms in BoP markets. Let's consider how Jacob can leverage the framework to make this opportunity happen.

The first principle is focus on outcomes. Practically, remaining focused on outcomes requires having a business strategy that resolves the tension between goals and resources. Understanding the needs they are trying to address and the context in which they operate is paramount to aligning strategies to the challenges at hand.

The clearer the desired outcome, the easier it will be to become creative. Such creativity must become the hallmark of their operations. This creativity is about ensuring the businesspeople fight the war with the army they have. Rather than continuously focusing on what is not possible, entrepreneurs must reorient, redesign, and execute.

Jacob's primary experience is in producing and distributing edible oils to his country and other central African nations. However, many aspects of his current plan go beyond this specific outcome. Jacob is not seeking capital to enter palm oil in a big way and get into sustainable energy and cosmetics. This could be a challenge.

To succeed here, the practice Jacob must rely on is to understand customer needs and the context. As discussed in Chapter 7, "Focus on Solutions," such an understanding is critical in moving beyond a fixed business plan toward an offering that is aligned with the way customers see their lives.

Jacob must focus on the outcome of becoming a leader in edible oil. Rather than planting 20,000 hectares at the beginning, he could buy some palm from existing suppliers. This would allow him to test how his current market reacts to palm oil. Afterward, he could decide to backward integrate into planting.

The second core principle is creativity. The principle of creativity must inform the operations of businesses serious about intelligent capital. Such capital can often show businesses ways to improve operations while optimizing their use of capital. It can also provide insights on ways to improve systems and processes.

An important aspect is the cash conversion cycle, which rests on operations. The cash conversion cycle measures how long it takes a firm to recuperate one dollar it invests in its operations. Intelligent capital can help firms in their bid to optimize their usage of cash. Any improvement will translate into happier customers and greater profits.

Jacob is embarking on an adventure that could seriously lengthen its cash conversion cycle. Not only is Jacob diversifying into a new product but he is also considering doing it at a scale that he has not experienced before. New palm tree plantations take up to four years before producing.

Intelligent capital partners would make such critical challenges and trade-offs in a way that would help him optimize his firm's operations. They would also challenge Jacob to be more creative, rethink his approach, and consider a focus that maximizes his return on investment.

To mobilize the required assets to apply resource-oriented thinking, the principle businesses must espouse is networking. This principle is about realizing that businesses are not islands. Solutions to challenges are often available in the context in which they operate.

Networking is about businesses seeking to plug in their ecosystems to find creative solutions to their challenges. By plugging into the ecosystem, firms can often find creative (and often nonfinancial) solutions to their challenges. Networking inspires businesspeople to begin collaborating with core stakeholders and other businesses.

Rather than focusing on getting money that is hard to come by, businesspeople can get some traction if what they ask for is assistance that is not necessarily a check for a specific amount. Applied to all stakeholders, this consideration can have a great impact on a business.

In deciding to produce palm oil, Jacob is potentially working with independent land owners and farmers who will have a tremendous impact on his ability to realize his dreams. An option he may consider is articulating an extension service scheme where he provides select inputs to farmers in exchange for a committed supply.

Another important consideration is skills. Operating two different locations and expanding into farming of palm oil will mean a perennial culture that is different from soy. An intelligent capital partner would probably point to different skills that Jacob must bring on board to bridge the leadership gap.

In addition, a critical challenge seems to be figuring out how to structure an investment. As it stands, Jacob wants an eight million euro loan to launch a new business that is three times the value of his existing firm. An intelligent capital partner can help him structure the deal, appropriately aligning assets and capital sources.

For the operating reality, it is important that businesspeople adopt a principle of trust. We discuss trust extensively in Chapter 6, "Build Trust." As it relates specifically to resource-oriented thinking, trust matters between businesspeople and their stakeholders. Such trust is the glue that makes stakeholders stand behind the business.

A tremendous opportunity exists for his venture to do well while doing good by sourcing its supplies from local communities. An intelligent capital partner can help Jacob see this opportunity, among others. As discussed above, Jacob can consider working with local landowners and independent farmers.

Intelligent Capital Partners Align Incentives to Transform Business Models

Intelligent capital distinguishes itself for its ability to transform business models and align incentives. These two dimensions must inform the search for intelligent capital.

The first dimension centers on key elements of successful business models. Businesspeople seeking intelligent capital must articulate concrete business objectives aligned along strategy, operations, assets, and operating reality. A clear understanding of why these four dimensions matter for intelligent capital is critical.

Ability to articulate concrete objectives aligned to a business model means that intelligent capital partners are not limited only to the usual financiers. Some banks and investment professionals with the right values can provide intelligent capital. What is critical is that such professionals consider the business in its entirety.

However, it does not stop with traditional financiers. In the context of BoP markets, the difficult operating reality provides an opportunity for other players such as successful entrepreneurs, multinationals, and regional pension funds to also offer intelligent capital. Such players have the understanding it takes to help smaller firms.

For SMEs and smaller firms, business development services (BDS) providers or experienced businesspeople will be in a pole position to provide intelligent capital. Skills and insights are critical to most small businesses. BDS providers and experienced businesspeople can provide the required insights along with financial capital.

A good example of an intelligent capital organization that combines BDS and financial capital is Raizcorp in South Africa. Profiled in Chapter 9, "Enable Prosperity Ecosystems," Allon Raiz and his team have developed a profitable incubation business model. They are now poised to expand beyond South Africa.

Another example of an intelligent capital partner is the Comcraft Group. As illustrated in the UST Global vignette at the end of this chapter, the Comcraft Group has emerged into a multibillion revenue conglomerate by empowering its executives to innovate under the Chandaria family values of humanity, integrity, and humility.

The second dimension is that of incentives. Incentives matter a great deal in the search for intelligent capital. Businesspeople want successful and profitable businesses. While objective measures of profits are easy to come by, definition of success is often personal. It is important for businesspeople to be explicit about their nonmonetary objectives.

Capital partners want returns commensurate with their risk within a specific time range. While businesspeople are tethered to a venture for the long term, most capital partners expect to exit their agreement. Again expected returns are often easy to outline at the onset of a relationship. Most complications arise around the exit.

Considering the fact that intelligent capital partners are not always usual financiers, there is an opportunity for successful businesspeople to incubate the next generation of business leaders by becoming intelligent capital partners themselves. This is an important consideration to solve the capital gap.

Local public financial institutions constitute another category of intelligent capital partners that can create tremendous value for foreign investors. Such capital partners often help foreign investors navigate the context and deliver their solutions in a way that benefits all stakeholders.

The Returns on Intelligent Capital

Businesspeople who seek intelligent capital stand to unleash the potential of their firms in significant ways. Three specific benefits make intelligent capital worthy of pursuit.

First, intelligent capital affords businesspeople significant support in scaling solutions. Capital partners such as banks or venture capitalists have attributes including skills, experience, and influence that extend beyond simply writing a check. Astute businesspeople seek to leverage those attributes for the success of their mission.

For instance, banks or business assistance providers will help a small firm implement better managerial systems such as financial reporting tools. Venture capitalists will bring a wealth of industry-specific business knowledge. The case of NSIA group discussed in Chapter 6 provides a good example.

Second, intelligent capital is often the best way for businesspeople to reduce their ultimate cost of capital. At first, this may seem like a paradox. Venture capitalists or business partners demand a high dollar on dollar return. Yet, attracting intelligent capital is critical to optimizing the capital structure for a specific venture or solution.

Consider Jacob. It is unlikely a bank will lend eight million euros for his venture. Bringing a venture capitalist on board improves his chances. For one, the equity staked into the project reduces overall risk. Next, the compelling business case required for the investor would go a long way toward convincing other financiers to lend.

As suggested earlier, the presence of intelligent capital reassures other capital partners. It reduces the risk of the venture because it increases the quality of business planning. It also reduces the perception of risk as other capital partners inherently trust that intelligent capital to select a venture with a sensible risk return profile.

Finally, intelligent capital removes a critical constraint for the growth of business in BoP markets. For entrepreneurs such as Jacob, limited venture capital puts a cap on growth prospects. For larger firms, the lack of local equity can expose a business to local political risks or exactions.

In allowing firms to scale their operations, intelligent capital is important in providing solutions for the bottom of the pyramid. In BoP markets, most micro and small scale entrepreneurs serve needs and create opportunities in their community. The firm's ability to grow translates into more solutions for the bottom of the pyramid.

Intelligent Capital in Action

Intelligent capital is critical in aligning financial capital to a firm's business model. When deployed astutely, intelligent capital can upgrade all aspects of a firm or an institution's business model, namely, the strategy, operations, assets, people, and the societal impact. How does intelligent capital deploy itself in action?

At the individual level, intelligent capital provides entrepreneurs, managers, and their collaborators with the confidence to make their plans work. This in turn unleashes innovation and helps entrepreneurs focus on delivering a solution. In this process, intelligent capital addresses one of the most pernicious effects of The Survival Trap.

At the firm level, intelligent capital translates differently according to the size of the business. Smaller firms will see their strategy improve and business systems strengthen from dealing with experienced capital partners. Larger firms get a better local acumen from national shareholders that can help navigate the challenging operating reality.

At the cluster level, intelligent capital increases overall competitiveness. Intelligent capital partners can bridge key gaps by targeting areas that are traditionally not financed such as inputs, guarantee funds, and so on. Capital partners also help in raising the overall capital absorption capacity of players in the cluster.

At the national level, intelligent capital addresses critical bottlenecks in resource mobilization and allocation. It ensures that viable opportunities do not go unfinanced. It also changes the nature of the national conversation. Instead of blaming lack of capital, capital partners identify real opportunities for improvement in the business model.

Intelligent Capital and Key Investments

In a global market where money is increasingly being commoditized, businesspeople have no excuse for failing to meet their business's or institution's capital needs. Rather than dwell on constraints, they must seek intelligent capital in their attempts to mobilize capital.

Beyond money, intelligent capital provides firms with the insights to unleash their solutions. Escaping The Survival Trap requires businesspeople to seek intelligent capital. Specifically, businesspeople must articulate their solutions in ways where capital needs are aligned with strategy, operations, assets, and operating reality.

Right before dinner, Jacob cornered me with a big smile on his face. Something had clearly changed: He had a new solution he wanted to test with me. "I am talking to a group who will not only help me develop a business plan but also help structure the project and raise the money." I was impressed.

The jury is still out on whether Jacob will raise his eight million euros. However, he is no longer stuck. He can either raise capital gradually according to a carefully designed plan or develop his palm oil factory organically the way he knows how. Rather than approach capital mobilization in a constrained way, he has viable options.

Beyond firms, intelligent capital can also unleash the potential of clusters and nations. It also allows stakeholders to address the mismatch between capital and strategy. It provides a unique opportunity to deliver great entrepreneurial solutions for prosperity. Ultimately, this is one of the keys to escaping The Survival Trap.

Vignette 8—Timeless Values in New Technology: UST Global

Values are expressed through traditions. A jar sits on the reception desk at the UST Global's offices in Trivandrum, India. UST staff knows it as the "Chairman's Sir Fund Jar." The tradition is simple: Everyone using the word "Sir" deposits money. Indian culture values hierarchy. The "Chairman's Sir Fund Jar" signals humility at all levels of the UST Global organization.

A leader in the fast-moving IT outsourcing industry, UST Global has leveraged its timeless values and traditions—new and old—to successfully implement a global customer-centric model of service delivery. UST Global offers some invaluable lessons to corporations straddling the BoP and developed markets.

Straddling BoP and Developed Markets

Headquartered in Aliso Viejo, California, UST provides comprehensive IT solutions for Global 1000 companies. Since its inception in 1999, UST has grown to more than 7,000 employees operating out of 18 locations across the world including England, India, Philippines, Chile, Malaysia, Singapore, Hong Kong, and various cities in the US.

Building a bridge between BoP and developed markets, UST has grown thanks to a strong customer portfolio with more than 95 percent of revenues coming from Fortune 500/Global 1000 firms. Analysts and media alike have recognized UST for its customer focus, innovation, and industry leadership.

In 2008, Gartner named UST one of 21 companies in the North American offshore applications services magic quadrant, which is an indication of service excellence. In 2007, the firm was ranked as the #1 ITO provider of legacy modernization and #7 top IT "green" outsourcers in India.

Globalization translates into specific business challenges for corporate leaders. First, operating in BoP markets heightens stakeholder expectations by emphasizing issues of corporate social responsibility.

Further, the importance of intangibles is increasing. Corporate leaders must find ways to foster one global corporate identity that translates well across cultures as diverse as Africa, Latin America, Asia, and the Middle East. Finally, nurturing competitive talent with the expertise to drive innovation in BoP markets is becoming a top challenge for corporations.

UST is a powerful illustration of a multinational that has successfully straddled BoP and developed markets by leveraging entrepreneurial solutions for prosperity.

New Technology, Timeless Values

My visit to the UST offices in Trivandrum started with a passionate discussion. That in itself is not surprising. What was unusual was that our conversation focused exclusively on UST's values. We had been speaking for 45 minutes before we discussed UST's offering.

It did not take me long to recognize that the values and culture that set UST apart are the same values that have informed the success of the Comcraft Group, UST's parent company. The values exemplified by Dr. Manu Chandaria and his family were at work: Interestingly, there was no Chandaria in sight.

The UST executive team emphasized how the firm's values of humility, humanity, and integrity shaped its culture, which itself informed UST's business model. One of the original employees, Arun Narayanan, UST's COO, shared how UST began as a crazy idea by the late G. A. Menon, a technology pioneer and associate of the Chandaria family.

Arun recalls how Menon instilled these values within the UST team. The "Chairman's Sir Fund Jar" is only a small way in which UST honors Menon's legacy. While Mr. Menon passed away in 2003, the values he instilled in UST are still flourishing.

When values run deep, they can spread far. Most of the current management never worked directly for Mr. Menon, much less the Chandarias. Yet, the values are still in force today.

The current chairman, Dan Gupta, insists on the importance of values: "Every location has this system of value mentorship. Our target is to have 1 value mentor for every 50 staff in India and 1 value mentor for every 30 associates in other locations. We very openly tell each and every associate that they must demonstrate an alignment with our values and culture and become role models for others in the company."

It is also a lesson that corporate leaders serious about straddling BoP and developed markets should emulate. Values are also critical in bridging the cultural gap that may exist in BoP markets.

UST Value-Driven Business Model

The UST leadership team made some counterintuitive strategic choices that paid off. Especially in services industries, client retention is a critical issue. This challenge becomes more complex in BoP markets due to lack of direct relationship to the ultimate client.

Most firms address this challenge by selling to more clients to spread risk. While this may make sense, it keeps some of these firms in The Survival Trap as the diluted focus hinders the provision of truly superior solutions.

In contrast, UST professes a belief in "fewer clients, more attention." This approach has differentiated the firm in its industry. The firm has pioneered a global customer-centric engagement model that ensures that it is close to clients while leveraging its global presence to deliver.

UST's unusual strategy of focusing on fewer clients has impacted growth. UST Global has grown fast. A major challenge has been maintaining its outstanding service levels. BPO being a talent-driven industry, the firm has made sure its new staff delivers consistently while espousing the firm's values.

The firm articulated the UST footprint into a model that translates the timeless values of humanity, humility, and integrity into five core competencies: living the values, putting the client first, inspire(d) people, passionate entrepreneurship, and execution mindset.

UST Global an Archimedean Firm

As illustrated above, UST Global is the archetype of a corporation that has leveraged the seven entrepreneurial solutions for prosperity. The firm's usage of four of the Seven Opportunities offers the most relevant lessons for corporations facing similar challenges in BoP markets.

Archimedean mindset: G. A. Menon—the iconic Founder Chairman of UST Global envisioned the firm as a successful business that would serve a higher purpose. UST Global still lives by one of his quotes: "We will listen, learn, be empathetic and help selflessly in our interactions with everyone."

This Archimedean mindset has helped UST build long-term relationships instead of focus on short-term transactions. When asked, the executive team suggests that the secret lies in the relationships UST has formed with key stakeholders.

Focus on solutions: UST's strategy of "fewer clients, more attention" means a clear focus on solutions. Building on the UST handprint, the firm's global customer-centric model illustrates how the firm brings the best it can muster to its client problems. This focus on solutions has also informed the firm's innovation drive.

Commenting on a report recognizing UST's performance, the CEO of UST Global, Sajan Pillai, remarked, "This report reinforces a major theme for UST, the importance of innovation for the advancement of global IT service delivery."

Enable prosperity ecosystems: Innovation has emerged as the preeminent issue in most boardrooms. UST creates innovative prosperity ecosystems through its Centers of Excellence, via partnerships with best-of-breed organizations that provide UST developers with access to new technologies.

Furthermore, the company's belief in the value of each and every employee has been at the core of innovation. The Apple Tree, *Eureka!*, and Open Minds are three such practices that have driven innovation at UST.

Intelligent capital: Since its inception in 1999, UST Global has remained part of the Comcraft Group. Growth is extremely capital intensive. By providing intelligent capital, Comcraft illustrates how conglomerates operating in BoP markets can incubate other conglomerates by availing intelligent capital. This is certainly an example that corporations must ponder as a way to make a difference while increasing their returns.

Bridge the leadership gap: IT services are characterized by high turnover. Thus, training and recruiting are sizeable costs. UST also recognizes the importance of retention to sustain its business strategy of "fewer clients, more attention." With a 95 percent plus retention rate over 24 months, the firm is bridging the leadership gap.

UST encourages a work culture characterized by a flat hierarchy where everyone is considered equal.

Arun Narayanan, UST's current COO, pioneered a unique corporate concept called Colors of UST Global that enables associates to work on organizational goals that are aligned with their personal goals. The result is a workforce that is committed beyond contract.

Profitability through Values

UST Global stands as a powerful testimony that timeless values generate profits. Since its inception in 1999, the leadership of UST Global has built a strong culture rooted on humanity, humility, and integrity. This culture has helped the firm emerge as a global leader in the competitive and fast growing IT industry.

Reflecting on the company's history, Dan Gupta, the current chairman of UST Global, remarks: "Values and culture can accelerate and enhance the top line and bottom line of any business. No company has grown like UST Global has in the past 10 years. 2009 was the worst year ever for the global IT industry, but UST Global saw a revenue growth of 19%. Our customers stayed on with us, while they reduced volumes with our peers in the industry."

Endnotes

[1] Roger Martin, "Embedding Design into Business," BusinessWeek Online, August 2005. http://www.rotman.utoronto.ca/rogermartin/EmbeddingDesign.pdf.

11

Bridge the Leadership Gap

A Bittersweet Promotion

Almost 20 years after joining a global pharmaceutical company, Alexandre de Carvalho reached the pinnacle of his career. After several management positions throughout the globe, he was now offered the Managing Director position for Africa.

On the one hand, drawn to Africa because of his paternal ancestry, Alexandre welcomed his assignment. On the other hand, given the not-so-notorious record of Africa as a "career booster" in his company, he was wondering whether this was a good move. A graduate of HEC Paris and Harvard Business School, Alexandre was extremely comfortable with the latest management techniques.

Through his vast experience, he had learned that good corporate citizenship hinges on a manager's ability to meet objectives, mostly financial. But no matter how much he looked into his "good" corporate citizen playbook, Alexandre was stuck.

The company's strategy required selling expensive drugs in Africa, a market with poor customers, inexistent social safety nets, and a focus on treatment instead of prevention. Very quickly, Alexandre realized he had inherited a "problem division."

Turnaround Through a Human-Centered Repositioning

But with the promotion, he faced a challenge like no other. A modern day Sisyphus, Alexandre felt drained at first. Sisyphus, in Greek mythology, was condemned to ceaselessly roll a rock to the top of a mountain, only to have the stone roll back down.

Alexandre could not help but feel that, despite all his hard work and willingness to change his division, his endeavors might prove futile. The situation was dire. The Africa division had not turned a profit in many years.

Sales were below targets in a market with great unmet needs. There was a growing rift between expatriate and local staff. Relationships with the community were not good. Africa was recurrently considered a division to close.

The solution came through a management program facilitated by a specialized consulting firm. Alexandre remembers: "I was deeply myopic as a 'good' corporate citizen. My challenge was reconciling my deep aspirations with my corporate responsibility. It took outside facilitators to help root my corporate vision on my human dimension."

Through the facilitated process, Alexandre and his management team introduced a human-centered vision from which they developed successful innovative strategies. This vision infused the ambition of creating in Africa an innovative pharmaceutical company, a pioneer in its comprehensive approach to healthcare, its performance, and its sustainability.

The turnaround was impressive. The company regained its leadership of the African market. Sales and profitability increased. Employee's morale and performance soared. The company's relations with local leaders improved greatly. Africa became a growth opportunity for the company.

Critical Leadership Gaps

Upon taking his assignment, Alexandre realized quickly that the poor results reflected critical leadership gaps he needed to bridge.

First, there was a vision gap. In spite of huge unmet health needs, the company does not envisage meeting these needs as its core mission. "Because of a focus on an exclusive branded medicine, growth potential in Africa was considered limited," Alexandre realized.

This vision gap is not limited only to Alexandre's company. Back in 2001, big pharma companies sued the government of President Nelson Mandela for seeking to provide generic drugs to address the HIV/AIDS scourge in South Africa.

Second, there was also a gap between the expatriate management and the local staff. He continues, "The company relied upon a management team made up of expatriates almost exclusively and was grossly unaware of a lack of motivation in the local team."

Similarly, some of the key managerial functions such as finance, HR, or marketing were being run from the central headquarters. Africa operations happened through HQs—"foldable" local legal entities.

Next, there was a gap between the company's strategy and the operating reality in Africa. Alexandre recalls, "The management team followed a top-down application of the company's global strategy and the overarching pursuit of the financial objectives predetermined by headquarters."

To compound the effects of the HR strategy described above, the company's operations and marketing strategies were not working. Operationally, the company was recurrently considering closing its factories in Africa. Furthermore, the priority in marking was to sell expensive/high margin products.

Finally, there was also a gap between the company and its key stakeholders. "Partnering with the local authorities wasn't considered, as these groups were focused on prevention. The company felt it could not sacrifice 'the golden goose' by promoting prevention instead it focused on treatment," recalls Alexandre.

Survival Business Revisited

In Chapter 5, "Foster an Archimedean Mindset," we discussed how the operating reality in BoP markets can lead firms to engage in Survival Business. Alexandre's division is a good illustration.

First, it was replicative as opposed to innovative. The top-down, copycat strategy was not working. It prevented the firm from seeing an exciting human-centered mission and any growth potential in Africa. Next, survival business can often be informed by pure opportunism. A sole focus on the "limited" market allowed is opportunistic. Paradoxically, not only did the firm not live to its claimed health mission, but it also left money on the table. Third, survival business tends to focus on short-cycle activities. This approach involved closing any sites that were deemed "nonstrategic" by the company. The company sought to minimize its investment.

Personal Costs of Survival Business

This situation put tremendous pressure on Alexandre as a human being. While he was doing everything his corporate and management training has taught him, Alexandre clearly sensed on a personal level that something was missing.

As a human being, Alexandre sensed a professional versus personal gap. This situation is not unlike that of many corporate leaders assigned leadership roles in BoP markets. Such leaders often feel like they are being asked to play a game with the wrong rules.

Such leaders may also feel powerless to bridge the gaps they are feeling between the management playbook and their personal values. This often puts tremendous pressure on these leaders as human beings.

Survival business can be tantamount to having to conduct business in a way that goes against their most profound human aspirations. It is also tantamount to being told to fight with their hands tied behind their backs.

Before bridging the leadership gap, it is critical such leaders take a personal stand. Because such a stand requires breaking away from routine, it can help to engage in a structured process or even enlist outside facilitation like Alexandre.

The Leadership Gap

These leaders must realize that the real challenge is the gap between their management playbook and their operating reality. In BoP markets, this gap is far from trivial: Human realities, market opportunities, and challenges are not traditionally bridged.

As a result, a brand new approach is required to meet basic unmet human needs, harvest opportunities, and respond to challenges. This approach requires managers to graduate from a traditional good corporate citizen to an ethical leader.

This type of leadership, as per the definition of the consulting firm that worked with Alexandre and his team, is about aiming at meeting fundamental human needs (from basic needs such as food, health to self realization, altogether). In providing solutions to such needs, economic performance ensues as a consequence.

Managers in BoP markets face a widening divide between human needs that translate into market opportunities and the capacity to meet these demands. This leadership gap materializes itself in two important ways. First, there is an over-reliance on management or strategy. The business playbook is often focused on management. Success is defined as meeting objectives, mostly (exclusively) financial, by delivering on a careful crafted business plan which outlines clearly the resources required.

Management is often focused on delivering on a pre-established script. Strategy is derived from these financial objectives and an underlying vision that makes little or no space for human value creation by meeting fundamental human needs.

Leadership differs from management inasmuch as it stems from a vision. As illustrated in Figure 11.1, rather than focusing on meeting financial objectives, leadership is about outcomes and value (human-centered) creation.

- Focus on Objectives
- Action Planning
- Script-Bound

- Vision
- Human Value
- Commitment, Rather Than Compliance

Figure 11.1   Minding the leadership gap

Leadership works in BoP markets because it creates commitment from stakeholders rather than mere compliance. It provides the business with the capacity to meet the stakeholders' (including BoP) needs and demands.

What is important for businesspeople to realize here is that leadership is about providing what's missing. Management alone is not enough. Management is best when the task at hand is relatively clear in a predictable environment.

In BoP markets, human needs are great, assets are limited, goalposts shift, and environments are unpredictable. Leadership works best in such conditions. Vision, innovation, and risk taking are required where stewardship is not enough.

What is required is a renewed focus on visionary, human-centered leadership. Such leadership creates the conditions for key stakeholders, especially employees, to share the vision and cocreate the corresponding strategies.

In the Alexandre's case, it is apparent how the focus on management and strategy had not delivered. While the headquarters offered a roadmap, the Africa division remains off the path.

Alexandre recalled: "I felt that we were suffering from the 'Beginner Golfer's Syndrome.' The harder one tries to hit the ball—that is, the more one focuses solely on financial results—the shorter and less accurate the ball may go; i.e., the poorer the overall performance and positive impact on stakeholders may be."

Second, focus on available talent as opposed to people's potential. This second aspect is about the so-called limited availability of top talent in BoP markets. In fact, companies believe in available talent and do not focus on people's potential.

Although this is changing for specific BoP nations such as India, it remains a problem of considerable importance for the poorest BoP nations, especially African countries. This has sustained an overreliance on expatriates.

In BoP markets, some historical factors have sustained this leadership gap. For example, in the case of Africa, three factors have a disproportionate impact on the leadership gap: a young population, limited investments in education, and a dependence on multinational corporations of previous colonizing countries.

To bridge the leadership gap that businesspeople face in BoP markets, the essence they must unleash is shared ownership. It is the leader's ability to share the vision with all stakeholders that will light the way. Through shared ownership, businesspeople are able to enlist everyone's help in meeting their objectives.

Shared ownership refers to the leaders' ability to articulate and communicate an inclusive and human-centered vision. It refers to the leaders' ability to muster loyalty and trust amongst the business's core stakeholders. It also refers to the leaders' ability to innovate in the face of challenges and opportunities.

An African folktale illustrates this concept best. As his death neared, a king decided that the smarter of his twin children should inherit the throne. The two children were given the same, extremely heavy, load to carry over a long distance. The challenge was to see who could get the weight to its destination the fastest.

The prince, who was the strongest, lifted the weight on his shoulder and took off running. After some thought, the princess decided to ask for help. As people saw the princess with the huge package, they felt compelled to help. She quickly managed to pass her exhausted brother and was declared the victor.

Businesspeople in BoP markets would be inspired to follow this example. In BoP markets, businesspeople carry a heavy burden of sustaining their businesses in difficult conditions. Being vulnerable is about managers coming out of the "good corporate citizenship" and confronting their desire to create human value.

Identifying needs and developing plans for shared responsibilities and shared rewards enables businesspeople to obtain the support they need. Shared ownership ensures that other stakeholders appreciate the challenges entrepreneurs face in such a way that they are compelled to share the burden.

What Mindsets Sustain the Leadership Gap?

At the root of the leadership gap are three critical mindsets that businesspeople must address. These mindsets are not unlike the ones that prevent collaboration and undermine trust. It helps to clearly identify these mindsets to resolve the tension that business leaders face.

The first mindset is the command and control mindset. By definition, business leaders are people with a track record of being in charge. Most develop a winning formula that seemingly allows them to triumph in the face of adversity. When it is not kept in check, this winning formula can breed overconfidence and disempowerment. This mindset carries three main risks. First, collaboration often brings better results. Second, counting only on oneself is a recipe for burnout. It invariably makes business leaders the bottleneck in their operations. Finally, they must realize that what was necessary to succeed yesterday is not enough today.

The management program described previously gave Alexandre a chance to get some feedback. At first, he did not like what he heard. Alexandre recalls: "My team said things like: 'when you speak with us like that, we really don't feel good.' Over time I came to understand the truth of what my associates were saying."

This management program helped Alexandre explicit some unproductive routines he was using. The tougher things became, the more convinced Alexandre became that "demanding" management was required.

A corollary of command and control, the second mindset is "knowing it best." Entrepreneurs and corporate leaders often have a sense that they know best. Not only is no one infallible but BoP markets offer complex operating realities. A knowing it best mindset is often the best way to alienate talent and stakeholders. Failure to acknowledge their potential contribution often leads to lack of motivation and poor relationships.

In the case of Alexandre, the top-down approach explains why the local direct reports felt hurt. At the beginning Alexandre tried to justify this situation by pointing to the need for improved results and the need for a demanding management style.

The last mindset is reverence for authority. This mindset plays out in two complementary ways. Traditionally, the culture in BoP markets, especially in Africa, features a great vertical distance. Those in positions of authority are often revered and even feared, as can be those who are older.

In larger organizations, senior managers combine both authority and seniority. As a result, subordinates bestow great respect upon leaders that borders on reverence. Subordinates often seek permission instead of just assuming leadership. This situation can be reinforced if the organization uses a top-down approach.

This attitude contributes to the gap by spreading disempowerment at all levels. Despite his seniority, Alexandre felt disempowered: "When faced with those higher up on the chain of command, I wasn't as assertive as I needed to be. I often found myself, in the most crucial moments, in a position of asking rather than being affirmative assertive," he recalls.

Mindsets contribute to creating the leadership gap. In the next section, we focus on diagnosing these mindsets.

Diagnosing Mindsets That Create the Leadership Gap

Bridging the leadership gap requires businesspeople to ascertain the presence of mindsets that create the leadership gap. This diagnosis must combine self-introspection and honest analysis at three levels: their own, authority, and stakeholders.

Leaders have a disproportionate responsibility in bridging the leadership gap. Given their positions, business leaders create the context for other stakeholders to play their part. Entrepreneurs and managers must begin with a healthy sense that they are responsible for the outcome.

In the case of Alexandre, the challenge came when the consultants challenged him as the head of a leading pharma firm—someone who could choose to make a difference. "It was then that I realized that if I didn't make a move, I would miss a tremendous opportunity to create human value," Alexandre says.

At the level of leaders, the diagnosis must focus on what we might call the mirror test. In the case of Alexandre, the consultants held the mirror. The mirror test consists of the leaders engaging in self-inquiry. They must ask themselves whether or not they fully own the operating reality and create the conditions for others to do the same.

When in a subordinate position, one must also assume his or her share of responsibility. Leadership can hardly be decreed. Rather leaders emerge by virtue of their willingness to embrace challenges and become part of the solution. Regardless of the environment, staff must strive to contribute to the challenges at hand.

In Alexandre's case, the staff did not necessarily engage with management productively until the opportunity of the management program came. To their credit, and that of the facilitator, the staff rose to the occasion where they were given an opportunity to share their feedback in a safe environment.

For staff, the mirror test would consist of analyzing their attitudes toward those in power. The key question here is whether one asks for permission instead of acting. Another way to frame the question is to ask whether or not one is acting as responsible for the outcome as opposed to remaining script-bound.

The third-level diagnostic is with stakeholders. Ultimately, bridging the leadership gap is about fostering shared ownership with all the business stakeholders. When this is achieved, the business thrives because all come together to further the mission that the leader and his or her team has established.

At this third level, the diagnosis must focus on the organizational culture and the firm's values. Questions to ask include whether the vision encompasses human value creation, the culture of the organization rewards obeisance or performance, and stakeholders are empowered to play their role.

Bridging the Leadership Gap

Bridging the leadership gap requires businesspeople to not only change their mindsets but also address the aspects of the operating reality outlined previously. Businesspeople must adopt a set of principles and practices that reposition the business on a human-centric vision that can significantly upgrade their business models.

Rather than being a one-time initiative, bridging the leadership gap is about rewriting a firm's business model so that it can reflect the essence of shared ownership (see Figure 11.2). It is therefore critical that business leaders focus on developing a new culture based on upgraded mindsets and human value as opposed to quick initiatives for a quick profit.

Essence	•Shared ownership			
	Strategy	**Operations**	**Assets**	**Reality**
Principles	• Empowerment	• Inclusive	• People Focus	• Continuous Change
Practices	• Reinforcing Shared Vision	• Delegating Responsibility	• Effortful Learning and Coaching	• Confronting Reality

Figure 11.2   Bridging the leadership gap to transform your business

The first principle is empowerment. Empowerment must inform business strategy. It is about sharing challenges and opportunities with key stakeholders. It is about empowering everyone to embrace a strategy that resonates with their own human aspiration.

Rather than seeking to solve everything or carry the burden alone, leaders must become adept at sharing the vision which often includes framing or defining challenges and opportunities for everyone to see and embrace.

Empowerment is about breaking down the overwhelming challenges into manageable parts through fundamental belief in people's potential. Identifying and being willing to make specific stakeholders responsible for overcoming a part empowers them by trusting and recognizing them as the most able to do so.

Empowerment bridges the leadership gap by making everyone a potential solution. Employees see themselves as owners. Customers give feedback or suggest potential innovations. Communities seek ways to support the activities of the business. Ultimately, empowerment breaks down the "us vs. them" mentality.

The practice that supports empowerment is reinforcing the shared vision. In Chapter 5, we identified a compelling vision as being an important tenet of an Archimedean mindset. Bridging the leadership gap requires that this vision not only be shared but also owned by all stakeholders.

Several initiatives can be considered to reinforce the shared vision. First, communication is critical to ensure everyone understands the vision. Second, aligning incentives is important. Businesspeople must establish a link between staff or stakeholders behavior and some form of compensation.

In the case of Alexandre, the facilitated training initiative gave him and his team an opportunity to redefine their vision. They define their ultimate vision as "Health in Africa, which included the notion of prevention as well."

Alexandre and his team shared this vision with everyone, all 170 employees, at a one-week seminar in South Africa. What was even more important to ensure the implementation of the new strategy was the division-linked compensation with this vision.

The second principle is being inclusive in managing operations. In fact, being inclusive is about giving appropriate opportunities, setting up systems and procedures, and working in a way in which stakeholders and employees feel part of the functioning of the business, invested in, and entrusted with its success.

The practice for being inclusive is delegating responsibility. Harvard's Jensen suggests that for delegation to be effective, decision rights must be aligned with competency. BoP markets are no exception. Businesses must consider either selecting the right talent and/or investing in that talent to upgrade its skills and know-how.

In the case of Alexandre, he implemented a more human-centered, yet ambitious system of management. This system made his team responsible for the ultimate fulfillment of the vision. Alexandre also started recruiting talented local managers who were attracted by the firm's compelling vision and inclusive operations.

Beyond the business, Alexandre and his team worked hard to improve their relationship with the local leaders. Specifically, they developed a series of activities around prevention that had them working in close partnership with the local leaders. The team was energized and began to see themselves as "health providers."

As it relates to assets, businesspeople must realize the focus should be on people. That is the third principle. In the developed world, customer-centered or people-centered approaches have become somewhat of a fad. While everyone professes to put employees and customer first, most businesses have not necessarily developed the appropriate mindsets.

A people focus is even more difficult to come by within businesses operating in BoP markets. On the customer side, this can be blamed partly on the lack of mechanisms and tools to engage BoP customers. On a stakeholder side, this can be blamed on bigger needs in the overall community that no businesses have enough resources to address.

A people focus is translated into reality thanks to a combination of effortful learning and coaching. Effortful learning deals with the need for businesspeople to continuously seek to learn about the needs of their stakeholders. Specific tools include feedback mechanisms that range from conversations to more involved changes processes. Such processes must aim at opening the businessperson's human dimension as well as redefining a human-centered vision and strategy.

Coaching is about providing people with the skills to bridge the leadership gap. This includes employee training. It also includes customer education to help them understand the company's promises. It can go all the way to skill transfer to partners in governments to increase their skills levels.

Alexandre and his team benefited greatly from the year-long training program that helped them address the challenges that they faced. Rather than focusing only on technical or business skills, this program brought a real transformation because it challenged Alexandre and his team to question their values.

Here business leaders must take a long-term view. Such a long-term view is critical in developing human resource systems that allow staff to rise through the ranks. Such a long-term view will also help corporations in supporting education and capacity building in the communities and nations where they operate.

This is an area where Alexandre did tremendously well. Not only did he replace all the expatriates in managerial positions with competent local managerial teams, but also when he was promoted to run India, his successor as head of the Africa region was for the first time not only a person of local contract but also a woman.

To complement this internal effort, Alexandre and his team engaged in road-shows. Conducted in partnership with the help of local public opinion leaders, therapeutic and preventative caravans (e.g., on malaria) gave them an opportunity to strengthen community relations.

Finally, as noted previously, BoP markets are characterized by unpredictable environments. Creating value in such environments requires a brand of leadership that can deal with continuous change. That is the fourth principle. Dealing with continuous change requires one to be alert to potential developments in the environment.

To embrace change, business leaders operating in BoP markets must be able to confront current reality. What is important here is for the leaders to be able to understand not only customer needs but also the reality in which they operate and include the human dimension. This distinction helps move businesses closer to outcomes.

In Alexandre's case, they were able to convince the headquarters to invest in their factories to raise the level of quality and ensure the development of a local line of product. The team also enriched its drug portfolio to include some generic that were more appropriate to the local reality. At the same time, the division rolled out access-to-medicine-program-based strategies for expensive products.

The Rewards for Bridging the Leadership Gap

Leaders who are able to bridge the leadership gap stand to be rewarded handsomely. In a nutshell, their reward is the opportunity to share the burden and reduce the weight that they currently carry. Specific benefits vary depending on the type of organizations these leaders are affiliated with. But a heightened ability to create value is often the result.

For entrepreneurs, bridging the leadership gap translates into growth and sustainability. It helps businesses mature from hand-to-mouth operations to thriving organizations and from informal entities to real businesses. Ultimately, bridging the leadership gap means building a real business.

For managers such as Alexandre, bridging the leadership gap translates into a greater ability to prevail over the challenges in the environment. They also gain a greater ability to execute their plans. It means better succession planning where nationals mature into leadership positions.

The leadership gap extends beyond business, and an important type of leadership gap is that which occurs at the national level. This matters because it undermines entrepreneurial solutions to prosperity to thrive. Nations able to bridge the leadership gap can reduce the burden on the public sector and increase the contributions of business and civil society to addressing societal problems.

Rewriting the Rules of the Game

The leadership gap is one the biggest challenges facing businesses people seeking to escape The Survival Trap face. To bridge the leadership gap, businesspeople must adopt the view of shared ownership. Such a critical view helps in accepting that other stakeholders must share the burden for everyone to succeed. It is also the key to being willing to give up some control. Rather than being a one-time activity, this must be a continuous practice.

Reflecting on his experience, Alexandre concludes: "I learned from my experience that all leaders have the potential for a vision with a human dimension. I now see success as the alignment of my aspirations as a business person with my aspirations as a human being."

In this regard, Alexandre and his team succeeded greatly. For the first time, the Africa division met its financial targets, by vigorously improving the sales and bottom-line trends, and teams were able to access their bonuses.

Alexandre became the first manager of African origin to lead the company in the buoyant Indian market. Alexandre was also named by a preeminent African business magazine as one of the "50 managers that are changing Africa" in 2003.

Reflecting on his experience, Alexandre concludes: "This is a process that every corporate leader in developing countries can go through because the needs are great. We can all do something that makes human sense."

Vignette 9—Redefining the African Entrepreneur: Eva Muraya

What strikes most people when they meet Eva Muraya is how approachable this leader is. The world has taken notice of this Kenyan woman entrepreneur. The Goldman Sachs/Fortune Global Women Leaders Award, and the Eve Woman Entrepreneurs Award are but a few of the accolades she has received.

These accolades are a testimony of her entrepreneurial success. The co-owner of Color Creations Limited, a medium-sized, Kenya-based business offering screen-printed and embroidered merchandise, brand strategy, and a charitable trust, Eva emerged as a business leader and role model for women entrepreneurs in Africa and beyond.

Accidental Entrepreneur

Eva attributes experiences in her personal upbringing as the foundation for her zeal, resilience, and character, key to her entrepreneurial success After graduating with a degree in journalism, Eva climbed the Nairobi corporate ladder, eventually leading sales and marketing for East Africa Courier Limited, a FedEx licensee.

Then, disaster struck: Eva's husband died suddenly in a car accident. Despite her education and professional success, Eva was a victim of discriminatory property rights laws at the time. As a woman, she was prejudicially prevented from inheriting the business her husband had painstakingly built.

In a fortnight, she found herself without a husband, without any assets, and with two young daughters to raise.

Eva's experience is illustrative of women's lives in many developing nations. Women often do not enjoy equal access to property rights, effectively making them second-class citizens for economic purposes, and translating into a major barrier to women's entrepreneurship in economies where access to finance is limited and most loans require asset guarantees.

Beyond property rights, another challenge women face in business is social censorship. Eva remarks: "Women are not often socialized to become entrepreneurs in our countries." This is significant in societies where there is strong pressure to conform. It often translates into women limiting themselves to survival business models, which do not require taking risks or making large investments.

The harsh operating reality women face contributes to keeping BoP markets in The Survival Trap. Most businesswomen in these markets operate at the fringes in informality. Undermining women in business amounts to writing off half the entrepreneurial potential of developing nations, leading to lost jobs and investments for the whole economy.

Furthermore, undermined women lead to disempowered families. Empirical evidence shows women are more likely to reinvest their income in their families and progeny. Such investments allow future generations in developing nations to receive proper education and develop to be productive citizens.

A second aspect of Eva's experience, which is unique, is her decision to leave a high-paying corporate job to start her own business. The prestige, security, and perks associated with most corporate jobs in developing countries are strong deterrents against any entrepreneurial venture. Eva was betting against the odds in many ways.

Yet, a corporate job is often a good vantage point from which to identify unique entrepreneurial opportunities. Many successful businesses were started when their founders decided to leave a comfortable job to fulfill a key unmet need in the market. Eva's experience shows that betting against the odds can pay off when one has the courage and foresight to follow through.

Betting Against the Odds

With her double loss still fresh, Eva took a dramatic step. She invested all her savings in top of the range screen-printing equipment previously belonging to an entrepreneur looking to immigrate to the US. "Everyone thought I was crazy, but deep down I knew it was the only thing to do!" she now remembers with a smile.

After she bought the equipment, she quit her job and started looking for her first order. That order almost ruined her business. Not only did Eva lack the money to buy supplies to fulfill the order, but she quickly realized that she was not an operations person. Yet, success in manufacturing requires operations.

Looking in her ecosystem for that expertise, Eva convinced one of her former suppliers who had significant manufacturing experience to become her business partner. Eva then went from bank to bank until a forward-thinking banking manager gave her the overdraft coverage she required to fulfill her first order.

One of Eva's first actions was to find a partner with strong production skills. Eva credits her business partner with the operational knowledge to run an efficient business. Working together, Eva and Arshad Mohamed Khan, her business partner, have built a superb team that has helped Color Creations thrive.

Eva turned her full attention to growing a sustainable business. By 2007, she had grown her business to more than 80 full-time employees. Today Color Creations Limited works almost independently from Eva as she focuses on building Brand Strategy Development Limited, the branding strategy subsidiary. This is a testament of how strong the Color Creation team has become.

Such achievements have come through hard work. "One of my first preoccupations was to reengineer our level of best practice," Eva says. Color Creations became the first business in its industry in sub-Saharan Africa to earn the coveted ISO 9001:2000 global management standard. This standard differentiated Color Creations in the competitive merchandising field.

It also poised the business for further growth. Color Creations upgraded its equipment, confident the investment would pay off. Just as the firm was ready, Kenya's scheduled 2008 elections occurred and the country disintegrated into chaos. The result was yet another challenge that could have ended Eva's entrepreneurial endeavors.

Redefining the African Entrepreneur

Color Creations was back in The Survival Trap. Timing and context matter tremendously in Survival Trap countries. Post-electoral violence almost turned Eva's dream into a nightmare. While many Kenyans were fighting for their lives, Eva's business went from thriving to struggling for survival.

As cash flow issues became acute, limited access to intelligent capital made things more difficult. Despite her business being victim of events outside her control, Eva was still not able to restructure her bank loans. Eva also realized that Color Creations sat at the end of a long value chain, instead of providing first hand broadbased solutions to customers.

One solution Eva recognized was investing in her own skills. At a time when many others would have shied away from the investment required, Eva decided to pursue a year-long advanced management program. This avenue gave Eva the skills, network, and fresh insight needed to take her business to the next level, but also with a passion to share her knowledge with her community.

Ultimately, Eva realized that to change the playing field, she needed to think differently. After years of operating in a product-based business, she decided to broaden her offerings through the inception of BSD (Brand Strategy Development) Limited in her group. In 2010, Eva successfully launched this arm of her business.

Eva reasoned that BSD would help her not only provide more comprehensive solutions to her customers but also shape the next generation of African businesses. This strategic offering allows her group to better serve existing and future customers. The market has welcomed this expansion in the scope of Color Creations Group.

What clearly distinguishes Eva are her core beliefs. Eva fundamentally sees any challenge as an opportunity. Commenting on a recent spatial image of the map of the world at night where Africa comparatively remained dark, Eva exclaimed: "Rather than worrying about lack of power, the real question is 'where is the African entrepreneur who will light this continent? There is huge opportunity here!'"

This opportunity mindset combines with a strong moral purpose. Reflecting on Africa's challenges, Eva redefined the African entrepreneur as a business leader inspired by courage, capability, character, commitment, and compassion. Eva herself models this framework.

In 2008, Color Creations launched a retail merchandising business program targeted at the skilled, unemployed Kenyan youth. In partnership with Equity Bank and relevant Kenya Government agencies, the Become Entrepreneur (BE) campaign will reach 22,000 youth over 40 months to help them establish their own businesses and acquire critical business skills.

In reinventing herself and her business, Eva's actions around three specific opportunities serve as inspiration:

Archimedean mindset: Eva has managed to draw inspiration from the challenges that life has thrown at her. From life tragedies, to political turbulence, each one was faced with an Archimedean mindset, helping her see opportunity where others see risk. Eva's mindset helps her see opportunity where others would give up.

Furthermore, the BE campaign is only one of the many ways in which Eva seeks to shape future generations. Eva serves as chairperson of the Zawadi Africa Education Fund, which gives impoverished Kenyan girls who demonstrate academic excellence and leadership potential an education at premier global universities including the US and Canada.

Focus on solutions: Combined with the resilience and vision that come with their Archimedean mindset, Eva and her partner Ashraf have an unwavering focus on solutions. This has allowed her business to evolve from a simple T-shirt business to a firm that provides both branding services and customized products.

The same ability has allowed Eva and her team to think of ways to address core challenges present in her operating reality. This is a hallmark of her leadership as she takes on community and national concerns. Eva was elected to serve as chairperson of the Kenya Association of Women Business Owners (KAWBO) to address some of the constraints she has faced.

Operate efficiently and sustainably: Eva has truly internalized this opportunity by making efficient and sustainable operations a core element in the fabric of Color Creations. Gaining the ISO 2000:9001 certification is not an easy process. Yet, the process and distinction helped the Color Creations Limited team move from a typical SME to a much stronger medium-sized business that is able to withstand challenges.

Eva and her team have also developed manufacturing processes that limit waste and as a result contribute to environmental sustainability. Environmental impact is an important challenge that business leaders, especially in the manufacturing sector, must address.

Turning the Tide

Eva could have resigned herself to be a victim. Instead, she chose a different path. Today, Color Creations has emerged as a successful medium size business. Through its BE campaign, the business is also preparing the next generation of entrepreneurs thanks to its focus on entrepreneurial solutions for prosperity.

Eva Muraya was featured as one of ten role models in a unique television series aiming to inspire and create mainstream women entrepreneurs. Such initiatives are critical to foster and enable entrepreneurial solutions for prosperity in BoP markets.

12

Insights on Mindset Change from Public Health

Missing in Action

Every generation is confronted with a major issue. The response to that major issue often shapes how it is remembered by future generations. In the 1960s, the issue was political independence. In the 1980s, HIV/AIDS emerged as one formidable issue. After many false starts, Africa is now making headway in curbing this pandemic.

Uganda is heralded as a pioneer in the response to the HIV pandemic. Threatened with this public health dilemma starting in the 1980s, Uganda's leadership realized that it needed to fight. After this realization, the HIV prevalence fell dramatically, from a peak in 1991 of around 15% among all adults, and over 30% among pregnant women in the cities, to around 5% in 2001.[1] The East African nation showed the rest of continent that decisive action can surmount the public health challenges posed by HIV/AIDS.

While Uganda's reaction to HIV/AIDS is well documented, no consensus exists on the triggering event that propelled Uganda's leadership to action. A turning point appears to have been the turning back from Cuba of Uganda's most promising officers, who had been sent for training after Uganda's war stopped. The heart of Uganda's army was being eaten alive by this disease. This situation reportedly shook the leadership to the core.

In their bid to escape The Survival Trap, executives could learn a great deal from social marketing experts who have operated in Africa since the early 1980s. Social marketing has matured as a discipline that aims to leverage best practices from marketing in addressing societal issues including HIV/AIDS. Progress against the global epidemic is no small feat.

A Trap of a Different Kind

Statistics fail to capture the full horror of HIV/AIDS in Africa. The cost in human life has been devastating, and the resulting impact on families and the community at large has been overwhelming. With this terrible societal impact comes negative economic impact as well, only accelerating the damage caused by this pandemic.

The disease has had devastating impacts and has given Africans a new appreciation of what it takes to survive. Despite the progress registered since then, an estimated 22.4 million are now living with the disease.[2] For communities, governments, and the international community, the pandemic means a huge drag on resources.

The biggest impact of the disease to business is productivity. Businesses lose valuable staff. Entire industries such as mining and tourism are hit particularly hard. Yet, the response to HIV/AIDS is a blessing in disguise for business executives serious about escaping The Survival Trap.

Since the 1980s, the vast resources invested to fight this pandemic amount to research and development for mindset and behavior change in Africa and other BoP markets. Some of the solutions developed give businesspeople and political leaders tools that can be applied to help them think and prosper in BoP markets.

Social Marketing and the Fight Against HIV/AIDS

Before diving into specifics, a definition of social marketing is in order. Alan R. Andreasen provides a useful definition: "Social marketing is the application of commercial marketing technologies to the analysis, planning, execution, and evaluation of programs designed to influence the voluntary behavior of target audiences in order to improve their personal welfare and that of their society."[3]

Two aspects of this definition must be underscored. Social marketing is about influencing voluntary behavior. This book has stressed the importance of the choices that executives and other leaders must make. Social marketing is also about specific target audiences. This important distinction helps in ensuring that mindset change results in action.

While progress has been made, the road remains arduous for HIV/AIDS programming. Two main approaches to disease prevention are currently vying for primacy: abstinence and contraception. Abstinence is often supported by faith-based organizations. Barrier contraception, specifically the use of male or female condoms, is seen as the pragmatic approach given people's behavior.

Yet, public health practitioners have won one of the hardest battles in this long war against HIV/AIDS, that of understanding the relationship between mindsets, behavior, and the disease. A broad consensus now exists on the fact that mindsets influence behavior when it comes to HIV prevention.

Such a consensus is one the biggest gaps that executives and leaders face in harnessing the Seven Opportunities to escape The Survival Trap. As discussed in Chapter 3, "Why Mindsets Matter," mindsets have remained taboo in the business and development discussions in BoP markets especially Africa.

Another element to keep in mind is the wealth of relevant experience social marketing brings to the conversation. Most of the progress registered by social marketers involved in HIV response happened in sub-Saharan Africa and other BoP markets in similar conditions to the ones facing executives and leaders in promoting entrepreneurial solutions for prosperity.

This wealth of experience suggests the specific skills and competencies needed to design and implement effective campaigns on enterprise solutions for prosperity already exist in Africa. Beyond the borders of businesses or institutions, executives and leaders should also leverage the competencies of social marketers to move the entrepreneurial solutions for prosperity agenda forward.

After defining social marketing and reviewing its most salient features, we look at specific opportunities that executives and leaders stand to benefit from in leveraging social marketing.

Creating Social Change for Entrepreneurial Solutions for Prosperity

Creating mindset and behavior change for prosperity are very similar. Before engaging in the process of learning from social marketing, executives and leaders must be clear about the opportunity that lies ahead and specific benefits for their companies and countries. Executives and leaders should keep three potential benefits in mind.

Social marketing borrows heavily from corporate marketing. Harvesting the Seven Opportunities through a marketing campaign lens will help focus the agenda.

The first thing executives and leaders can learn from social marketers is how to build a sense of urgency on the challenges inherent to the operating reality. As discussed throughout this book, most stakeholders in developing countries are skeptical about the intentions of business. This lack of trust pervades the international community as well.

Executives and leaders must find a way to create a sense of urgency around removing constraints to enterprise solutions to poverty. J. P. Kotter stresses the importance of having a clear sense of urgency for any change process in his study of change processes in 100 businesses.[4]

Over the past couple decades, social marketing has managed to build coalitions around whichever issues it has tackled. Such issues include HIV/AIDS, microfinance, and the environment. Today, executives and leaders must build a similar coalition on the importance of mindset and behavior change toward entrepreneurial solutions for prosperity.

Leveraging Social Marketing for Entrepreneurial Solutions to Prosperity

Here we must begin with a clear vision. Once this vision has been defined, it matters to understand the distinctive contribution of social marketing.

To mainstream entrepreneurial solutions for prosperity, our vision must be to change mindsets of key stakeholders toward a dual recognition. First, world-class businesspeople exist in BoP markets. Second, business can do well for society while generating profits. This mindset change must be accompanied with behavior change that embraces this new mindset.

Such vision must be translated into specific measurable results for all stakeholders. Business must be able to see how this vision will impact profitability. The BoP should see rising wages and greater opportunities. Nations should see growth in investments, exports, and the economy as a whole.

The Seven Opportunities provide anchors for a vision of entrepreneurial solutions for prosperity. Progress around each opportunity can be measured and related to specific variables that are relevant to business and stakeholders.

While embracing the Seven Opportunities will lead to quick wins, mindset and behavior change delivers its full benefits in the medium term. The mindsets and behaviors keeping stakeholders in The Survival Trap are deeply ingrained. Executives and leaders must therefore commit to a sustained effort as opposed to a one-time event. Several of the case studies outlined in this book show how keeping the commitment pays handsomely.

In their quest to mainstream entrepreneurial solutions for prosperity, executives and leaders have several approaches at their disposal. A comparative analysis of these approaches can be helpful in enriching a leader's toolbox. In his book *Marketing Social Change,* Andreasen offers a rigorous comparison of four approaches for mind-set and behavior change.

The first one is the education approach. As its names suggests, this approach consists of providing information to target audiences in a way that makes them change their mind. Executives looking to educate employees on quality would be using such an approach.

While this approach sometimes successfully changes behavior,[5] it lacks several important components. First, it does not focus on behavioral change. Second, it ignores the effect of social pressure. Third, delivering facts to change behavior may have a boomerang effect. Furthermore, it makes it difficult for executives and leaders to track progress.

Second is the persuasion approach. The goal of this approach is to discover the careful arguments and motivational hot buttons. The problem with the persuasion approach is one of getting the customer to adopt the persuasionist's view of the world. It is what marketers would call a selling approach, and it is what gives marketing a bad name because it is organization centered.

While powerful, the persuasion approach is not without significant risks. Executives and leaders resorting to this approach can appear manipulative. This approach can seriously backfire for entrepreneurial solutions for prosperity given that trust can be low in developing countries, and most stakeholders are suspicious of the intentions of business.

Next, the social influence approach, argues that campaigns directed at influencing community norms and collective behavior are the most cost-effective way to reach and change individuals and families.

The social influence approach is often privileged in BoP markets. It leverages one core cultural attributes prevalent in BoP markets, namely the importance of the community and social acceptance. The main shortcoming of this approach is its failure to empower individuals who at the end make the decisions.

Andreasen then goes on to identify seven features of social marketing. Given their familiarity to business, we list these seven features here:

1. Customer behavior is the bottom line.

2. Programs must be cost-effective.

3. All strategies begin with the customer.

4. Interventions involve the Four Ps: product, price, place, and promotion.

5. Market research is essential to designing, presenting, and evaluating intervention programs.

6. Markets are carefully segmented.

7. Competition is always recognized.

The social marketing approach appears to offer the most comprehensive framework for mindset and behavior change. Next, we provide an overview of best practices from social marketing.

Best Practices from Social Marketing

Social marketing has a track record in BoP markets, which makes it a discipline to learn from in changing mindsets and behavior around entrepreneurial solutions for prosperity. Much like the five stages outlined in Chapter 4, "A Framework to Escape The Survival Trap," social marketing uses analysis, planning, and execution techniques rooted in business thinking. Both approaches are based in the pursuit of specific measurable results.

Beyond this common root, social marketing offers seven best practices that are of specific relevance to executives and leaders:

- **Focus on individuals as the locus of choice and action**   A target-centric approach is essential to delivering sustainable results. Focusing on an organization or ill-defined targets has doomed more than one social marketing initiative to failure.

    Both in his definition of social marketing and the techniques described in his work, Andreasen emphasizes the need to begin with a clear target audience whose needs, beliefs, and associations are clearly known.

- **Set clear aspirations for new behavior** Ultimately, the only access to results is through the behavior of targeted individuals. Social marketing therefore puts an emphasis on identifying specific behaviors linked to desired results.

  Executives and leaders have a responsibility to set clear aspirations. Adopting the Seven Opportunities provides an example of clear behaviors that executives and leaders must embrace to escape The Survival Trap. In the absence of such clarity, our attempt to escape The Survival Trap and promote entrepreneurial solutions for prosperity may fail to fulfill their potential.

- **Tell stories to inspire target audiences** Stories can be a powerful tool to set clear aspirations for new behavior and to inspire target audiences to change their behavior. Good storytelling is both an art and a science. The art refers to the ability to craft powerful metaphors to touch the heart of the audience. The science is about grounding such stories on credible evidence.

  Howard Gardner suggests that for large populations to change minds effectively, leaders make particular use of two tools: the stories that they tell and the lives they lead. In terms of our levers of change, the "resonance" that exists—or doesn't—between those stories and those lives speaks powerfully.[6]

- **Provide clear role models** This best practice leverages the power of the demonstration effect. This effect has been known to increase the believability of the change required. The emergence of prizes and competitions are a good example of the power of the demonstration effect. Role model choice is an important factor for increasing impact.

  Role models have proven particularly effective with entrepreneurs and businesspeople. This is particularly true in developing countries where social influence remains a big driver of behavior.

- **Create opportunities for social reaffirmation of behavior** Individuals are more likely to embrace and sustain a new behavior when this behavior is reaffirmed in their community. Ignoring this effect can often undermine social marketing campaigns.

Such social reaffirmation is likely to be a major factor in the case of enterprise solutions for prosperity. Currently, trust levels toward business are low in developing nations. In Chapter 6, "Build Trust," we amply discuss how this contributes to perpetuating The Survival Trap. Building social reaffirmation can help in increasing trust toward business and their intentions.

- **Leverage the power of consistency through commitments** According to Robert Cialdini, psychologists have viewed the desire for consistency as a central motivator of our behavior. But is this tendency to be consistent really strong enough to compel us to do what we ordinarily would not want to do? There is no question about it.

  Executives and leaders can look to opportunities for target individuals to commit to act in a way that either removes constraints to business or empowers the private sector to create prosperity. Cialdini suggests that commitments are most effective in changing a person's self-image and future behavior when they are active, public, and effortful.[7]

- **Use one of Gardner's seven levers for mindset change** Howard Gardner identifies seven factors that could be at work in all cases of a change of mind.[8] As it happens, each factor conveniently begins with the letter "R": reason, research, resonance (affective component), representational redescriptions, resources and rewards, real-world events, and resistances.

  Beyond the six best practices outlined above, executives and leaders must develop their skill at recognize which one of the R's is most relevant to move their agenda forward. In most cases, experience suggests that a mix of levers is more effective to drive mindset and behavior change than the mere use of one lever.

Social Marketing to Unleash Entrepreneurial Solutions for Prosperity in BoP Markets

Best practices from social marketing can help executives aiming to build vibrant businesses and leaders committed to prosperity to create a new model for business and economic transformation in BoP markets.

This model is unlike anything BoP markets, especially Africa, have seen so far. First, the model will be self-correcting. Holding mindsets up to scrutiny will allow executives and leaders to adapt their solutions to the most pressing issues facing their businesses or nations.

Next, this new model puts the onus on BoP markets' decision-makers to solve their region challenges. Business executives and other leaders are empowered to drive economic transformation through their choices and behavior. This second feature is critical in relieving the international community from what Easterly calls the White Man's Burden.

The social marketing best practices outlined previously can give these individuals better control of their economic destiny. As suggested in Chapter 3, most stakeholders at the bottom of the pyramid operate in micro- and small-scale businesses.

Escaping The Survival Trap requires a clear roadmap for the bottom of the pyramid. Shared with the BOP through appropriate social marketing initiatives, the Seven Opportunities could help transform the lives of these microentrepreneurs by helping them improve their businesses in a systematic way. It could also help them see the value they contribute through their activity.

Specifically, this new model puts an emphasis on the role of businesspeople in building great firms that not only deliver outstanding returns to their owners but also deliver societal value. One of the biggest gaps in the development discussion is the exclusion of entrepreneurs and managers from the development agenda.

Addressing this gap can have the same impact on the development conversation that including women in the workforce had in the West in the early 20th century. This is important because it can unleash top human talent on the continent's biggest development challenges. It is important to note that the impact goes beyond executives and leaders.

In developing countries, most clusters are underdeveloped in at least three ways. First, cluster members do not see themselves as part of the same reality. Second, understanding of competitiveness and what is required to succeed differs greatly. Next, critical links or institutions in the cluster are often missing. These three gaps can be addressed in part through best practices from social marketing.

At the cluster level, social change campaigns can make a great difference by providing a language to address common issues such as strategy, skills, standards, societal impact, and so on. When properly executed, social change campaigns can help cluster members build a sense of oneness that matters to foster collaboration.

At the national level, it is important that individual, business, and cluster efforts get national resonance for maximum impact. Our previous discussion highlighted ways in which social marketing tools can help in creating a sense of urgency, building coalitions and availing key skills for mindset and behavior change toward entrepreneurial solutions for prosperity in BoP markets.

National leaders must lead campaigns around the role of business and entrepreneurship in prosperity creation. The type of commitment required is not unlike that of the leadership of Uganda when its response to the AIDS epidemic commenced.

At all levels, best practices from social marketing can make a difference in the adoption, diffusion, and implementation of entrepreneurial solutions for prosperity.

No Shortcuts to Prosperity

Social marketing offers a host of best practices and tools that executives operating in BoP markets especially Africa can borrow from in their attempt to harvest the Seven Opportunities. These best practices deserve special considerations because of their business roots, their relevance to BoP markets, and the track record at building a global coalition for change.

The single most important contribution of social marketing is the emphasis on driving mindset *and* behavior change in specific targeted individuals. While this may sound obvious to some business executives and leaders, experience shows that very few adopt a stakeholder-centered approach in a systematic way. Yet, a stakeholder-centered approach is paramount for success.

In the 1980s, Uganda made a choice to confront the HIV/AIDS scourge through mindset and behavior change. The leadership decided to confront the issue publicly, going against taboos of the time. However, not all African leaders demonstrated similar foresight. In South Africa, the Mbeki administration ignored the disease at the peril of the people.

There are no shortcuts to prosperity. Today, BoP markets, especially its business executives and leaders, face a choice on whether to address the Seven Opportunities for prosperity. While this choice demands commitment and resolute action for all involved, evidence suggests that the prize for both the businesses involved and society as a whole is worth fighting for.

Vignette 10—Dr. Paulin Basinga: Acting Out Against HIV/AIDS

The last in a series of speakers at TEDx Kigali, Dr. Paulin Basinga faced a considerable challenge. Each luminary before Basinga leveraged all the tricks in the public speaking playbook to mesmerize the audience. Yet, 90 seconds into his talk, pure excitement replaced restlessness.

As he steps on stage, the audience begins to wonder what Dr. Paulin Basinga can teach about HIV/AIDS that they do not already know. No stranger to restless audiences, Dr. Basinga takes the stage with the ease of an experienced actor. He has acted out for thousands of African youth against HIV/AIDS.

Forum Theatre to Fight HIV/AIDS

"We are going to do a little exercise! Every time you recognize a number in what I say, shout it out loud." Without further delay, Basinga begins rattling off the fun story of a typical courtship in an

African high school: A beautiful young girl meets the school's most eligible boy.

As the doctor tells his story at a speed that suggests great practice, the crowd shouts numbers aloud, glued to his every word. What began as a promising and heady courtship tale degenerates quickly into a horror story, to the dismay of the listening audience. Soon, the two teenagers have destroyed their lives.

Without even realizing it, the audience had been taken down a road where they were not only entertained but also were taught. Dr. Basinga made his point in the subtle way only art can. People begin to wonder how this doctor became an actor. Or rather, how did this actor become a doctor?

If George Clooney was African, he would look exactly like Dr. Basinga: handsome, articulate, and charming. This is where the similarity stops. Clooney has made millions starring in Hollywood blockbusters. Basinga is attempting to save millions of African youth by delivering gripping high school productions.

Drawing Inspiration from One's Reality

Dr. Basinga grew up the elder child in a large family in the war-torn region of the Ituri in eastern Congo. A refugee and an orphan, Basinga developed a strong sense of imagination to help forget the daily hardships he faced. Paulin still remembers how his family was treated as second-class citizens because of their Rwandan origins.

After the 1994 genocide, Dr. Basinga returned to Rwanda to find that his brother, sisters, and most people in his extended family had been decimated. The Rwanda he had fantasized about as a refugee had been destroyed. Even for a child having grown up in one of the world's most dangerous places, the horror he was confronted with was unbearable.

He attributes these horrors with his decision to consider medicine. During his medical studies at the National University of Rwanda (NUR), Basinga developed an interest in acting. Without any outlet for his creative energy in medical school, he decided to start the Beacon of Hope, an acting troop with some classmates colleagues at the National University of Rwanda.

What began as a hobby developed into a full-fledged, all-consuming passion. Soon Dr. Basinga was wondering whether to become a professional actor. Practicality got the better of Dr. Basinga. Acting does not pay in Rwanda. As the second and in charge child in his family, he needed a real job to meet his obligations to care for his siblings.

While he accumulated scholarships that allowed him to complete his Masters in Science and his Ph.D., Dr. Basinga's passion for acting never receded. When he shared this passion with his thesis advisor, the advisor refused and proposed instead a topic on tuberculosis.

After completing his thesis, Basinga started studying the effectiveness of forum theatre and published an article in a reputable journal later.

Then something happened. Just when Rwandans thought the worst was behind them, people started dying again. This time the culprit was HIV/AIDS. The genocide perpetrators had used rape as a war tactic, thereby infecting millions of women and children in the process. In the face of this tragedy Dr. Basinga decided to make the fight against pandemics such as HIV/AIDS, maternal and child help as well as health financing, his life quest.

Reinventing HIV/AIDS Prevention

HIV/AIDS is a pandemic that has wreaked havoc on Africa's socioeconomics creating a loss of productivity, reducing average life expectancy, and leaving millions of orphans in its wake.

For people living with HIV/AIDS, life is often reduced to a constant struggle for survival. HIV/AIDS keeps them and their families focused on the task of making it through today. The impact of this Survival Trap is felt by current and future generations.

In an attempt to reach this critical generation Dr. Basinga realized his skills as a doctor would not be enough. Youth with access to important information about HIV/AIDS were still making decisions that led to dire consequences. Instead of focusing on standard dry techniques of information dissemination, he looked to integrate his passion for theater into his outreach.

Forum Theater was the perfect solution. The technique was developed by actor Augusto Boal and was aimed at breaking the actor-audience division. By allowing actors or audience members to stop a scene and suggest a different course of action, the production unfolds as a participatory exercise.

The result is a change in the direction of the play. Uniquely, the audience is able to see how the rest of the production plays out based on their decisions. Such a solution is perfect for youth, who evidence shows, are prone to change their behavior through participation and group influence.

By using this method to engage youth, Dr. Basinga is able to move past the memorization of key facts that most HIV/AIDS education campaigns promote. Instead, individuals preview typical situations where the choices that influence their lives are made, and the positive or negative impact of those choices. Building students' pattern recognition in this area preempts poor choices in day-to-day lives.

As researchers work to develop effective treatments, it grows increasingly important to prevent the spread of the HIV/AIDS pandemic. In prevention, one of the biggest challenges HIV/AIDS practitioners face is the Knowing-Doing Gap: What people know about the scourge does not necessarily translate into the actions they take.

This is particularly true with young adults who are likely to have a sense of invincibility. Combined with social pressure, experimentation, and substance abuse, this sense of invulnerability makes young people prime targets for HIV/AIDS. Forum Theater allows the youth to experiment with characters, rather than their own lives.

Another key challenge is trust. Youth often perceive adults as outsiders who lack an understanding of their reality. Acting gives Dr. Basinga instant credibility and a certain "coolness factor," and engaging the youth in the process allows them to participate in demonstrating their reality.

The result is that youth leave these Forum Theater sessions better equipped to face HIV/AIDS. Dr. Basinga becomes a role model that differs not because of the temptations he has faced in his life, but because of the positive choices he has made.

Test results on the effectiveness of the program have been promising. High school students from schools where Forum Theater has been demonstrated were more likely to change behavior than the general population. This is important because knowing information without acting on it is not enough. This is the core issue of mindset and behavior change.

Acquiring information is not enough, a shift in mindsets is essential and is the only true method to influence and change behavior. This is equally evident when reflecting on The Survival Trap. For many BoP citizens stuck in The Survival Trap, it is about giving them an opportunity to question some of their behaviors and the impact it can have on their lives.

Mindset Change Through Participation

While the current applications are with HIV/AIDS, Forum Theater could be used to discuss gender issues, economic choices, and societal issues. The power of Forum Theater lies in its participatory approach, which makes the target of any mindset and behavioral change program a participant in the change process.

Similarly, our experience working with businesspeople in BoP nations shows that most of them know not only what their challenges are but also what potential solutions might be to those challenges. However, knowing does not necessarily translate into different actions. Experience is so strong that entrepreneurs often keep the same routines.

Dr. Basinga's approach to addressing HIV/AIDS leverages two entrepreneurial solutions for prosperity.

Focus on solutions: By understanding the shortcomings of existing educational programs, Dr. Basinga has been able to develop a program that goes deeper than typical HIV/AIDS education initiatives. He has been able to address the Knowing-Doing Gap in a way that few others have been able to.

Basinga has also been able to find a way of incorporating his passions and his skills into his work. The result is not only fulfillment and success for him, but also significant impact on a generation that is facing the one of the deadliest diseases the world has ever known.

Build trust: Trust is a key issue in the health field, but in particular when dealing with youth. This is particularly true for any issue considered taboo by the stakeholders dealing with it, such as sexual behavior. Building trust is essential to preventing the spread of HIV/AIDS.

By engaging youth in a way that is equalizing and diminishes the expert-power dynamic, they are able to participate in the process. The result is youth are able and willing to address the mindsets that put them at risk, and work to change them.

Reinventing HIV Prevention

Dr. Basinga's ability to think innovatively has allowed him to see an opportunity to integrate different fields into a sustainable solution to a complex problem. The main innovation in Basinga's approach is to have integrated diametrically opposed fields—science and art, medicine and theater, prevention and acting.

As he reflects on his experience experimenting with new methods for HIV/AIDS prevention, Dr. Basinga credits the leaders of the healthcare sector in Rwanda with fostering an atmosphere where the focus is on outcomes, new ideas are welcome, and collaboration is possible.

This integration is built on the knowledge transmission process, which is an important and successful technique offering a unique avenue to ensure that youth will move beyond information to being prepared to make critical choices in using that knowledge in their lives.

Endnotes

[1] Avert.org, "HIV and AIDS in Uganda," http://www.avert.org/aids-uganda.htm.

[2] Unaids.org, "AIDS epidemic update December 2009," http://data.unaids.org/pub/Report/2009/JC1700_Epi_Update_2009_en.pdf.

[3] Alan R. Andreasen, *Marketing Social Change: Changing Behavior to Promote Health, Social Development, and the Environment* (San Francisco: Jossey-Bass, 1995), 7.

[4] J. P. Kotter, *A Force for Change: How Leadership Differs from Management* (New York: Free Press, 1990).

[5] N. K. Janz and M. H. Becker, "The Health Belief Model: A Decade Later," Health Education Quarterly, 11 (1984) 1–47.

[6] Howard Gardner, *Changing Minds: The Art and Science of Changing Our Own and Other People's Minds* (Boston: Harvard Business School Publishing, 2008), 17.

[7] Robert B. Cialdini, *Influence: The Psychology of Persuasion* (New York: William Morrow, 1993) 92.

[8] Howard Gardner, *Changing Minds: The Art and Science of Changing Our Own and Other People's Minds* (Boston: Harvard Business School Publishing, 2008), 17.

13

Societal Innovations Through Mindset Change

Turning Back the Hands of Time

Since returning from Accra to the village to visit, Koffi felt he had turned back the hands of time. His oldest brother Atta Kwesi said, "I am thinking of taking a second wife. I need more children to nurse me in my old age!"

Despite framing the discussion as a choice under consideration, Koffi knew Atta Kwesi had made his decision. Koffi did not know how to respond. Respect was an important value in the Akan tradition. As the eldest brother, Atta Kwesi had supported Koffi throughout his studies.

Now the tables were turned. As the one with a job in Accra, Koffi sent money to the village each month to support the ever-growing family. Crops were failing for lack of fertile land and commodities prices were in free fall. Koffi had just learned that Atta Kwesi's son had failed his school exams because he had no light to study by.

While this situation sounds surreal to most Westerners, it is one that most Africans routinely face. A small number of individuals carry the heavy burden to help the whole society survive. Consider the surge of the remittances industry. Our investigation of The Survival Trap thus far has focused on the realms of business and economics.

Yet, the same vicious cycle that informs The Survival Trap is also at work on other major societal issues. Energy, population, markets, technology, and the environment are five issues of great relevance to prosperity that are directly impacted by failure to change mindsets.

A Fresh Look at The Survival Trap

The Survival Trap is not only an economic construct; it manifests in other societal issues. Consider this vicious cycle through the lens of a prism: When each issue is observed individually, the same relationship between context, mindsets, actions, and results is at play that influences the overall society.

Lifting the bottom of the pyramid out of poverty is the challenge of our generation. As discussed throughout this book, The Survival Trap is a major factor in the predicament of the BoP economic struggles. Nowhere is the challenge clearer than in Africa. We therefore use the example of this continent in the rest of this chapter.

The mindsets held by the bottom of the pyramid, the leadership, and the international community contribute to making a difficult situation worse. For instance, most at the bottom of the pyramid are led to believe that the solutions to their woes rest in the capital city or in the hands of outside experts. Sometimes leaders seeking to increase their power or experts aiming to secure their jobs reinforce this mindset.

Figure 13.1 illustrates how a change in mindsets that is accompanied by a change in behavior can lead to progress on social issues.

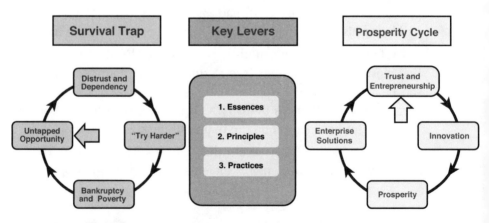

Figure 13.1   Bringing social change through mindset change

Ensuring that the bottom of the pyramid is empowered to solve its own issues is critical. The Survival Trap also underlies the preponderance of violent conflicts on the African continent. Since the 1960s, 38 out of a total of 53 African nations have had some form of conflict.[1]

Most of these conflicts are intrastate wars such as represented by Darfur, the Niger Delta, and the Rwandan genocide that destroy the very fabric of society in the nations in which they occur. Such conflicts destroy fundamental human values such as trust.

Conflicts are often fuelled by one problematic mindset: the belief that natural resources equate to wealth. Despite ample proof that natural resources alone have never propelled a people to prosperity, a significant proportion of leaders engaged in conflict do so in part to control natural resources. This is yet another example of mindsets at work against human progress.

Healthcare is another good example of how mindset change influences The Survival Trap. The continent is prey to pandemics such as malaria, tuberculosis, water-borne diseases, and HIV/AIDS. Public health research suggests that pandemics are driven mostly by mindsets behavior, especially at the bottom of the pyramid.

What is important to note is that knowledge alone is not enough. The operating reality also needs to be different to enable sustainable behavior change. In this particular case, even when the mindset is there, any gaps in the environment can undermine progress.

Today, we can safely assert that everywhere a nation has progressed against the HIV/AIDS pandemic it has done so thanks to profound mindset change. Public health specialists have mounted effective campaigns to change mindset around one of the most taboo subjects: sex.

In short, the pervasive nature of The Survival Trap means that the only way to fully address its negative impact in Africa is to mount a comprehensive solution that addresses its most important facet: mindset. Such a solution requires that Africa's leadership focus on key issues that can act as levers to lift the continent out of poverty.

What Levers Must Mindset Change Efforts for Africa Focus On?

Escaping The Survival Trap is about enabling every citizen to achieve prosperity and dignity. It is about making business and economics work for the benefit of the majority. It is about allowing Africans to defy the circumstances that surround them and have a life guided by the choices they make. It is about changing the mindsets on issues with the greatest potential to enable progress.

Leaders must focus on the levers with the greatest potential to transform the prevailing context in Africa. Energy, population, markets, technology, and the environment can become five of such progress levers.

A sustained commitment to addressing this is possible only when leaders understand why these levers are so important in their bid to drive progress. These five levers are the roots of modern and post-modern economic life. Technological breakthroughs in the energy sector were fuelled by the nineteenth-century industrial revolution in Europe.

Most prosperous nations have smaller yet better-educated populations. Markets have supported specialization and globalization. Mankind's relationship to the environment will shape our future. Empirical evidence suggests that these five issues have the greatest impact on economic transformation.

The World Development Report suggests that these five issues combined account for most of the suffering that plagues the bottom of the pyramid on the African continent. For example, climate change is likely to reduce the amount of arable land in sub-Saharan Africa by 9 percent to 20 percent over the next 70 years.[2]

With an increasing population still highly dependent on agriculture to survive, there needs to be a mindset that looks to these types of issues to plan for an inevitable future. This mindset must also consider the impact of such challenges on the large proportion of Africans living on subsistence agriculture.

These five specific issues can be addressed through change focused on the Seven Opportunities outlined earlier in this book.

Stakeholder collaboration and a focus on solutions are particularly critical for activating all five levers. The long-term and complex nature of these issues requires intelligent capital to be unleashed.

Last but not least, these levers are illustrations of societal challenges for embracing entrepreneurial solutions for prosperity. The ubiquity of these challenges combined with their potentially transformative impact creates an incentive for businesspeople to innovate and find solutions.

Energy: The Dark Continent

Almost one-third of the estimated 1.6 billion people living without access to electricity worldwide live in Africa, Azanaw Abreha, Vice Chairperson of the Commission on Sustainable Development (CSD), said in Addis Ababa as African countries began to review the region's input to the 14th session of CSD.

Electrification levels in Africa are low, especially when compared with Europe and North America. South Africa and Egypt have the continent's highest electrification levels at approximately 70 percent, while the average for the Southern Africa Development Community (SADC) region is only 20 percent. A NASA photo of the world taken at night with a "dark" Africa makes this point.

This statistic has great social repercussions. Harvested agricultural crops go bad, medicines cannot be refrigerated, and children fail at school for lack of electricity to study by.

Sadly, the lack of power has made the 19th-century characterization of the continent factual. In short, modern life is difficult for most Africans residing on a continent gone dark. Furthermore, the lack of energy caps economic growth. Firms operating in Africa lose competitiveness and industrialization is extremely difficult.

In an Experts' Group Meeting, convened in the capital, Lilongwe, by the United Nations Economic Commission for Africa a working document stated "that recent studies show that the poor state of infrastructure in sub-Saharan Africa cuts national economic growth by two percentage points every year and reduces business productivity by as much as 40 per cent."[3]

An Outdated Model

At the heart of the energy issue is the gap between supply and demand that rests on the model that has prevailed in the energy sector in Africa. The crux of this model has been a mindset that favors large investments financed through development assistance. With a growing population living in overcrowded cities, this model has shown its limitations.

Another mindset at play has restrained the emergence of sustainable energy solutions. The international framework that privileges multilateral agreement has shown its limitations in Copenhagen. Instead of creating the breakthrough expected, it generated a typical reaction of developing countries wanting a form of aid to do the right thing.

Shifting from Investments to Solutions

Our focus must shift toward the provision of energy solutions. In thinking about the energy market in Africa, leaders must realize that a new approach is required on both the demand and supply sides. Demand is characterized by limited purchasing power. Supply lags behind in both generation and distribution.

Such solutions must begin with the understanding of the energy needs and usage patterns of individuals, businesses, and communities. Such an understanding would help the continent adopt a mix of technology and also reduce the required investments to bridge this gap. This shift would allow greater private sector involvement.

Practical Considerations

Most energy users make choices based on their perceptions of cost and benefit. Beyond large public-private partnerships, the energy sector is ripe for entrepreneurs looking to provide targeted solutions to clearly delineated customers.

Such entrepreneurs are not only able to have tremendous social impact, but they also generate enormous personal wealth. This alignment of incentives should provide an impetus for the entrepreneurs to innovate.

On the demand side, it is critical to promote energy efficiency, especially in the private sector, which consumes a large part of all energy in Africa. In looking at the adoption of energy efficient solutions by manufacturing firms, Paul Kleindorfer identified perception of risks as a major constraint.[4]

Population: Young, Crowded, and Divided

The average African family has seven people. Fifteen percent of the global population lives in Africa. It is estimated that this percentage will grow to 21 percent by mid 2050. Africa is a youthful continent, 41 percent of Africa's nearly one billion citizens are under 15 years old. Projections put this number at nearly one-third of the world's total youth by 2050.[5]

This implies that African youth will be a major source for labor for the world. BoP markets are the only societies where three societies are clustered in one. Most young city dwellers exemplify a postmodern society connected to the Internet. Mostly urban, affluent adults represent the modern society. The bottom of the pyramid, urban or rural, lives in a pre-modern society. The societal implications of these observations are great.

Medicine Advances Beat Reproductive Behavior

At the heart of BoP markets' frightening demographics is the fact that reproductive behavior has not caught up with medical advances. Africa has historically been plagued with extremely high mortality rates. Child mortality in Africa is still ten times that of the average in developed countries but has still declined.

In 2007, the rate had dropped to 157/1,000 from 184/1,000 in 1990.[6] Maternity death rates are also steadily, albeit slowly, declining. Although not a single challenge in and by itself has changed drastically, the aggregate of the progress means that more people are living longer.

While large families made sense with high mortality rates and an agrarian society, they do not make sense anymore. Yet, the average woman continues to bear seven to eight children in Africa. A factor that compounds the crisis is the limited education for women, which prevents them from making informed choices. Mindsets must change on this issue for the continent's sake.

Unleashing Human Capital

Today, BoP markets especially Africa nations are characterized by high fertility rates and dwindling resources. In 1798, English economist Thomas Malthus suggested that societies would collapse when their population grew to exceed the resource base of the society.

Today, BoP markets are at risk to personify this cycle of resource absorption to the point of collapse in the decades to come. Unleashing human capital begins with women's education. This factor is critical to reducing the average size of African families. Educated women can transform their families by educating their children.

The continent must realize that it cannot grow out of poverty while ignoring half its population. As stated in the 2007 UNICEF 2007 World Report, "gender equality will not only empower women to overcome poverty, but also their children, families, communities and countries. When seen in this light, gender equality is not only morally right—it is pivotal to human progress and sustainable development."

Enterprise-Based Solutions to Population

Family planning and contraception discussions have traditionally been led by government and development partners. An estimated $10 billion is spent annually in developing countries on family planning and contraception. Yet, the *population momentum* dictates that population growth will continue until the proportion of young and old is in equilibrium.[7]

The population momentum suggests that any further delay in action will only make the issue of population for Africa worse. Innovative and decisive action is required. We must realize that a collapse would create instability and destroy the fabric of society.

Environment: A Ubiquitous Challenge

The environment is closely related to both energy and the population. An estimated 80 percent of rural African families depend on biomass for working and heating.[8] A fast-growing population puts tremendous pressure on the environment.

Despite these staggering statistics, the average BoP citizen has a lower impact on environmental degradations than the average US citizen, who consumes eight times the amount of energy of an African. In their bid for prosperity, China and India are populous nations that are using environmental resources, especially energy, at an alarming pace.

Impact on Africa

Africa is the most affected by this challenge. In 2003, the World Bank noted in its World Development Report that: "Air: polluted, Fresh Water: increasingly scarce, Soil: being depleted, Forests: being destroyed, Biodiversity: disappearing, Fisheries: declining." The report further noted that Africa would be the most affected by this situation.

The 2010 World Development Report notes that while adverse climate does not discriminate by income, better off people can more successfully manage the setbacks. The report also notes how women who tend to be the most vulnerable stakeholders in BoP markets are more negatively impacted by climate change.

Mindsets at Play

Most human beings do not draw a direct relationship between their lifestyle and the environmental crisis. Africans are no exception. A cocoa farmer, Atta Kwesi still burns vast expanses of forest to clear the way to plant his crop. Yet, he would be hard pressed to articulate the impact such antiquated farming practices has had on his failing crops.

The disappointing outcome of the Copenhagen summit suggests that overreliance on government and development partners to address the climate challenge is the wrong path. Global leadership failed to rise to the occasion by refusing to take decisive actions and instead engaging in a blame game. A new approach is required for progress.

Equipping Individuals

To complement ongoing efforts by government and development partners, individuals must be equipped to make sensible choices about the environment. Such equipment includes education, access to alternative technologies, and clear incentives. This equipment moves the conversation away from big debates toward day-to-day choices with global impact.

In the absence of a blanket solution for all involved, enterprise has an opportunity to help individuals make the right choices around the environment. It is estimated that the global environmental technology market was more than $1.2 trillion in 2005 and is expected to grow 5 percent annually to $2.7 trillion in 2020.[9] Information, alternative technologies, and innovations represent a chance for daring entrepreneurs to help address this challenge.

Technology: Beyond the Digital Divide

Since the term "digital divide" was coined in the mid 1990s and used by Bill Clinton and Al Gore on the campaign trail, this issue has dominated the debate on technology in Africa's development. The literature about the digital divide is staggering.

According to the International Telecommunications Union (ITU), the Internet remains a major challenge in terms of Internet and broadband uptake and stands at less than 0.5 percent in Africa, with Internet use being the lowest in the world with only 5 percent of the population online.

The continent represents a very small share of the booming global IT industry. In its focus on information technology, the literature about the digital divide only paints a small part of the total picture. Agricultural technology and healthcare technology are also problematic. The divide is not only deep but also wide.

The Emergence of Free Technology

Technology rollout in Africa has focused on large operators; both government and private sector institutions that roll out technologies are based on scale. Often this large investment is ill focused for it provides blanket solutions that are not always adequate. Furthermore, it requires large amounts of capital that the continent does not have, fuelling dependence on aid.

In his book *Free*,[10] Chris Anderson argues that information technology challenges business models, allowing a large number of valuable services to be offered to users for free. An illustration of his powerful point is how Google has built one of the world's largest companies based on giving its customers access to information free of charge.

The ABC Solution

Bridging the technological gap requires that leaders change perspective. Instead of focusing on technology supply, the priority must be to understand and serve demand. As illustrated with the energy issue above, it is critical that the cost-benefit ratio to individual users be addressed. Ultimately, this ratio is the key driver for it matches self-interest.

To make the most out of large infrastructure investments, business leaders must offer solutions that improve *Access*, increase *Benefits*, and reinforce *Capabilities*. This ABC solution is critical in all areas where technologies can make a difference. This solution will also need entrepreneurs.

The Next Technological Revolution

By focusing on *Access*, *Benefits*, and *Capabilities*, African businesspeople push the technological frontier. Such focus allows them to articulate solutions that address the most pressing needs of various users in Africa. This focus on solutions is important to ensure that individual users realize maximum benefits and willingly invest in technology.

Because of the digital divide and lack of appropriate skills, the continent also lags behind in taking advantage of free technology. Entrepreneurs such as the founders of Google need to find ways to use technology to address the biggest challenges facing Africa in a cost-effective way. This would create transformative business models.

Markets: Failures All Around

Well-functioning markets are critical for Africa to escape The Survival Trap. Energy supply, population, the environment, and technology are all impacted by markets. Beyond, other critical aspects of life such as jobs, commodities, education, and healthcare are also regulated by markets. Yet, most of Africa's markets have failed to mature and fulfill their promise.

Objectively, African markets are characterized by failure all around. Financial markets are underdeveloped. Job markets show an oversupply of underqualified youth. Most commodities have seen their real price decline over the long run. Technology, except mobile telephony, has yet to reach its potential.

Distorted Perception of Markets

To make matters worse, stakeholders have distorted perceptions of markets. Many wrongly focus on physical markets in a world where markets have gone virtual. Failure to move toward virtual markets contributes to keeping transaction costs high in Africa.

Since 2008, the near meltdown of the global financial markets has created a backlash against markets. Globalization skeptics use the crisis as evidence that Africa should not trust markets.

The issue is not whether markets can be trusted. No matter what stakeholders think, markets are a critical part of our lives. Furthermore, markets are here to stay. What matters is how Africa can make markets work for its own prosperity creation agenda.

Making Markets Work

Making markets work is a priority for the continent. A well-functioning energy market will see the gap in both power generation and delivery addressed. Financial markets will help entrepreneurs scale their businesses and create jobs. Well-functioning environments and technology markets avail the intelligent capital required to bring a significant leap forward.

Making markets work is also extremely important for the poor. As suggested by Paul Collier, in the *Bottom Billion,* failure to participate in global markets increases likelihood of poverty. Here agricultural markets play a disproportionate role. In real terms, rural areas have seen their incomes decline, effectively making rural societies dependent on urban dwellers and the international community.

Reducing Information Asymmetries

Reducing information asymmetries is the first step in making markets work for Africa and its poor. Such information asymmetries are a big factor in the lack of supply of satisfactory services to the economic BoP. As a result, the economic and social costs of such asymmetries must not be ignored.

By virtue of their position at the nexus of most markets, executives have a unique role to play in enabling this. The good news is that well-functioning markets help such executives reach their own business objectives in the long run. While some businesses have been built around asymmetries, such as in the trading sector, the societal cost is high.

Leadership as the Business of Mindset Change

Mindsets matter for society in Africa because they give us access to innovative solutions for economic transformation. In fact, most of these challenges have persisted not because the leaders involved are not trying hard enough. Rather, the operating reality drives mindsets to influence actions that fail to produce desired results.

Along with business and government executives, most African leaders have failed to understand the full impact of mindsets on their ability to articulate effective and sustainable development solutions. Instead of confronting reality, these leaders grow comfortable in applying the Washington consensus on development half-heartedly. This choice keeps Africa poor and robs the continent of its dignity.

The few enlightened African leaders preaching mindset change must manage important risks. These leaders often risk sounding hollow or appearing to lack integrity. First, they sound hollow when their discourse is divorced from action. Second, they seem to lack integrity when they profess mindset change for others without doing the same for themselves.

As illustrated in the previous chapter, leaders who are serious about leveraging mindset to change their nations must articulate and deliver effective mindset campaigns. Such campaigns must combine public relations, provision of tools, and incentives to affect new behavior, as well as provide the institutional support required to support this change.

Entrepreneurs have a particular role to play in this agenda by finding ways to profitably solve the challenges facing Africa. Corporate managers can leverage their organizations to provide specific skills and resources and roll out effective solutions. The continent's leadership must reclaim their role on these issues from political leaders and development partners.

All leaders must take their mandate to change mindsets to heart. Why is it so important for all leaders to embrace mindsets to change Africa?

Mindset Change at Work for Africa

All leaders at all five levels must change their mindsets to have a significant impact in this vital area of society.

At the individual level, access to energy, a smaller and educated population, functioning markets, adequate technology, and sound environmental strategies will help the bottom of the pyramid connect to the global economy. Addressing these five issues ensures that people struggling to escape The Survival Trap do not fall back into it because of contextual factors beyond their control.

At the firm level, mindset change creates tremendous entrepreneurial activity around these five issues. Not only will a new class of successful entrepreneurs emerge, but also these entrepreneurs will draw satisfaction from their societal impact. This in turn strengthens the fabric of society.

The cluster level impact builds greatly on that of enterprises. A focused approach to mindset change on these five issues creates opportunities for local stakeholders to address these issues' profitability. Clusters surrounding energy, technology, financials, and the environment would emerge. This would result in specific countries exporting their solutions to other nations facing similar issues.

At the national level, mindset change on these five levers would relieve government leaders from tremendous pressure to solve these challenges. Instead of the prevailing overreliance on dwindling government resources, it would increase ownership of these issues by all stakeholders. This would unleash not only innovation but also capital to address these issues.

Mindset change on these five issues could have positive repercussions at the global level. It would reduce the continent's dependence on aid. It would instead support a shift toward enterprise-based solutions to poverty. This would result in a breakthrough in the fight against poverty and for human dignity. It would help change Africa.

Fast Forward

Energy, population, markets, technology, and the environment are five issues of great relevance to prosperity that are hampered by the failure to change mindsets. Three overarching solutions must be implemented: a focus on mindset change, a greater involvement of enterprise, and bridging the leadership gap with appropriate knowledge.

As Koffi's case illustrates, the situation is not only difficult for rural families but also puts tremendous pressure on their relatives living in towns and abroad. This can create a situation where urban families can never save enough to get out of The Survival Trap. The national impact of this situation can be felt through weak financial markets.

By extension, this situation puts tremendous pressure on the international community that must provide ever-growing resources to solve poverty. It perpetuates the aid model in the presence of substantial evidence that aid alone has never helped any nation get out of poverty.

Endnotes

[1] US Department of State, Humanitarian Intervention Unit, 2010; Paul Collier, Oxford University.

[2] World Development Report 2010, "Managing Land and Water to Feed Nine Billion People and Protect Natural Systems," http://siteresources.worldbank.org/INTWDR2010/Resources/5287678-1226014527953/Chapter-3.pdf, p.146.

[3] African Union Commission, African Development Bank, Development Bank of Southern Africa, Infrastructure Consortium for Africa, the New Partnership for Africa's Development, and the World Bank, "Transforming African Infrastructure Will Require an Additional $31 Billion a Year and Huge Efficiency Gains," MIDRAND, South Africa, November 12, 2009, http://www.infrastructureafrica.org/aicd/highlight/Highlight-test-03.

[4] Kleindorfer, Paul R., Risk Management for Energy Efficiency Projects in Developing Countries (March 29, 2010). INSEAD Working Paper No. 2010/18/TOM/INSEAD Social Innovation Centre. Available at SSRN: http://ssrn.com/abstract=1579938.

[5] United Nations Population Fund, 2010, Population Division of the Department of Economic and Social Affairs of the United Nations Secretariat, World Population Prospects: The 2008 Revision, http://esa.un.org/unpp, accessed Sunday, August 22, 2010.

[6] United Nations "Millennium Development Goal Progress Report 2008,"New York, NY 2008, http://www.un.org/millenniumgoals/pdf/The%20Millennium%20Development%20Goals%20Report%202008.pdf, p. 22.

[7] Julie DaVanzo, David M. Adamson. "Family Planning in Developing Countries an Unfinished Success Story," Rand Institute: International Family Planning 1998, Santa Monica, California, http://www.rand.org/pubs/issue_papers/2005/IP176.pdf.

[8] UN Economic and Social Conference, Economic Commission for Africa, "Reports on Selected Theories on Natural Resources Development in Africa: Renewable Energy Technologies for Poverty Alleviation," August 2003, Addis Ababa, Ethiopia www.uneca.org/estnet/eca_meetings/CSD3/RETs_Paper.doc, p.7.

[9] Roland Berger Strategy Consultants, "Environmental Technology—Growth Market and Industry of the Future," http://www.rolandberger.com/expertise/industries/environmental_technology/index.html.

[10] Chris Anderson, Free: The Future of a Radical Price (London: Random House Business, 2009).

14

Rwanda's Homegrown Solutions

Zen Revelations

Walking into the compound of Zen restaurant with Francis felt like stepping into another world from the hustle and bustle of Nairobi streets with the honking, smoking matatus, and young men and women shouting to rustle up business. A manicured garden, deeply set lighting, and water springs created a sophisticated and tranquil décor.

To enter, we passed through the Zen lounge, where legions of Nairobi's beautiful people enjoyed martinis and sashimi. As we ate, the conversation drifted naturally to our work in Africa and our views on what that meant. I shared my experience in Rwanda with him.

Francis looked at me carefully. "Eric, Rwanda is not really Africa!" My heart missed a beat. Removing Rwanda from Africa is tantamount to tearing out the continent's heart. The breathtaking and hilly nation sits squarely at Africa's center of gravity.

He continued, "Look, I have done business all over Africa. I tell you Rwanda is not Africa! What Rwanda has done in such a short time is amazing. But Rwanda is *not* Africa!"

Seeing the puzzled look on my face, Francis explained about a Rwandan project he was considering investing in that caused him to develop his unlikely thesis. "For one, Rwanda does not tolerate corruption. No one asked for anything when I was looking at this deal. Second, systems actually work there. Not to mention, the country is so clean!" Francis's comments rang familiar.

He rested his case: "The rest of Africa cannot replicate what Rwanda has achieved!" Other well-meaning Africans had argued the same before. While Francis's perception of Rwanda rang true, his conclusion was disturbing.

A successful Kenyan entrepreneur who had returned from the diaspora, Francis is dedicated to doing business in a way that is changing the lives of thousands of Africans. He, like many on the continent, is striving to make a difference, but the prevalent belief is that these accomplishments are being achieved against all odds and that it's a testament to these unique people's dedication and drive. These people are seen as the exception rather than the rule, just as Rwanda is.

How is it that this country, which once represented the worst of Africa, has been transformed into what is arguably the best in Africa, to the point where people see it as beyond the rest of the continent's reach? Having witnessed this transformation from a unique standpoint, I felt obliged to share with Francis why I know Rwanda is the heart of Africa, why its metamorphosis could be the catalyst for transforming the rest of the continent.

Rwanda's Homegrown Solutions

There is something powerful about art. Art is an intrinsic part of culture and oftengive a unique window into the soul of a nation. Often, we learn more about a people through their art than by almost any other means. It is through the beautiful basket, called the Agaseke or Rwandan Peace Basket, that we learn about Rwanda.

Beyond its striking patterns and swirling designs, the baskets are amazing for how they are crafted. The aesthetics of each basket are unique, handcrafted products. Traditionally, the Agaseke carried great symbolic importance in Rwandan culture—signifying virtue and thereby an intangible foundation for the future. Finally, the environment in which these baskets are produced is important; women, young and old, gather together to weave, socialize, and bond. Agaseke are the fruits of collaboration.

It is therefore not surprising, when we consider Rwandan culture through this lens, that they have taken a unique approach to how the nation's problems are solved. It is not enough to fix something that is broken; the country takes it to the next level by collaborating to make the problem into the source of the solution, and making something new and better. It is about the approach: Industriousness is turned into competitiveness, ability into skills, and survival into vision.

In 2001, news of my relocation to Rwanda incited panic among my friends. Today, when I tell people I live in Rwanda, the reaction is completely different. Instead of concern, what I see is genuine curiosity, and some are even envious. Everyone wants to learn one thing about Rwanda: What is her secret?

In answering this question, the Agaseke is what first comes to mind. The Agaseke tells us three things about the soul of Rwanda and gives us unique insight into the country's economic transformation. Just as each Agaseke is unique, the story of Rwanda is like that of no other nation. Unlike most nations, Rwandans invest in crafting their own story, rather than following the script that was written for Rwanda.

Even today, Rwandans continue to put a big emphasis on intangibles. Rather than focus on natural resources, the country appreciates its citizens, its human capital, as its single most important asset. This focus on intangibles has been critical to the success of Rwanda. Finally, Rwandans from all walks of life come together to weave their future. From the simplest citizens to the seniormost leaders, Rwandans come together to build their country. Like the Agaseke, the Rwandan nation is the fruit of collaboration.

Beyond Relief Toward Prosperity

Less than ten years after my arrival, in 2010, Rwanda ranked 67th in the World Bank's Doing Business Survey, and, according to the World Bank, "Rwanda is the star and the world's top reformer of business regulation...it marks the first time a Sub-Saharan African economy is the top reformer."

In one year alone, Rwanda jumped 76 spots thanks to its drive to make business easier, ranking 11th when it came to starting a business and 27th in protecting investors. Besides being the world's top reformer, the country ranked ahead of African economic powerhouses such as Kenya, Egypt, and Morocco.

Three specific elements have led to this change. The first is purposeful development of a product portfolio based on strategic choices and competitive advantage. The second is the leadership's targeted focus on reducing the costs of doing business in the nation. The last is investing in human capital.

Rwanda's strategic choices have paid off over the past ten years. Exports have grown more than five times to reach over $350 million. Average wages have grown more than 30 percent per annum over the decade in key sectors such as tea and coffee.

Since the leadership believes that business is the building block of lasting prosperity, it has invested in improving the business environment in several ways, which led to its making life easier for businesspeople in three ways. First, it now takes one day to register a business compared to six in the United States. Second, the country tremendously improved protection of investors with a 144 rank change. Finally, Rwanda has improved access to credit.

Not only has Rwanda made it easier for businesses in terms of employing workers, but it is also making it easier to find skilled employees. Last year, Rwanda graduated 5,200 people from university, more than the 2,160 total graduates in the 30 years that followed independence. Furthermore, 30 percent of the national budget is to be allocated, among others, to a universal nine-year program with a curriculum geared toward technology and graduating young adults equipped with skills to enter the workplace.

Economic theory illustrates that doing business in a landlocked nation surrounded by countries experiencing insecurity is not trivial. Nonetheless, Rwanda has managed to achieve this remarkable feat. Beyond underscoring the reality of Rwanda's transformation, this feat also points to the fact that this transformation is far from being only physical.

While the country is still far from its objective to become a middle-income nation, empirical evidence, as illustrated in Figure 14.1, suggests that Rwanda has started to escape The Survival Trap.

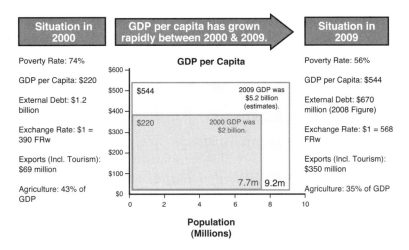

Figure 14.1   Rwanda's ongoing metamorphosis

A Mindset-Driven Metamorphosis

While many have told Rwanda's story, few have successfully addressed the most important factor in its transformation: mindset. This is the real secret of Rwanda's metamorphosis. Yet, to any careful observer, it is a secret hiding in plain sight. Most of Rwanda's national conversation is about mindset.

This is apparent in speeches, on billboards, in community activities and in programs such as Umuganda, the national civic service day that occurs the last Saturday of every month, in which the entire country, including President Kagame, clears brush and cleans the streets. Another one of such programs is Ingando where youth learn about the history of the country.

Consider a recent example where the country embarked on a national debate to improve its customer service. It all started with one disgruntled visitor who provided candid feedback on his Rwanda visit. The visitor recounted how he had to wait hours for a brochette he ordered in a local restaurant. The article was circulated widely.

Anyone familiar with the continent knows Africa's distorted relationship with time. Yet in Rwanda, this feedback became the impetus of a national debate to improve customer service. At first, the campaign focused exclusively on the hospitality industry. Very quickly, it also came to include the service that government provides to businesspeople and the rest of society.

While the campaign is still underway, the real feat is that it started at all.

These examples are illustrative of how mindsets are the underpinning of Rwanda's metamorphosis. In 2000, Rwandan leadership realized it needed to start with mindsets. The core mindset they embraced was the need to look within for solutions. Once they began looking, they realized Rwanda needed a lighthouse: a very powerful force that would guide them to their destination.

The leadership sat together to articulate Vision 2020. This vision states that Rwanda can become a middle-income nation in one generation. Today it all seems possible; back in the late 1990s, it was a wild dream. Rwanda made this wild dream, its goal, and in turn has begun to realize the dividends.

Once the vision was in place, three attitudes emerged:

1. Prosperity of the average citizen is what matters.
2. Entrepreneurship is the best way to create prosperity.
3. Collaboration becomes the mechanism to make this happen.

Rwanda was willing to face uncomfortable truths about business and its society by looking within, and was thus able to find solutions from within, solutions that otherwise could not be seen. Rwanda was able to harvest opportunities out of the same set of facts that were the makings of its challenges. Seizing these opportunities are gradually helping Rwandans escape The Survival Trap.

Having a mindset where we don't merely see what is there but what is possible is at the core of the country's metamorphosis. The mindset has changed the face of the country's economy, because of how it is leadership has chosen to change the business environment. With this change, people are shifting from surviving in the environment through toil to thriving in it through entrepreneurship.

A Leadership Mindset of Innovation and Competitiveness in Rwanda

Success in competitiveness requires both doing and thinking differently. Rwanda tasked the OTF Group to implement the Rwanda National Innovation and Competitiveness (RNIC) program. The program was structured around three goals: Create a culture of innovation and competitiveness, foster public-private dialogue, and identify and enhance key industries.

As discussed in Chapter 3, "Why Mindsets Matter," the prosperity of a nation is strongly dependent on the mental models (attitudes and beliefs) of its economic actors. The primary objective of creating a culture of competitiveness is to change attitudes toward wealth creation, competition, and the respective roles of the public and private sectors.

True economic development cannot be realized without a change in the mental models of participants. Rwanda's leaders sought first to embrace the principles of competition and cooperation to make complex decisions. They were able to do this because they recognized that wealth is not finite, that it can be created for one person without it being taken from another, and that it happens faster with helping hands. These beliefs make cooperation possible.

Rwanda deliberately promoted a culture of innovation and competitiveness throughout its leadership and population. Not only were policies and regulations changed to remove barriers, but businesses were encouraged through, for example, the yearly Rwanda Private Sector Federation Business Plan competition. Furthermore, national leaders championed the creation of the Academy for Leadership in Competitiveness and Prosperity (ALCP), which gives young leaders from the government and private sector the opportunity to step out of their daily lives to learn about the principles of competitiveness and put them in practice.

Rwanda realized that it would achieve its economic goals only if all parties engaged in a structured dialogue around the region's economic and social objectives. An important component of this is addressing the mental models of the country's leaders and citizens. Neither the public sector nor the private sector alone is or should be responsible for economic development. Both have complementary roles to play to achieve maximum impact and growth.

This objective was important in Rwanda due to the relatively new nature of the current government. Mechanisms of public-private partnership are essential to ensure that new legislation, policies, and investments are targeted in an economically driven manner. The RNIC was one of a handful government led initiatives to foster such dialogue within the context of specific industries through structured meetings.

At the essence of the three points mentioned above is the fact that the leadership took deliberate action. Failing to choose is often choosing to fail. Strategy, at its core, is about making choices, and a key choice facing Rwanda was the need to focus at first on a few, targeted industries. The country's leadership made this important choice on the basis of three criteria: leadership, strategic potential, and impact on prosperity. With limited resources to deploy, efforts must be focused where they can do the most good.

Coffee, tourism, and tea emerged as priority clusters. The heart of competitiveness is the development of industries that compete on value-added, differentiated products and services offered to targeted customers. The RNIC established and facilitated industry workgroups to foster collaboration within the industry.

While the RNIC is just one example of how Rwanda leveraged such initiatives, we can focus the lens through which we examine the nation's progress using the seven key mental models to escape The Survival Trap.

Creating a Mindset of a Shared Future in Its People

What makes Rwanda different from so many countries is that its people allow themselves to dream, and they dream together. Rwanda's Vision 2020 aspirations might seem unattainable to outsiders, but for Rwanda it's a tangible goal post that is apparent in every Rwandan's everyday life. No matter where in the country you go, you are likely to find numerous businesses with the words "Vision 2020" in their name, whether it is a barber shop, a restaurant, or a tiny corner grocery store.

There is not a child in the country who hasn't grown up seeing the aspirations as promises to their generation from this one. Consider the example of Sarah, the daughter of a friend of mine. A Rwandan girl from a middle-class family, Sarah attended primary school in the capital. The youngest child in a family of five, Sarah was cherished. One evening when her parents were asleep, she snuck out of her bed to watch TV.

The next morning, Sarah woke her parents up; her mother noted that something was amiss. She admitted to having watched TV at night. After a quick reprimand, it became clear the young girl had something more to share with her parents.

The night before, Sarah had seen a preacher on an evangelical channel foretell the end of the world for 2015. Sarah was obviously worried: "Daddy, Mommy, if the world ends in 2015, what about Vision 2020?" Her parents could not help but burst into laughter at the little girl's surprise. Sarah's dilemma is just one small illustration in an ocean of evidence that demonstrates the commitment of Rwanda, its people, and its leadership to a prosperous future for all Rwandans.

Since the vision has taken root in its people's DNA, the nation works as one to reach its future. The community dream and spirit are not new to Africa, but it is one that had taken a back seat to modern individualism in the years since colonialism. Rwanda revived that value.

This mindset is evident in numerous societal innovations such as Gacaca, Umuganda (mentioned previously), and Imihigo. Gacaca is a community court justice system inspired by tradition and established in 2001 as a humane and just way to deal with genocide-related crimes. The Gacaca was traditionally a framework to settle village and family disputes, where respected elders were elected to mete out justice, which aimed toward reconciliation and reparation rather than punishment. That spirit guides it today where accord, acceptance of contrition, and collaboration between the judges and spectators is given high importance.

Umuganda, literally translating to "contribution," is a Rwandan tradition that predated colonialism. It is a platform where all able-bodied persons over 18 engage in community work every last Saturday of the month. This phenomenon has received international recognition and become part of the country's brand. It reminds people that they achieve things by combining efforts and that the individual's good is furthered by the community's good.

Umuganda is used to do community labor but also to discuss events and concerns, to celebrate national events, and as a platform to sensitize the population on economic development and poverty reduction strategies. Thus, not only is a traditional mindset revived and reinforced through this activity, but it is taken to the next level and used as a springboard to foster new mindsets and learning.

Imihigo is another old cultural practice where two individuals set themselves targets with a clear deadline and where failure led to dishonor to the individual and the community. Today, the country has institutionalized the tradition as a way to empower people from the bottom up, to enhance local government and catalyze development.

Principles that guide the Imihigo include local population welfare, sustainability, employment creation, and promotion of social cohesion to name a few. Again, Rwanda has been able to take its own traditions and translate them into the present as a unique tool to achieve its goals.

Each of the preceding examples shows how the country looked within to find the answers and tailor its solutions. Using such traditions to solve current issues helped the leadership leverage deep-rooted Rwandan values to solve difficult problems. Rwanda's societal innovations are now being studied, shared, and used by many other nations.

Rwanda has been able to adapt its mindset, not only to change the fabric of its society but also that of its economy by using challenges as opportunities. To truly understand the impact of the mindset shift in Rwanda, it helps to see how these opportunities are aligned with the some of the seven key mental models to escape The Survival Trap.

Opportunity 1—Foster an Archimedean Mindset

Rwanda clearly decided to foster an Archimedean mindset. As illustrated by Rwanda Vision 2020, the country has made its moral purpose to transform the life of the average Rwandan citizen explicit.

The country embraced a series of initiatives to address this gap in a facilitated fashion.

As with the other mindsets the country fosters, the Archimedean mindset is rooted in values. Rwanda's leadership has created a platform for such entrepreneurs to realize their potential. Many Rwandans have discovered the role they can play and have seized this opportunity.

Rwanda's entrepreneurial mindset is apparent in the transformation of the country's private sector. Rwanda's private sector now numbers more than 70,000 entities, several times the number in 1994. Beyond sheer numbers, the quality of business, as evidenced by the doing business data highlighted earlier, has improved greatly with many international firms seeking to operate in Rwanda.

Opportunity 2—Build Trust

Rwanda started with a very low trust basis. Rwanda has sought to foster a safe environment where physical security is the best in Africa. This has meant that professionals are increasingly comfortable making Kigali their home. A sense of security is especially critical in the country's bid to foster knowledge sectors.

Policies have been put in place to engender trust. Zero tolerance on corruption means businesspeople are confident in their dealings. Bad governance can be a real deterrent for business as it increases the cost of doing business. Rwanda's adherence and implementation are internationally recognized and lauded; according to the United Nations Conference on Trade and Development (UNCTAD) "the low incidence of, and a zero-tolerance policy towards, corruption, [differentiates] Rwanda from regional competitors."

Institutional delivery has engendered trust. The war saw the destruction of public institutions, forcing the new leadership to reinvent the nation from scratch. Rwanda is now investing in strong institutions that offer a dependable and consistent experience to investors.

Opportunity 3—Focus on Solutions

Rwanda has prioritized specific products, creating many entrepreneurial opportunities and improving incomes at the bottom of the pyramid. Rwandan bourbon coffee is a strong brand in specialty coffee circles. Sold in Starbucks and other high-end outlets, Rwandan bourbon coffee has helped the wages of 500,000 coffee growing families rise at 30 percent per annum. Over 150 washing stations are the small enterprises leading this revolution.

Beyond coffee, tourism is transforming lives in Rwanda. Discerning tourists now pay $500 to spend an hour with Rwanda's mountain gorillas in the Virunga National Park. Tourism has now emerged as the country's top foreign exchange earner. Many hotels have been built, and numerous tour operating companies have sprung up.

Product and service choices are guided by principles of sustainability, job creation, and environmental impact.

Opportunity 4—Enable Prosperity Ecosystems

Many firms in developing countries focus on the competition they can see: their neighbors. Exacerbated competition results in lack of trust and loss of market shares. Yet, most businesses in developing countries could address some of the challenges they face through cooperation. Establishing issue-driven workgroups is often a mechanism to achieve collaboration.

Rwanda's leadership has invested in establishing facilitated industry workgroups through. This unique initiative has helped businesspeople, farmers, producers, and government leaders come together to agree on joint investments to develop specific products.

Rwanda's tourism workgroup is a good illustration of this approach. The tourism workgroup articulated the national tourism strategy, led the marketing of the destination, and worked together to establish standards. While stakeholders are not always of the same mind, a collaborative approach has helped enterprises thrive.

Opportunity 5—Operate Efficiently and Sustainably

In its bid to operate efficiently, Rwanda embarked on a decentralization program that helped the country take service delivery closer to its citizens. An important element in this approach has been the use of ICT through an innovative e-government platform to foster better service delivery and more efficient government.

As suggested in the "Rebuilding Rwanda's Tourism Industry" vignette (in Chapter 8, "Operate Efficiently and Sustainably"), the country strives to articulate a responsible approach to economic development. Rwanda has become a model for its innovative approaches to conservation in tourism. This has gone a long way toward allowing the nation to register astounding progress in the conservation of mountain gorillas. Beyond this, the country adopted innovative sustainability policies such as the ban of plastic bags, terracing, and forward thinking environmental management policies.

Opportunity 6—Seek Intelligent Capital

Underscoring her transformation is the fact that Rwanda has vowed to foster enterprise as a solution to poverty. This stand has translated into concrete actions within the country and outside. Within the country, the leadership has vowed to see a private-sector-led growth. After a vigorous privatization program, the country has sought innovative partnerships to increase private sector involvement.

Furthermore, the country established the Rwanda Development Board (RDB) in 2009. Modeled after the Economic Development Board of Singapore, the mission of RDB is to provide business with an effective platform in its dealing with government. While the institution is still in its infancy, it will become a tool to fast track the development of Rwanda.

Finally, President Kagame has taken a stand in the raging debate of aid over trade. Being the first African head of state to take such a stand, the President is sending a powerful message, adding a powerful voice to those who believe business should be facilitated to drive prosperity creation. This is important in changing this global mindset.

The importance that the country puts on human capital as its most valuable asset, means that Rwanda is seeing a brain flow. Professionals from the diaspora and other countries' citizens are flocking to Rwanda. Internationally leaders such as, Michael Fairbanks, Michael Porter, and Joe Ritchie come to the country regularly to exchange thoughts. Rwanda is fast becoming the think tank for escaping The Survival Trap.

Opportunity 7—Bridge the Leadership Gap

Rwanda aims to become a middle-income country within a generation. Visions often are to countries what New Year's resolutions are to individuals: lofty goals pushed aside as soon as reality sets in. Rwanda's leadership is steering the country on a different path: demanding that policy, strategies, programs, and investments actually be measured against Vision 2020.

Vision 2020 states clearly that Rwanda needs private-sector-led growth. This important maxim has translated into real opportunities for daring entrepreneurs. It has also meant that public servants are sensitized to support the private sector. The leadership of the country is not afraid to listen to the private sector and invite it to the table.

The scale of devastation meant that Rwanda lost many of its best minds during the 1994 genocide. The country therefore had to start with a "clean slate." This has meant that most of the country's leaders are relatively young. While youth can bring inexperience, it also has brought commitment, energy, fearlessness, innovation, and a tolerance for failure in the case of Rwanda.

Recognizing this challenge, the country has embarked on a variety of initiatives to train its young leaders. These programs range from trial by fire to graduate education under scholarships to short-term courses such as the Academy for Leadership in Competitiveness and Prosperity. The country has invested tremendously in fostering a sense of ownership.

No Excuses for Africa

As Francis and I considered Rwanda's tremendous achievement one critical conclusion emerged. If Rwanda has been able to metamorphose itself, the rest of the African continent has no excuses. While the small African nation is not out of The Survival Trap yet, leading indicators suggest it is on the right path.

The key to Rwanda's success has been mindset change. The country has fostered unique mindsets rooted in its in own value systems and translated them to make unconventional choices to drive its metamorphosis. Rwanda's merit has been to keep its commitment even under challenging circumstances. Concrete homegrown initiatives such as the Doing Business Initiative and Societal Innovations have helped.

The exciting news is that this means that African leadership and businesses are not condemned to settle for less. Instead, they can set their eyes on the highest ideal, prosperity, and strive for it. Escaping The Survival Trap requires nothing short of such a commitment. It also requires a better understanding of how the Seven Opportunities Rwanda has leveraged can be applied to specific cases.

Epilogue: A Call to Action: Embrace Entrepreneurial Solutions for Prosperity

Enugu, Nigeria, April 2000. I had flown to Nigeria to help facilitate consultations on the country's economic priorities. Little did I know that lunch with an old man would challenge me to become a fighter for Africa's prosperity!

This man was the Iyase of Benin, Prime Minister of the Yoruba Kingdom in Nigeria. Our lunch started on an unusual footing. "You don't look like the consultants they usually send. Where are you from young man?" A dozen questions followed in a quick burst.

After his due diligence, the Iyase opened up about his own story. At the call of his people, the Iyase had voluntarily quit his job as senior police officer. When I asked why, he replied: "It was the right thing to do!" His integrity moved me.

What began as a conversation took a solemn turn. Taking my hand, the Iyase looked into my eyes as if to imprint his words on my soul: "Our generation freed Africa politically. Your generation must free our countries economically." Something told me that his message applied to all emerging nations.

The Iyase's words sent butterflies to my stomach. African traditions are oral, and elders speak their will. I felt the Iyase had entrusted me with part of his will. His was a challenge that my generation, our generation, has no choice but to accept.

Poverty, war, disease, and other woes exist in Africa and other BoP regions. Yet, these issues do not define these regions. The Iyase's call was for all young leaders from BoP nations to embrace new ways of thinking, to employ the most effective tools available, and to ensure that self-determination is at the heart of our respective region's economic transformation. The Iyase would no doubt encourage us to embrace enterprise solutions to poverty.

What Are Enterprise-Based Solutions to Poverty?

The idea that enterprise is the solution to poverty is far from trivial. It's certainly not the accepted modality, although its prominence in the global discussions is increasing. Most argue the business of business is profit. We must therefore clarify this concept.

The essence of entrepreneurial solutions for prosperity is to evolve businesses that create value for all stakeholders involved. As previously discussed, Michael Fairbanks's COW-F model is a good way to frame our understanding of the stakeholder relationship. This model suggests that enterprise must create value for four core stakeholder groups: customers, owners, workers, and the community/ future generations.

A clear distinction must be made between entrepreneurial solutions for prosperity and social entrepreneurship. Enterprise-based solutions to poverty recognize the social contributions made by regular entrepreneurs building businesses, creating jobs, and attracting foreign currency.

Social entrepreneurs apply some business concepts to the challenges of solving social problems. While social entrepreneurs typically mean well and often have impact, most social entrepreneurs ultimately fail for lack of a sustainable or scalable business model. Sustainability and scale are often a function of capital accumulation that originates from healthy profits.

Beyond social entrepreneurship, entrepreneurial solutions for prosperity are about the implementation of hybrid strategies that transform business and society. Such solutions build on the importance of profit as the driver for entrepreneurial activity. Beyond profits, hybrid strategies address fundamental needs of core stakeholders making the business transformative.

Entrepreneurial solutions for prosperity integrate the pursuit of profit to the private sector's social imperative. In the absence of this integration, prosperity fails to materialize. As a result, the bottom of the pyramid remains poor. The Survival Trap is perpetuated, affecting individuals, firms, clusters, nations, and the world.

What Stakeholders Must Embrace Entrepreneurial Solutions for Prosperity?

Five stakeholder groups matter for entrepreneurial solutions for prosperity: local entrepreneurs, managers, government leaders, development partners, and civil society.

Local entrepreneurs and managers have been grouped in the same category throughout this book. In embracing entrepreneurial solutions for prosperity, it is important to recognize that these two sets of private sector operators have different roles to play. This differentiation is mostly a function of the background each group brings to the challenge.

Government leaders have an important role to play in setting the environment where firms compete. First, they often set the national development agenda. Second, public leaders contribute in shaping mindsets. They also enact policies and strategies that impact business.

The last two groups are development partners and civil society. Development partners include development finance institutions (DFIs), international nongovernmental organizations (NGOs), and foundations. Through injection of large resources, they greatly influence the broader agenda. Civil society, especially the media, must fully realize its important role as a shaper of mindset. Embracing entrepreneurial solutions for prosperity without civil society is much more difficult.

Embracing entrepreneurial solutions for prosperity requires mindset change and decisive action from a variety of stakeholders. Imagine, if you will, that each of the cases illustrated in this book had a chance to sit with the Iyase as I did that day. How would he advise different stakeholder to embrace new thinking? Figure E.1 offers an integrated virtuous cycle that can help businesspeople and other leaders articulate, implement, and benefit from entrepreneurial solutions for prosperity.

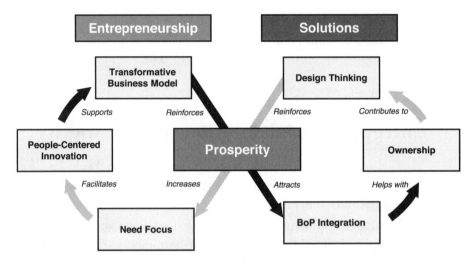

Figure E.1   Embracing entrepreneurial solutions for prosperity

Themba: The Local Entrepreneur

Local entrepreneurs such as Themba have a paramount role to play in making entrepreneurial solutions for prosperity a reality. Their role is crucial in delivering solutions directed at the bottom of the pyramid, creating jobs and fostering prosperity at the community level.

The Bottom of the Iceberg

BoP markets, especially Africa, ignore the bottom of the iceberg in their private sector at their peril. Most private sectors have the shape of an iceberg with an overwhelming number of micro- and small-scale firms at the base with a few visible large businesses at the top. A World Bank report estimates that such micro- and small-scale firms contribute respectively for 53 percent and 18 percent of employment in low income nations.[1] Yet, few support services exist for these entrepreneurs. As a result, these businesses are often stuck in The Survival Trap.

Invisible Yet Crucial

Local entrepreneurs trapped at the bottom of the private sector iceberg are invisible (see Figure E.2). Most leaders and executives fail to recognize the role of such local entrepreneurs as full-fledged economic operators. The perception of informal business as a sub-class of firms is yet another illustration of this sad reality.

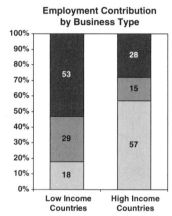

Employment Contribution by Business Type

☐ Formal SMEs ■ Informal Sector ■ Large firms

Figure E.2   The private-sector iceberg

Source: Ayyagarri, Beck, Dimurguc, "SMEs Across the Globe," World Bank, 2003.

Embracing entrepreneurial solutions for prosperity is about recognizing and unleashing local entrepreneurs. While few might mature into larger firms, most local entrepreneurs remain stuck in The Survival Trap. As discussed throughout this book, this reality breeds mindsets in the entrepreneurs that shape behavior, which is counterproductive for the firms concerned and society as a whole.

Archimedean Entrepreneurs

Stuck in The Survival Trap, local entrepreneurs learn quickly to focus on their immediate needs first before anything else. This often leads to shortcuts that can be damaging not only to the firm itself but also to all stakeholders involved. A good example of such shortcuts is the reluctance to invest in training, product development, or even lack of suitable standards.

Becoming an Archimedean entrepreneur is the best way for a local entrepreneur to fully embrace entrepreneurial solutions for prosperity. Local entrepreneurs must build businesses that fulfill the needs of all stakeholders.

Graduating from Survival

Escaping The Survival Trap requires that local entrepreneurs harvest the Seven Opportunities outlined in this book to make this situation real for all businesspeople. This book puts the onus on entrepreneurs to own the metamorphosis process that can make these opportunities real. It also illustrates how such entrepreneurs can change *both* mindsets and behavior to graduate from survival.

While local entrepreneurs must own their predicament, it is important to recognize the role of other stakeholders in supporting their development. The rest of this epilogue provides some concrete ideas. Unfortunately, certain development and government projects show how a paternalistic attitude can undo the noblest intentions while leading to waste of valuable resources.

Jaime: Business Managers

Business managers such as Jaime bring a wealth of knowledge and a vast amount of resources that are linked to their positions. Such managers have a big role to play not only in upgrading their businesses but also in leveraging the platform these businesses offer in enabling entrepreneurial solutions for prosperity.

The Top of the Iceberg

Business managers include national and international executives leading larger firms in Africa. Typically, such managers combine a strong educational pedigree with good experience. Furthermore, their higher income puts them at the top of the pyramid, giving them social influence. Such managers sit at the top of the private sector iceberg.

Despite their privileged position, business managers often face myriad challenges not unlike those of local entrepreneurs. While they operate stronger organizations, such executives are also negatively impacted by The Survival Trap. The poor operating reality translates into lower profitability, lost opportunity, and great frustration for all involved.

International Executives

International executives represent a unique subset of managers that must be discussed separately. For one, most international executives begin with a limited familiarity either with BoP markets or the culture of the country they are dealing with.

Next, such executives often bring a wealth of knowledge translating into potential for unique contribution to society through skills transfer or the leadership of specific initiatives.

One example of such unique contribution is through their connection to international networks of productivity. Simply defined, such networks encompass unique access to world-class know-how or capital that can strengthen a specific business.

An Unsuspected Fulcrum

Business managers, including both local and international executives, can be a unique force to lift BoP markets such as Africa out of poverty. As discussed previously, such executives lead institutions with enormous reach and wide scope. Such executives also have unique knowledge and experience that can help other stakeholders not only in understanding but also acting on the Seven Opportunities outlined throughout the book.

Yet, most managers are often underused as a fulcrum. The managers themselves and the other stakeholders must share the blame for this fact. First, very few are the business managers who embrace their role in improving the operating reality. This is a result of short-term focus. Second, other stakeholders are untrusting toward managers, which further limits their involvement.

Reinforcing the Entrepreneurial Ecosystem

Managers can have a disproportionate impact on BoP markets embracing enterprise-based solutions to poverty if they elect to invest in the entrepreneurial ecosystems of the countries where they operate. Leading the charge in advocacy for specific business reforms and investment is an important contribution to the entrepreneurial ecosystem.

Another set of contributions relates to their ability to act as mentors to local entrepreneurs. Such investments in the local community can take several forms from supplier relationships to sharing experiences on business issues to mentoring young entrepreneurs. Given their experience and education, managers can also influence other stakeholders, especially government leaders and development partners.

Ijeoma: Government Leaders

Government leaders are extremely important in the operating reality of BoP countries. Beyond shaping the operating reality through policies, government leaders also play a great role in shaping mindsets through their positions as leaders.

Sharing the Burden

BoP markets, especially African countries, face myriad challenges with limited resources. Traditionally, governments have been at the forefront of the economic development agenda. This has been exacerbated by the vast amount of aid invested in such nations. Despite all this aid, most government leaders have the experience of too many competing priorities and not enough money to go around.

Government leaders take an active role. In Chapter 9, "Enable Prosperity Ecosystems," we already discussed how learning to collaborate can make a difference in bridging the leadership gap. Working together is critical for BoP markets, especially for Africa, to meet their development agenda. Such sharing of the burden begins with embracing enterprise as a solution to poverty.

Mindsets at Play

Lack of trust is the first mindset that undermines a full embrace of enterprise-based solutions to poverty. In Africa, government leaders are often suspicious of the intentions of businesses, especially foreign ones. When asked to support the private sector, one government leader replied: "Why should we invest our scarce resources in the businesspeople that are rich as opposed to helping the poor?"

The second mindset is overreliance on aid. Most government leaders often measure their own performance through the ability to mobilize aid. Such leaders also lack a clear understanding of how the private sector can contribute to prosperity creation throughout society. This mindset is a corollary of short-term focus as opposed to long-term investments.

Leading the Charge of Mindset Change

The foremost responsibility of government leaders is in shepherding mindset change toward enterprise-based solutions to poverty. Using their authority and power of persuasion, government leaders can convince civil society, communities, development partners, and even some entrepreneurs. Chapter 12, "Insights on Mindset Change from Public Health," illustrates how such efforts benefit from systematic communication campaigns.

A critical success factor in such a mindset change campaign here is in matching words with deeds. Government leaders must realize that speeches divorced from action will only breed skepticism. The campaign must be closely coordinated with new behavior that demonstrates concrete impact for local firms and international business.

New Behavior

Mindset change can only be measured through behavior change. The Washington consensus offers a host of measures that government should adopt to support business, including infrastructure investments, education, and business climate reforms. Specific development partners have fostered interest in such areas. Such initiatives are necessary but far from sufficient.

Concrete actions to build trust between the public and private sectors are often missing in Africa. First, entrepreneur incubation and business development services are an area where government leaders can make a difference. Second, an overall respect for time translated into clear service charters for the private sector from government leaders would also help in making a difference.

Rob: Development Partners

The role of development partners in the current operating reality cannot be underestimated. Their biggest potential contribution is in adopting a mindset that BoP markets must become economically sustainable through entrepreneurial solutions for prosperity.

An Outdated Model

Let's focus on the case of Africa. The continent's economic agenda is greatly influenced by development partners through the vast amount of aid they provide. In 2008, total net official development assistance (ODA) from members of the Organization for Economic Cooperation and Development's (OECD) Development Assistance Committee (DAC) rose by 10.2 percent in real terms to USD $119.8 billion. This is the highest dollar figure ever recorded. It represents 0.30 percent of members' combined gross national income.[2]

While development partners come in many forms, most operate through governments of recipient countries. Yet, this vast amount of aid is also the problem of development partners: They provide their aid through governments of recipient countries. Moyo[3] and Easterly[4] outline how such aid breeds corruption, ineffectiveness, and lack of accountability. Empirical evidence exists that such aid can even undermine the local private sector.

New Players, Same Formula

As new players, institutions such as the Gates Foundation have generated great excitement in Africa. This excitement comes with great expectations. Expectations around capital have yet to be met despite the multibillion dollars that large foundations such as the Gates Foundation have in endowment. Yet, the real test is whether such foundations are going to revolutionize the existing development formula.

Unfortunately, foundations have so far espoused the same formula informed by charity. This is even more disappointing considering that most patrons of foundations are entrepreneurs themselves.

Yet somehow they believe that what has worked for them as individuals and the developed world does not work for BoP markets, especially Africa.

Enterprise Not Charity

The Golden Rule states that people should do to others what they want done unto to themselves. This rule is a central tenet in most of the world's religions. Most western nations have centered their development agenda on charity.

Charity has its place in international relations in specific cases such as natural disasters or certain projects. The first side of the problem is when it morphs into a belief that large infusions of capital must be the only way forward.

The second side of the problem is how this aid gets deployed. In the *Aid Trap*,[5] Hubbard and Dugan advocate for injection of aid capital to support local businesses. The Marshall plan did just that for post-World War Europe. It is paramount that development partners look for ways to inject capital in such a way that unleashes the private sector.

Catalyzing the Private Sector

Development partners can unleash the private sector in two practical ways. The first is through prioritization of cross-cutting investments that support the private sector. Such investments include targeted roads, power projects, and training of specific relevance to business. This action can help in reducing the operating costs for private firms.

The second area where development partners can make a difference for business is through intelligent capital. While we discuss this opportunity in great detail in Chapter 10, "Seek Intelligent Capital," development partners already have existing initiatives to inject skills and capital in the private sector in Africa. An important improvement should be on ensuring such efforts are managed with a business mindset.

Civil Society

Although we have not discussed civil society much throughout this book, our omission should not be interpreted as a neglect of the important role that civil society has to play if entrepreneurial solutions for prosperity are to become a reality. As other stakeholders work to adapt the Seven Opportunities, civil society has a great role to play. Upholding honesty and integrity among all stakeholders is just one way civil society can contribute to developing entrepreneurial solutions to prosperity.

Inherent Lack of Trust

A definition of civil society is a useful starting point. Our definition of civil society includes the media, NGOs, and religious groups. While it gets included in social issues, civil society often is ignored for business and economic development. Poor behavior of entrepreneurs and international managers toward workers, suppliers, and communities has also damaged perception.

This situation has resulted in mistrust from civil society toward business and economic development. Such mistrust is apparent in how the press reports on business issues. Skepticism toward foreign investors is an additional problem. Without addressing this lack of trust, civil society will not be in a position to play its role in embracing entrepreneurial solutions for prosperity.

Keeping Everyone Honest

Embracing entrepreneurial solutions for prosperity is a major challenge due to the often conflicting natures of incentives for all stakeholders involved. Even after embracing enterprise, the four previous stakeholder groups—local entrepreneurs, international managers, government leaders, and development partners—often find it difficult to align their practices given a long history of diverging agendas.

The unique contribution of civil society, especially the press, is in keeping everyone honest. Specifically, civil society must evaluate progress on tangible impact for communities as a whole and the bottom of the pyramid particularly. It must then provide specific feedback to the various stakeholders to help them improve their behavior as it relates to enterprise-based solutions to poverty.

Ruthless Compassion

To effectively play its role in keeping all stakeholders honest, civil society must demonstrate ruthless compassion. Ruthlessness empowers civil society to provide honest feedback even when the truth is hard. Compassion relates to the need for civil society to recognize the hardships that stakeholders face not only in upgrading their mindsets but also in changing behavior to improve their business models.

With the mandate of ruthless compassion comes the responsibility to better understand business strategy. The status quo is that most members in civil society have a limited understanding of business. This contributes to the aforementioned challenge of distrust from civil society toward business. It also contributes to the low receptiveness that other stakeholders have of civil society.

Embracing Enterprise to Monitor Business

Civil society must embrace enterprise if it is to become effective in playing its role of keeping everyone honest. This requires a mindset change from the distrust that we observed previously. Rather than believe without data, we invite civil society to begin with skepticism and investigate testimony from workers and the community about business's impact.

Frequent interaction and continuing education are two powerful avenues to understand business strategy. Frequent interaction is the essence of understanding business. It will help move away from myths toward hard facts about specific stakeholders. Continuing education has potential to not only help civil society better manage its activity but also to help with learning about business through immersion.

Upgrading Africa's Prosperity Software

As discussed throughout the book, escaping The Survival Trap begins with recognizing the role of mindsets in shaping our actions that keep us stuck this vicious cycle.

After they recognize the importance of mindsets, stakeholders must choose to change behavior. Rather than being a one-time event, this commitment must translate into a new culture that stakeholders adopt. This in turn allows stakeholders to challenge specific mindsets over time and improve the performance of their business as a result.

Such commitment to mindset change and the resulting behavior may seem an ordeal to most. However, benefits abound for those executives and leaders who make this commitment and take the necessary actions. The Rwanda case study discussed earlier in the book, along with the other examples outlined throughout this book, provides a good illustration of what is possible.

A Path out of The Survival Trap

Africa's foremost imperative must be to escape The Survival Trap. Mindset change in Africa is necessary for prosperity creation—beginning within firms and extending to all stakeholders, driving real change in business models and transactions.

Addressing this imperative requires that Africa's leadership embrace enterprise solutions to poverty. President Kagame and the economic transformation that he has led in Rwanda is an excellent illustration of enterprise solutions to prosperity in action. The Iyase's call for this generation of economic freedom fighters now calls to you: Are you prepared to make a difference?

Endnotes

[1] Ayyagarri, Beck, Dimurguc, "SMEs Across the Globe," World Bank, 2003.

[2] Organization for Economic Cooperation and Development, 2009.

[3] Dambisa Moyo, *Dead Aid* (New York: Farrar, Straus and Giroux, 2009).

[4] William Easterly, *The Elusive Quest for Growth* (Cambridge, MA: MIT Press, 2001).

[5] R. Glenn Hubbard and William Duggan, *The Aid Trap: Hard Truths About Ending Poverty* (New York: Columbia University Press, 2009).

Bibliography

Africa the Good News. May 21, 2009. "MTN Dedicated to Battling Malaria in Africa." http://www.africagoodnews.com/health/mtn-dedicated-to-battling-malaria-in-africa.html.

Aldas, Kirvaitis. *World Wide Major Stock Exchange Links*. Lithuania. http://www.tdd.lt/slnews/Stock_Exchanges/Stock.Exchanges.htm.

Andreasen, Alan R. 1995. *Marketing Social Change: Changing Behavior to Promote Health, Social Development, and the Environment*. Washington, DC: Georgetown University.

Argyris, C. 1993. Knowledge for Action. A guide to overcoming barriers to organizational change. San Francisco: Jossey Bass.

Argyris, C., and Schön, D. 1974. *Theory in Practice: Increasing Professional Effectiveness.* San Francisco: Jossey-Bass.

Argyris, C. 1978. *Organizational Learning: A Theory of Action Perspective.* Reading, MA: Addison Wesley.

——. 1996. *Organizational Learning II: Theory, Method, and Practice.* Reading, MA: Addison Wesley.

Argyris, C., Putnam, R., & McLain Smith, D. 1985. *Action Science: Concepts, Methods, and Skills for Research and Intervention*. San Francisco: Jossey-Bass.

Argyris, Chris. 1985. *Strategy, Choice, and Defensive Routines*. New York: Harper Business.

Ayiteh, George. 2005. *Africa Unchained: The Blueprint for Africa's Future*. New York: Palgrave MacMillan.

Bandura, Albert. 1986. *Social Foundations of Thought and Action*. Englewood Cliffs, NJ: Prentice-Hall.

Banfield, Edward. 1958. *The Moral Basis of a Backward Society*. Glencoe, IL: Free Press.

Bill and Melinda Gates Foundation. "Malaria Overview." http://www. gatesfoundation.org/topics/Pages/malaria.aspx.

Bosma, Niels, Levie, Jonathan, and Global Entrepreneurship Research Association (GERA). 2010. "Global Entrepreneurship Monitor 2009 Executive Report." Babson Park, MA: Babson College, Santiago, Chile: Universidad del Desarollo, and London, UK: London Business School. http://www.gemconsortium.org/download.asp?fid=1055.

Brafman, Ori, and Rom Brafman. 2009. *Sway*. New York: Broadway Business.

Brendenbruger, Dam M., and Barry J. Nalebuff. 1996. *Co-opetition*. New York: Doubleday.

Collier, Paul. 2007. *The Bottom Billion: Why the Poorest Countries Are Failing and What Can Be Done About It*. New York: Oxford University Press. http://comtrade.un.org/db/dqBasicQueryResults.aspx?px=S4&cc=6618&r=156&y=2008.

"Country Forecast, Sub-Saharan Africa, Regional Overview." December 2009. The Economist Intelligence Unit. New York. http://store.eiu.com/product/1930000193SS.html?ref=featuredProductHome.

De Lorenzo, Mauro. January 1, 2008. "The Rwandan Paradox." AEI, American Enterprise Institute for Public Policy Research. http://www.aei.org/article/27476.

Doing Business. "Economy Rankings." http://www.doingbusiness. org/economyrankings/.

——. "Enforcing Contracts in Africa." http://www.doingbusiness.org/ ExploreTopics/EnforcingContracts/.

———. "Enforcing Contracts in the United States." http://www.doingbusiness.org/ExploreTopics/EnforcingContracts/Details.aspx?economyid=197.

———. "Reforms in Africa, 2008-09." http://www.doingbusiness.org/Reformers/Africa2009.aspx.

Donner, J. C. 1998. "Making Mental Models Explicit: Quantitative Techniques for Encouraging Change." In *Monitor Company Seeds for Change Series*.

Easterly, William. 2001. *The Elusive Quest for Growth*. Cambridge, MA: MIT Press.

"Enterprising Rising: Signs of a Recovery." 2004. http://www.economist.com/node/2338542.

Etounga-Manguelle, Daniel. 1991. *L'Afrique a-t-elle besoin d'un programme d'ajustement culturel?*. Ivry-sur-Seine: Editions Nouvelles du Sud.

Fairbanks, Michael and Stace Lindsay. 1997. *Plowing the Sea*. Cambridge, MA: Harvard Business School Press.

Fairbanks, M. 2000. "Changing the Mind of a Nation: Elements in a Process for Creating Prosperity." In L. E. Harrison, & S. Huntington, *Culture Matters: How Values Shape Human Progress* (pp. 268-282). New York: Basic Books.

Feltman, Charles. 2008. *The Thin Book of Building Trust*. Bend, OR: Thin Book Publishing.

Fukuyama, Francis. 1995. *Trust: The Social Virtues and the Creation of Prosperity*. New York: Free Press.

Gardner, Howard. 2006. *Five Minds for the Future*. Boston: Harvard Business School Press.

Green Peace Canada 2008. *The Congo Basin Rainforest*. http://www.greenpeace.org/canada/en/recent/greenpeace-opens-africa-office/the-congo-basin-rainforest.

Hammond, Sue Annis. 2004. *The Thin Book of Naming Elephants: How to Surface Undiscussables for Greater Organizational Success.* Bend, OR: Thin Book Publishing.

Hampden-Turner, Charles. 1993. *The Seven Cultures of Capitalism.* New York: Currency Doubleday.

Harrison, Lawrence. 1992. *Who Prospers? How Cultural Values Shape Economic and Political Success.* New York: Basic Books.

Harrison, L. E., & Huntington, S. P. 2000. *Culture Matters: How Values Shape Human Progress.* New York: Basic Books.

Hayden, Goran. 1983. *No Shortcuts to Progress: African Development Management in Perspective.* Berkeley: Univ. of California Press.

Hofstade, G. 1991. *Cultures and Organizations: Software of the Mind.* New York: McGraw-Hill.

Hubbard R. G., Duggan W. 2009. *The Aid Trap: Hard Truths About Ending Poverty.* New York: Columbia Business School Publishing.

IFC and the World Bank. Washington, D.C./New York, NY. http://www.doingbusiness.org/documents/fullreport/2010/DB10-full-report.pdf

Inkeles, Alex. 1997. *National Character: A Psycho-social Perspective.* New Brunswick, NJ: Transaction Publishers.

International Telecommunication Union. 2009. "Information Society Statistical Profiles 2009." Africa. Printed in Geneva Switzerland. http://www.itu.int/ITU-D/ict/material/ISSP09-AFR_final-en.pdf.

Kay, John. 2004. *Culture and Prosperity: Why Some Nations Are Rich but Most Remain Poor.* New York: HarperCollins.

Kotler, Philip. 1989. *Social Marketing.* New York: Free Press.

Johnson-Laird, P.N. 1986. "Mental Models: Towards a Cognitive Science of Language, Inference, and Consciousness." Cambridge, MA: Harvard University Press.

——. 2009. *How We Reason*. New York: Oxford University Press.

Landes, David. 1998. *The Weather and Poverty of Nations: Why some are so rich and some are so poor*. New York: W.W. Norton.

Lindsay, S. 2000. "Culture, Mental Models and National Prosperity." In L. Harrison, & S. Huntington, *Culture Matters: How Values Shape Human Progress* (pp. 282-296). New York: Basic Books.

Lippman, Walter. 1922. *Public Opinion*. New York: Free Press.

Mahajan, Vijay. 2008. *Africa Rising*. Upper Saddle River, NJ: Wharton School Publishing.

McLelland, David C. 1961. *The Achieving Society*. New York: Irvington Publishers.

Monitor Group. 2009. "Paths to Prosperity: Promoting Entrepreneurship in the 21st Century." http://www.compete.monitor.com/ App_Themes/MRCCorpSite_v1/DownloadFiles/ NED_report_final.pdf.

Moyo, Dambisa. 2009. *Dead Aid*. New York: Farrar, Straus and Giroux.

Mukaaya, Eddie. January 25, 2009. "Rwanda: Business Round-Up." *The New Times*. http://allafrica.com/stories/200901261124.html.

Ndikumana, Leonce, and Sher Verick. 2008. Working Paper, "The Linkages between FDI and Domestic Investment: Unravelling the Developmental Impact of Foreign Investment in Sub-Saharan Africa." The Institute for the Study of Labor.

Organisation for Economic Co-operation and Development, *Emerging Economies*, volume 2009, no.15, p. 102.

Porter, Michael E. 1990. *The Competitive Advantage of Nations*. New York: Free Press.

Prahalad, C. K. 2006. *The Fortune at the Bottom of the Pyramid*. Upper Saddle River, NJ: Wharton School Publishing.

"Prostitution v Constitution: A Challenge to America's Anti-AIDS Policy." 2005. *The Economist*. New York. http://www.economist.com/displayStory.cfm?Story_ID=E1_QNJNGDR.

Ramachandran, Vijaya. 2009. *Africa's Private Sector: What's Wrong With the Business Environment and What to Do About It*. Washington, DC: Center for Global Development.

Rapaille, Clotaire. 2007. *The Culture Code: An Ingenious Way to Understand Why People Around the World Live and Buy as They Do*. New York: Broadway Books.

Rwanda Development Gateway. January 12, 2007. "Rwanda among World Bank Anti-Corruption Sample." http://www.rwandagateway.org/article.php3?id_article=4010.

Sabel, Charles. 1992. "Studied Trust: New Forms of Cooperation in a Volatile Economy." Cambridge, MA: Massachusetts Institute of Technology.

Sachs, Jeffrey. 2005. *The End of Poverty*. New York: Penguin Press.

Sala-i-Martin, Xavier. Global Competitiveness Report 2009, the World Economic Forum. Geneva, http://www.weforum.org/pdf/GCR09/GCR20092010fullreport.pdf.

Senge, P. M. 1990. *The Fifth Discipline: The Art and Practice of the Learning Organization*. New York: Currency Doubleday.

Senge, Peter, A. Kleiner, C. Roberts, R. Ross, and B. Smith. 1994. *The Fifth Discipline Fieldbook: Strategies and Tools for Building a Learning Organization*. New York: Currency Doubleday.

Senge, Peter, et al. 2008. *Presence: Human Purpose and the Field of the Future*. New York: Crown Business.

Smith, David. October 22, 2009. "Africa Calling: Mobile Phone Usage Sees Record Rise after Huge Investment." Guardian.co.uk. http://www.guardian.co.uk/technology/2009/oct/22/africa-mobile-phones-usage-rise.

Sowell, Thomas. 1994. *Race and Culture: A World View*. New York: Basic Books.

Telecommunications Industry Association. "2009 ICT Market Review and Forecast." www.tiaonline.org.

Thomas, Gareth, DFID Minister of State for International Development (speech). February 9, 2010. http://www.dfid.gov.uk/Media-Room/Speeches-and-articles/2010/ Remittances-and-financial-inclusion-conference/.

United Nations Statistics Division. 2010. *United Nations Commodity Trade Statistics Database*. http://comtrade.un.org/db/dqBasicQueryResults.aspx?px=S4&cc=66 18&r=156&y=2008.

United Nations. "World Population Prospects: The 2008 Revision Population Database. Africa, Population aged 0-14, Medium Variant 2005-2010." AND "Africa, Population aged 15-24, Medium Variant 2005-2010." http://esa.un.org/unpp/.

Wilson, E. O. 1998. *Consilience: The Unity of Knowledge*. New York: Knopf.

Wind, Yoram (Jerry), Colin Crook, Robert Gunther. 2005. *The Power of Impossible Thinking: Transform the Business of Your Life and the Life of Your Business*. Philadelphia: Wharton School Publishing.

World Bank. 2009. "Doing Business Report 2010." A copublication of Palgrave Macmillan,

World Bank. July 2010. *World Development Indicators Database*. http://siteresources.worldbank.org/DATASTATISTICS/Resources/ GNIPC.pdf.

World Health Organization. April 2010. Malaria: Fact sheet N.94. http://www.who.int/mediacentre/factsheets/fs094/en.

INDEX

W Wharton School Publishing

In the face of accelerating turbulence and change, business leaders and policy makers need new ways of thinking to sustain performance and growth.

Wharton School Publishing offers a trusted source for stimulating ideas from thought leaders who provide new mental models to address changes in strategy, management, and finance. We seek out authors from diverse disciplines with a profound understanding of change and its implications. We offer books and tools that help executives respond to the challenge of change.

Every book and management tool we publish meets quality standards set by The Wharton School of the University of Pennsylvania. Each title is reviewed by the Wharton School Publishing Editorial Board before being given Wharton's seal of approval. This ensures that Wharton publications are timely, relevant, important, conceptually sound or empirically based, and implementable.

To fit our readers' learning preferences, Wharton publications are available in multiple formats, including books, audio, and electronic.

To find out more about our books and management tools, visit us at whartonsp.com and Wharton's executive education site, exceed.wharton.upenn.edu.